The
Keelboat Age
on Western Waters

The Keelboat Age

on

Western Waters

—

LELAND D. BALDWIN

UNIVERSITY OF PITTSBURGH PRESS

THIS BOOK is one of a series from the Western Pennsylvania Historical Survey sponsored jointly by The Buhl Foundation, the Historical Society of Western Pennsylvania, and the University of Pittsburgh.

Published by the University of Pittsburgh Press, Pittsburgh, Pa., 15260
Copyright 1941, University of Pittsburgh Press
Copyright 1969, Leland D. Baldwin
Feffer and Simons, Inc., London
Manufactured in the United States of America

First printing 1941
Second printing 1960
Paperback reissue 1980

LC 41-10342
ISBN 0-8229-5319-6

Contents

Illustrations

Preface

THIS monograph in its original form was submitted to the faculty of history of the University of Michigan in partial fulfillment of the requirements for the degree of doctor of philosophy. In its preparation a score of important collections of sources of western history were visited and a proportionate number of librarians and historians gave cheerfully of their time and accumulated knowledge in gathering together the bits that have gone to make up the mosaic. The unfailing patience, courtesy, and interest encountered everywhere have done much to smooth the way and make pleasant the memories of an arduous task. Some special acknowledgments are in order.

Mr. Walter B. Briggs, assistant librarian of the Harvard College Library, and Dr. Clarence S. Brigham, director of the American Antiquarian Society, were especially generous in opening the way to the use of the fine collections of early western newspapers in their charge. At New Orleans, particular mention should be made of Miss Cerf of the Louisiana Historical Society, who aided in the use of the resources of the Cabildo, and of Mrs. E. D. Fredericks of the city archives, who kindly allowed the use of the only extant file of the *Louisiana Gazette,* together with the two surviving volumes of the old New Orleans wharf register. At the same time should be remembered Dr. Robert J. Usher of the Howard Memorial Library, who showed his interest by the loan of a collection of photographs of Lesueur sketches. Mrs. N. H. Beauregard, archivist of the Missouri Historical Society permitted examination of that society's varied collections, and Mr. Otto

PREFACE

Rothert, the secretary, and Miss Ludie J. Kinkead, the curator, made available the material in the Filson Club.

In addition should be mentioned Miss Wilby, curator of the Historical and Philosophical Society of Ohio; Dr. Louise Kellogg of the Wisconsin Historical Society, in which is kept the extensive Draper Collection; Mrs. Butler, curator of the Ayr Collection in Newberry Library; and Miss Ver Nooy, reference librarian of the University of Chicago and in charge of the Durrett Collection. Miss Irene Stewart, former reference librarian of the Carnegie Library of Pittsburgh, very kindly opened the Craig Papers to research. Messrs. Franklin J. Meine and Walter A. Blair, placed before me the results of their researches on Mike Fink, now issued in book form. I am also grateful to Doris Corbett and Elisabeth M. Sellers for their painstaking care in editing and preparing the manuscript.

It is my particular desire to express to Professor Dwight L. Dumond of the University of Michigan my gratitude for the many ways in which he has aided me. Also, as seems inevitable with the historian, I must mention my wife, whose patience and care in copying, typing, and doing reference work during the long hot summer days practically halved the time necessary for research.

LELAND D. BALDWIN.

University of Pittsburgh

The
Keelboat Age
on Western Waters

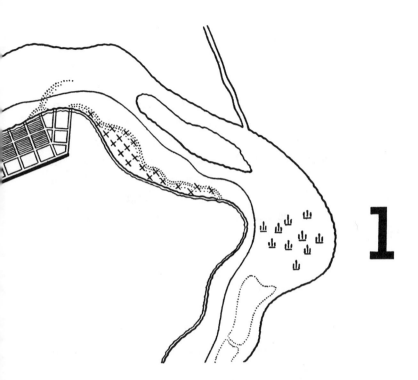

The Role
of the Western Waters
in American Expansion

WHEN the Pennsylvania pioneers first topped their laurel-clad mountains they had already developed many of the characteristics that were to become known as typically western. Foremost of these was that love of elbow room, and of the security and independence that went with it, that constituted for them the alpha and omega of life. They had learned that the man trained in frontier ways or able to adapt himself to them could go out into the wilderness with his ax, his rifle, and a bag of seed corn and win a spacious home for himself. Perhaps the settler might have to pay tribute to a pettifogging land dealer or to a none-too-generous government, but if he "humped" himself he could at least keep beyond the reach of "law and physic," which in his eyes characterized the stifling atmosphere of the crowded East. The westerner might be ostracized by his neighbors, he might lose his scanty possessions to the land shark, his children to fever or milk sickness, or his wife to the Indian scalping knife, yet as long as there was land farther west, life was still worth the living. "Whatever turns up," wrote Anthony Trollope in grudging admiration, "the man is still there; still unsophisticated and still unbroken."[1]

The story is told that about the close of the eighteenth century Louis Philippe, forced to travel by the exigencies of revolution in his own land, made a stop at a tavern in the squalid little village of Cincinnati. When he went to pay his bill, there arose a difference of opinion between him and the landlord, and the scion of French royalty, drawing himself to his full height, announced haughtily:

"One who is destined to become king of France cannot stoop to bandy words with a common backwoodsman."

That was too much for the democratic landlord, who, jumping over his rude bar, seized the customer by the seat of his royal pants and the scruff of his neck and booted him out of the tavern and into the gutter.

"There!" he cried, dusting his plebeian hands, "You're to be a king, are you? Well, we're all kings over here."[2]

The tale may well be apocryphal, yet it neatly characterizes the dwellers on the western waters. Such a state of mind did not come about through chance. Those were the days when the old men dreamed dreams and the young men saw visions. The men and women who launched their frail arks at the headwaters of the Ohio and the Tennessee and literally fought their way against man and nature to the fertile bottoms down river were consciously seeking to begin a new chapter in human history. They came from North and South alike, echoing in the half-mute, half-profane way of the common man the sentiments expressed in the lines of Philip Freneau:

> The east is half to slaves consign'd
> And half to slavery more refin'd.

Behind them were high rents, slavery in mine or factory, and an overstringent law made and administered by a coastal aristocracy; before them, down the course of the forest-bordered stream, were rich, black lands to be had almost for the taking, and freedom from meddling laws and extortionate overseers. The disillusioned modern, coddled and kicked in turn by that plutocratic stepmother known as the Industrial Revolution, in looking back upon the floating pigsties that brought to the West those crude pioneers, cursed with fever and ague and ridden by lice and itch, cannot help but envy them their self-reliance, their chance to battle against purely physical odds, and their almost childlike faith in the future of America.

It is the misfortune of this later day that no contemporary with the genius to do it justice saw the epic possibilities in this transit of civilization and depicted the scene for future generations. Here and there a voice rises from the throng of westward-bound pioneers: a frontiersman exults in a shot well aimed against the foe; a lover captured by savages writes a note and, tossing it into a boat, sets it adrift with the prayer that it will reach the hands of his beloved;[3] a missionary mourns for wife or child laid to rest between sullen river and darkling forest; or a land speculator records the planting of a village destined to become a metropolis. But most of the pioneers were men of action who looked upon the note-scribbling traveler with contempt and who spent their evenings in caucus or with cards and bottle rather than with a useless diary.

Even when these hardy men had found a resting place and "made a crop," there was still the long journey to be undertaken to the New Orleans market. The immigrant into the West embarked in the ark to seek his home, and his prosperity was built up by the sale of goods taken to market in the ark. The difficulty of communication with the East was one of the factors that produced a simple civilization that found expression in a simple, direct, equalitarian theory of government. At the same time, paradoxically, the prosperity of the West was dependent upon the markets furnished by Europe and the eastern coast, and the westerner was thoroughly alive to world events. In an age when the square, boxlike ark was the chief means of transportation, there grew up the psychology of the Middle West, which for good or ill has become the psychology of the country. Perhaps it is not too much to say that out of the womb of the ark was born the nation.

The West for some distance beyond the lower Mississippi River was settled and had come of age before the steamboat had won its supremacy. The states bordering on the Ohio and the lower Mississippi (with the exception of Arkansas) had taken their places in the Union by 1821 and had already developed the institutions and the men that were to be their peculiar contributions to the American social, economic, and political system. Also, the West as such began to lose its native freshness and vigor, together with its naïveté, as the ark and the long, gondola-like keelboat were displaced by the steamboat and the railroad. The Northwest, as it began to adopt the Industrial Revolution, became increasingly like the East, and the old Southwest became linked to the South. As the lower West more and more approximated the economic system of the South, the middle westerner's eyes became fixed upon it as the market for his flatboat load of flour and pork. Ten thousand young men were leaving the upper waters each year for the trip to New Orleans, and the middle westerner found that the Union guaranteed his market; but what was more, he saw the vast expanse of his country, and a natural pride developed in him a concept of national solidarity. The southern common man, conversely, rarely leaving his native county and seeing America only through the eyes of faith, did not feel as strongly that old "Mrs. Sippi" with her thousand tentacles had bound the nation into an indissoluble union. But so she had, and these bonds were to survive even the blood and fire of the War between the States.

It was in this pioneer economy that the keelboatman found his niche. Minimize the volume of his cargo as one will, it was he who prevented the expanding young West from losing contact with the East and who was most responsible for the development of the western country. When the southern mountains were as yet unopened to wagons and when the journey overland was too long to be profitable, the boatman's herculean muscles brought from New Orleans and Pittsburgh to the crude villages of the West some of the comforts and fashions of life, as well as the necessities. In the gallery of American *genre* paintings the boatman deserves a place along with the pioneer, the steamboat pilot, the cowboy, and those other types that have enriched American life and lore.

The fur traders, French and English, who first penetrated the western wilderness were the forerunners of the boatmen and the pioneers. They explored the advance ground, learned the languages and customs of the aborigines, and finally, by the introduction of civilized vices, so weakened the Indians that they were rendered an easier prey to the march of civilization.[4] During the middle years of the seventeenth century the Iroquois, in order to keep beaver hunting in their own hands, had driven out the tribes of the territory that is now Ohio, Kentucky, and western Pennsylvania and had maintained that region as a huge hunting preserve. With the decadence of the Iroquois, however, the Shawnee, Delawares, Ottawa, and Miami began, between 1720 and 1750, to filter from East and West into Ohio and western Pennsylvania. The Pennsylvania traders who had dealt with the Shawnee and Delawares east of the mountains loaded their pack horses and followed their customers through the passes of the Alleghenies into the Ohio Valley. Before the outbreak of hostilities with the French, these traders had traversed the Old Northwest as far as the Wabash and had established a number of trading posts, among them one at Logstown, about eighteen miles down the Ohio from the forks, and one at Pickawillanee, or Piqua, a Miami town on the Scioto.[5] The first active opposition on the part of the French to this westward extension of the Pennsylvania trade came in 1749, when Céloron made his famous voyage down the Allegheny and Ohio rivers and ordered the English traders to leave Logstown. Three years later the destruction of Piqua by the French and the rapid advance of their military forces on the Allegheny put a temporary end to the English trade northwest of the Ohio.[6]

During the war that followed, the course of the Ohio became more than ever before a scene of activity. Flotillas with troops were continually traversing the Allegheny and to some extent the Ohio. Yearly convoys of provisions came to Fort Duquesne from New Orleans and the French settlements in the Illinois country across the river from St. Louis. In the spring of 1756 Captain Coulon de Villiers ascended the Ohio and in July attacked Fort Granville, on the site of Lewistown, Mifflin County. Here he captured about forty prisoners, including three women and seven children, and sent them to

Fort Chartres in Illinois and then to New Orleans. The next year the rumor of a British plan to invade the Mississippi country from Carolina via the Tennessee River caused the French to rebuild Fort Massac on the lower Ohio, and soon afterward the commandant, Charles Philippe Aubry, led a force of forty men up the Tennessee River to invade the country of the Cherokee. In March of 1758, Aubry, with seventeen large bateaux, reprovisioned Fort Duquesne, and he was in the retreat in November when the fort fell before General Forbes. The next spring he led four hundred men from the Illinois country back up the Ohio and Wabash rivers to Lake Erie, but was defeated near Niagara by General William Johnson.[7]

The British victory and the French surrender of the territory east of the Mississippi, far from solving the problems of the Pennsylvania traders, seemed for a period of nearly two years to complicate them. The Indians for various reasons were slow in deserting their French alliance and under the great organizer, Pontiac, captured every British post in the West except Detroit, Fort Pitt, and Ligonier. Colonel Henry Bouquet's expedition in 1763 quieted the Ohio Indians, however, and the traders filtered back to their old stamping grounds. The fact that Detroit was largely supplied from Fort Pitt in the transition years made the Allegheny River-French Creek route to Presque Isle important for the carriage of food and munitions.[8] Since the large, flat-bottomed skiffs, known by the French as bateaux, furnished the quickest and cheapest means of transportation, they began increasingly to displace pack-horse trains in the economy of the West, and this tendency was accentuated as watercraft became lighter and the boatmen grew more expert in their use.

The British occupation of the Illinois brought to the merchants of Philadelphia golden dreams of the wealth to be gained by opening a trade with that fruitful country. The Philadelphia firm of Baynton, Wharton, and Morgan was the first to enter the Illinois trade. Twenty wagons were engaged by the company in hauling goods to the mountains, and six hundred pack horses were used in the mountains. The firm's youngest partner, George Morgan, went to Fort Pitt to supervise transport facilities, and there he erected a structure to serve as a company headquarters and for the convenient storage of goods. Sawyers and boatwrights were brought from Philadelphia and set to building bateaux; Morgan planned to have 65 bateaux and 315 men engaged in the river commerce by the fall of 1766. The first shipment was sent in March of that year, when five company boats departed for Kaskaskia. Morgan followed in June.[9] The crews were composed of twenty-two men to a boat, and many of their provisions were supplied by hunters from the game along the banks. Few of the boats returned up the Ohio, for it was soon found that the expense of rowing them back to Pittsburgh was greater than the original cost. The result was that the company's peltry and other exports were sent down the Mississippi, and the crews returned east by way of Pensacola or walked across country to Pittsburgh.[10]

The Baynton, Wharton, and Morgan venture in the Illinois proved unsuccessful for a number of reasons. Goods, and often British goods at that, were brought up the Mississippi by the French and Spanish traders more cheaply than they could be shipped through Pittsburgh; and even more disastrous from the business viewpoint, a new "concern" of Pennsylvania merchants, Franks and Company, entered the trade and sent a Scotch soldier named William Murray to represent them in the Illinois. Baynton, Wharton, and Morgan had complained of the trade as early as 1766 that "the Enormous Expenses attending it at Times makes us almost Sick," and now they must have felt even worse as the Scotchman's good sense and good humor began to make his business thrive —with the support, it might be said, of the British commandant in the Illinois, who had become Morgan's enemy. Finally in 1771 Morgan sold his firm's western stock to Franks and Company. Murray continued to represent his "concern" in the Illinois until the outbreak of the Revolution.[11]

Business and settlement on the lower Mississippi, meanwhile, were thriving—a fact that eventually was to prove of importance to the farmers and petty manufacturers at the head of the Ohio. The merchants of Natchez, then the western metropolis of the British possession of West Florida, had to take their goods up the Mississippi from the mouth through Spanish territory, and they took advantage of the opportunity to supply the needs of the Creoles along the river, accepting produce in exchange and allowing liberal credit. "Floating stores," which seem to have been boats fitted with shelves and counters, plied the river, stopping at every landing where there was a chance for a sale. Creole boats going north took on a few articles at New Orleans but received most of their cargoes in West Florida. In this way the British built up a business that, according to the calculation of a Spanish officer, consisted of about 85 per cent of the total commerce of Louisiana.[12] This prosperous trade, coupled with the fertility of the soil, soon drew numbers of permanent settlers to the Mississippi River shore of West Florida. From 1764 onward, settlers were crossing the mountains to the village of Boatyard (now Kingston, Tennessee) on the Holston River and drifting down to Natchez. In 1770 there were said to be three hundred inhabitants from Virginia and the Carolinas in the region, with three to four hundred families expected by the end of the summer. The Ohio River had its share of this emigration to the South, for in 1773, according to one account, four hundred families came to Natchez by way of that river.[18]

The western waters were in an unprecedented state of turmoil during the Revolution. The passes of the Alleghenies were fairly thronged with immigrants moving to the West, many of them Tories fleeing from Whiggish tar and feathers, or neutrals evading military service. Land speculation and its attendant political strife flourished. Indian bands haunted the rivers and forest paths; and armies, British and American, marched and countermarched assiduously, but produced, for all the expenditure of money and strength, remarkably few results. Still, it was in the midst of this chaos that the real foundation of American nationality in the West was laid. Among the outstanding figures of those days, George Rogers Clark deservedly ranks first, but soon after him should come George Morgan. As a trader in the Illinois, Morgan had become conversant with the Indians and had gained knowledge that stood him and the country in good stead during the Revolution, when he was Indian agent at Fort Pitt. His experience as a trader was utilized in building at Pittsburgh the little navy of gunboats to "secure the navigation of the Ohio River from Post to Post." It was apparently Morgan who, in the spring of 1776, suggested that the colonists could draw supplies and munitions from New Orleans by way of the Mississippi and Ohio rivers.[14]

The first powder expedition was undertaken at the order of Virginia and was led by Captain George Gibson and Lieutenant William Linn. Disguised as common traders, they departed from Pittsburgh in the summer of 1776 in two boats with about twenty-five men and arrived at New Orleans without serious trouble. At that place Oliver Pollock, an American merchant who had zealously embraced the Revolutionary cause, prevailed upon Governor Unzaga to furnish them with powder from the royal magazine. Spain, however, was not yet at war with Great Britain, and the suspicions of a number of British residents were aroused. In consequence Gibson was thrown into prison, and Linn hurriedly and quietly loaded the powder and started up river. A little later Gibson was released and departed by sea in charge of an additional shipment.

Linn left New Orleans about the last of September with ninety-eight barrels of powder. The commissary had neglected to lay in proper supplies, and in consequence of this lack the party suffered from exposure and hardship. Linn dictated a letter to Pollock in which he said that half the men were obliged to help the other half off the boat every night and to carry some in blankets to the fire. They arrived at the mouth of the Arkansas on November 26 and were kindly received by the Spanish commandant, who agreed to let them remain until they had recuperated. From New Orleans, Linn had sent to Virginia for help, his messengers traveling up to the region of St. Louis and then across Illinois and Kentucky to Pittsburgh. As his party was further weakened by the exertions of the trip, he now sent to the Spanish commandant at St. Louis to ask for provisions to be sent to the mouth of the Ohio about the sixth or seventh of March. Reflecting upon the New Orleans incident, however, and fearful lest the Spanish might try to hinder them again, the members of the party made every effort to pass that point ahead of time and succeeded by three or four days—thus, it was claimed, escaping an instigated Indian attack. It appears certain that Linn was at the mouth of the Ohio on March 3 and there purchased eighteen bags of corn from the agent of the Illinois merchant, Thomas Bentley. Meanwhile Governor Henry of Virginia had sent out a relief expedition that may have met Linn near the Wabash. At least, according to British reports, Linn had one hundred men when he passed that river. At the

Falls of the Ohio, now Louisville, the party carried its gunpowder, contained in 156 kegs, around the falls and dragged the boats through. They arrived safely at Wheeling on May 2, 1777. Linn's cargo of gunpowder was a very welcome help in the defense of the West, and part of it was probably used by Clark on his expedition to the Illinois.[15]

In the period just before the opening of the Revolution, James Willing, scion of a prominent Philadelphia family, had engaged in trade at Natchez. Now, about December, 1777, he received through the influence of Robert Morris a commission that authorized him to bring five boatloads of goods from New Orleans. He departed from Pittsburgh in January, 1778, in a gunboat called the "Rattletrap," with about thirty-five men. The British had placed two outposts along the Mississippi, but Willing succeeded in slipping by them and meanwhile recruited his company to a strength of about one hundred. On February 20 he arrived at Natchez and under cover of night sent out parties that seized several prominent pro-British residents of the vicinity, among them Colonel Anthony Hutchins. As soon as Willing passed the southern boundary of the neutral Natchez district, his progress became an orgy of plunder—plate, Negroes, and provisions were seized, and much other property was burned. As it proceeded, the company was increased until it numbered between three and four hundred men, and it was able to seize, at Manchac, the British vessel, "Rebecca," which was armed with several swivels and sixteen fourpounders on carriages. After its arrival at New Orleans the band also captured the British brig, "Neptune," below the city.

The booty secured in this raid was sold in New Orleans with the assistance of Oliver Pollock. A period of inaction followed, during which Willing formulated a plan to return to Natchez and treat it as the country down river had been treated. Upon learning this, Colonel Hutchins managed to escape and warn the settlers, who, consolidated against Willing and the American cause by the raids, organized an "armed association" of three hundred men. As Willing's fleet approached White Cliffs, twenty miles below Natchez, it was forced by the strength of the current to pass to the west. A skiff with a flag of truce was sent across to treat with the associators, and the latter agreed to receive Willing in a friendly manner if he meant to keep the peace. Upon the return of the skiff, Willing fired three shots, the signal agreed upon as denoting peaceful intentions, and he dispatched a barge, under the direction of Lieutenant Harrison, across the river. According to the account of an associator, as Harrison approached the shore he ordered his gunner to load the boat's swivel gun with musket balls, and the men of Natchez, overhearing the order, seized their rifles and threatened to shoot the gunner if he obeyed. Upon this, Harrison clapped his pistol to the latter's head and forced him to fire. Several of the shore party were wounded but returned the fire with such vigor that at least five of the barge crew of thirty-five were killed and the rest captured. The American account was that the Natchez men, urged on by Hutchins, fired first.

Willing gave up his plan and retreated down river. A few weeks later he crossed over to the Tensaw settlements above Mobile in an attempt to enlist the settlers in the American cause, but he was likewise unsuccessful there. British reinforcements had meanwhile been rushed to the Mississippi, but the danger from Willing was over. Late in the fall his men started up the west side of the river under Lieutenant Robert George to join Clark in the Illinois, while Willing himself departed by sea for the East. He was captured by the British and, after narrowly escaping hanging, was paroled and finally exchanged.[16]

THE KEELBOAT AGE

Willing's raids had the effect of cutting off Natchez' lumber exports to Pensacola and the West Indies; on the other hand, they definitely aligned the Natchez settlers against Congress. When Spain entered the war and Governor Gálvez of Louisiana, after a whirlwind campaign in September, 1779, conquered the Natchez region, the settlers remained loyal to Great Britain. In April, 1781, they proposed to hinder Gálvez' siege of Pensacola by raising a revolt at Natchez, and acting under Colonel Hutchins they captured Fort Panmure by a ruse. Their efforts were in vain, however, for they were soon confronted by a fleet of five Spanish barges filled with veteran soldiers and at the same time heard the news that Pensacola had fallen. Then followed one of the strangest odysseys in history as the leaders of the revolt fled with their families from the victorious Spaniards. The remnants of a band of one hundred, after incredible suffering, succeeded in reaching the British army at Savannah. Another party found refuge in the Cumberland country. Others were massacred by the Choctaw or captured and taken to New Orleans, and a few settled among the friendly Chickasaw.[17]

Those rebellious settlers who fled to the Chickasaw entered upon a course of harassing Spanish and American commerce. Their leader was a trader named James Colbert, who had been adopted into the Chickasaw nation and had become the father of four sons, all of whom were to play important roles in Chickasaw history. The depredations continued for an indeterminate length of time. Between September, 1780, and May, 1781, no boats came up the river past Fort Jefferson, where Robert George was in command. In August, 1782, Gálvez wrote that navigation between Arkansas and the Illinois was interrupted by "the union of the Chies Indians with the fugitives of Natchez and the roving traders who have remained after the conquest of the English settlements in those provinces." The first important raid of which an account has been left was that in which a boat belonging to Captain Pourée, a merchant of St. Louis, was captured on March 19, 1782. The seizure was made by eleven Englishmen and three Negroes under the leadership of a Juan Toorner, or John Turner. Four hours later the captured crew revolted and threw their captors into the water, killing eight of them with oars. Only Turner and five others escaped by swimming to a pirogue and making off.

Western tradition has amplified the account in what, after all, may be an authentic manner. The encounter was supposed to have occurred at Cottonwood Creek, where Captain Pourée, nicknamed *Beausoleil*, was captured with a load of valuable merchandise, and he and his crew were thrust below deck. Pourée's Negro cook, Cacasotte, appeared delighted to be thus released from slavery; he laughed, sang, and danced about the boat and sprang to render every service to the rebels, so that it was not long before they ceased to watch him and let him go on with his regular duties. He then communicated to his two Negro helpers a plan for freeing them all from their captors' power. At the dinner hour the Englishmen assembled on deck, some of them gathering in the bow and stern, and others seating themselves on the gunwales. Cacasotte singled out a big rebel and at the dinner signal suddenly lunged against him and pushed him overboard; he then ran from one dumbfounded man to another, thrusting them backward into the water. At the same time his companions were following his example, so that within a few seconds the entire company was struggling in the water. The victors then seized oars and struck on the heads those who attempted to climb back on board, or picked them off with shots from the rifles that were lying about.

There may have been half a dozen or more boats captured

by the Natchez rebels in the winter of 1781–82. In May, 1782, the wife of Governor Cruzat of the Illinois was captured with her four sons and a crew of ten boatmen near Barrancas de Margot (modern Memphis) and, after being held for nineteen days, was released upon the promise of ransom. As late as May, 1783, the rebels were still active. In that month the traders Lacassagne and Tardiveau, who had come down the river from Pittsburgh, were met by Colbert and seventy of his men in three boats. The fugitives fired three shots from the swivel gun and then surrendered. For eleven days they were kept prisoners, and then were given one of their own canoes and allowed to go on to New Orleans. Eventually the pacific policy of the Spanish colonial government toward the rebels resulted in their pardon and return to their homes.[18]

Meanwhile George Rogers Clark had undertaken his expedition to the Illinois. He left Redstone, on the Monongahela River, on May 12, 1778, with 150 men and about 20 families of immigrants. His flotilla consisted of six boats lent by the Continental authorities—probably bateaux or keels, for part of them had been brought upstream from Wheeling—and an unknown number of other boats built for the occasion at Redstone. After planting a settlement at the falls, he set off on the famous expedition to Kaskaskia, abandoning his boats at Massac for the overland route. It is probable that Clark could not have retained his conquests had it not been for the help of Oliver Pollock. The latter kept up the American credit in the Illinois by paying Clark's bills of credit with silver and, in addition, sent several cargoes of supplies up the river.[19] As part of his force for the reduction of Vincennes, Clark fitted out a small row galley with two fourpounders and four swivels. The "Willing," as he called his craft, was placed under the command of Captain John Rogers and with a crew of forty-six men was ordered to ascend the Wabash to the mouth of White River, about thirty miles below Vincennes, and await Clark's coming. The "Willing" left Kaskaskia on the fourth of February, 1779, and arrived at Vincennes on the twenty-seventh. By that time, as one of the participants expressed it, "mear Hunger then forced us to attact the Fort before the arivel of our boat . . . we wounded sundray of their men through the Portholes which Caus'd them to surrender themselves and Garrison, to the great Mortification of Our Boats Crew who had not the Opportunity of makeing use of their Cannon." After the capture of Vincennes, three boats, each armed with a swivel, were manned with fifty men under Captain Leonard Helm and sent to meet ten British boats that were on their way down the Wabash. Seven of the British boats were captured, together with forty men and a welcome supply of provisions and baled goods. On March 19 six boats, including the "Willing" and a small craft called the "Running Fly," were started for Kaskaskia with some of the prisoners, and with that voyage the "Willing" disappears from the records of the West.[20]

Within a few months after Clark had won his victory at Vincennes the series of disasters to the American cause began. The first was the taking of Colonel David Rogers' powder boats on their way from St. Louis in October, 1778, with sixty or seventy men and several bateaux. At a point just below the mouth of Licking Creek a party of Indians was seen crossing the river above, and Rogers' party foolishly landed on a sand bar and started in pursuit. They had hardly scrambled through the willows before they were surrounded by Indians. Two men escaped with one boat and reached the falls in safety, and a few others succeeded in breaking away. Most of the band, including Rogers, were killed or captured.

The worst disaster, however, was yet to come—the ambush and capture of Colonel Archibald Lochry's force not far below the place where Rogers had been attacked. Lochry had raised a company of 107 men in western Pennsylvania and had purposed to join Clark, who was preparing an expedition to the West. Clark, however, left Wheeling before Lochry arrived, and the latter, almost destitute of ammunition, hastened to overtake him. Lochry's men traveled in four or more boats, one of them a horse boat carrying thirty-two horses. Several men whom Lochry sent ahead to Clark with letters detailing his situation were captured by a British and Indian party under Joseph Brant, who accordingly planned an ambuscade. Brant had already allowed Clark's flotilla to pass unmolested. On the morning of August 24, Lochry's men, who had killed a buffalo, landed on the north shore to cook breakfast. Some of the men were building fires and others were still in the boats when the Indians suddenly opened fire. Thirty-six men were killed, several of them being kicked to death by the horses. One boat got away but was captured by Indians on the opposite shore. There was no effective resistance, since the men had but little ammunition, and they were forced to surrender on the second or third volley. Brant reported that he took sixty-four prisoners. A number of them were killed by the Indians soon afterward.[21]

Meanwhile, smaller raids by the British and Indians continued unabated, and the enemy crossed the Ohio when and where they pleased. To meet the situation, a committee of the Virginia House of Delegates reported, without daring to advocate, an ambitious plan to build a little navy of eight gunboats of the row-galley type. Unfortunately Virginia was on the verge of bankruptcy, and Clark was forced to boil the project down to the construction of one galley, the "Miami," and two small gunboats. These were built at the Falls of the Ohio under the direction of James Asturgus, who received eventually the munificent sum of two Spanish dollars a day.

Workmen were scarce, and this fact caused considerable delay. There was also much difficulty experienced in finding ropes; they finally had to be made from papaw bark. The cannon had to be brought over the mountains to Redstone and floated down the river. When completed, the "Miami" was calculated to be seventy-three feet in keel, propelled by forty oars, and armed with one sixpounder, six fourpounders, and one twopounder. The gunwales were four feet high and bullet proof, and false gunwales fastened by hinges could be raised above them, making the sides so high that there was no danger when the galley approached within pistol shot of the shore.

The galley was ready to set out for its appointed patrol in July, 1782. Her crew, which was supposed to total 110 men, presented difficulties. The nucleus was made up of a company of marines under Captain Jacob Pyatt, composed largely of discharged men who had been tempted into the service by the promise of a suit of clothes and ten dollars a month. According to the pay roll, they served from March 9 to September 9, 1782. In addition, detachments of militia were assigned to duty with the boat; the first was composed of Captain Robert Patterson and thirty-seven men. Captain Robert George, who appears to have commanded the "Miami," had his hands full. To begin with, Patterson demanded double rations of flour, asserting that "he would be dam'd if any of his men shod stay on Board" unless the rations were granted. George gave in perforce, but the next morning the militia, backed by their captain, refused to come on board, saying that they would not be made into sailors. The point was gained and they marched on shore, escaping the labor at the oars. Not satisfied with this, however, most of them deserted that night. The next month another detachment under Captain Chenoweth probably served on the "Miami."[22]

As deterrents to the passage of the rivers by Indian raiders, armed boats were probably not worth the money it cost to build them. On the other hand, no gunboat or convoy, so far as is known, was ever attacked by Indians. Cannon seem to have inspired a healthy respect in the savage mind. If there had been more cannon, the war in the West could have been more successfully prosecuted because the navigation of the rivers would have been more practicable. Next to the scarcity of money and the apathy of the people, it was the difficulty and peril of navigation in the face of the enemy that made the record of the Revolution in the West a long series of sufferings and disasters shot through only now and then with a ray of triumph.

During the Revolution, Spain relaxed her restrictions sufficiently to allow a traffic in military supplies to be opened with the struggling English colonies. Trade also began between Kentucky and the Illinois country, and by 1782 the settlements along the Monongahela were sending cargoes of flour down river to New Orleans. Writing from Pittsburgh on April 29 of that year, General William Irvine reported that he had given permits for ten boatloads of flour to be exported to New Orleans and Kentucky, and estimated that they carried at least three hundred tons. His information was that another fleet of ten or twelve boats of even larger burdens would soon arrive. A few days later he described the flour trade as if it were a business of long standing. The seasons for exporting were from the middle of February to the first of June and from the first of November to the last of December. A boat carrying forty tons would cost about forty pounds. Five men, each receiving from three to four pounds a month, were enough to work a boat. One supercargo could serve for a fleet of several boats. It may have been one of the boats mentioned by Irvine that fell into the hands of the Delawares on March 22. The crew, who lost three hundred barrels of flour by the capture, reported to the commandant at Detroit that other boats were to follow. In April or May, British irregulars on the Mississippi captured an American "huckster" with a load of flour. In the three years from 1782 through 1784, ten American flatboats landed cargoes aggregating 2,640 barrels of flour at New Orleans, and there is no way of learning how many cargoes may have been sold at other points along the Mississippi, particularly at Natchez.[23]

The only man who can be identified with these ventures in 1782 was Jacob Yoder, a Pennsylvania German. He was born in Reading in 1758 and was a soldier in the Revolutionary army in 1777–78. In 1780 he emigrated to western Pennsylvania and two years later left Redstone with a flatboat laden with produce. In May, 1782, he landed his cargo in New Orleans and sold it to the Spanish commandant, who gave him a draft on the captain general of Cuba. At Havana he invested in furs and hides and sold them in Baltimore at a profit. The next year he repeated the venture, but it was not a financial success. He removed to Kentucky in 1785 and perhaps continued to engage in the New Orleans commerce. In the winter of 1782–83, two Frenchmen, Barthelemi Tardiveau and John Honoré, made trading voyages from Redstone to New Orleans, apparently in partnership but on different boats. Both men had trouble with the Indians, and the former was robbed. Tardiveau later had business connections in the Illinois country and at New Madrid and was influential with Harmar and St Clair. Honoré, according to one account settled in Louisville and lived there until well toward the middle of the next century.[24]

The little port of Louisville at the Falls of the Ohio must have been the scene of considerable business during the latter years of the war. Colonel William Linn brought two or three thousand dollars' worth of goods from Kaskaskia and sold them at the falls—not a large enterprise but perhaps indicative of others. In October, 1782, Clark, anxious to obtain supplies for his expedition against the Shawnee, deeded thirty-five hundred acres of his own land to Tardiveau in exchange for "Seventy thousand weight of flower." There were then about four thousand kegs of army flour there, besides the cargoes that traders put ashore to lighten their boats for the descent over the falls; and certain malcontents took advantage of the confusion to accuse Clark of abstracting flour from the army stores to sell in New Orleans. Banking after 1780 was carried on by John Sanders in a houseboat anchored at the river front. In this "keep," traders and hunters deposited their furs and received certificates that passed as money and were redeemable upon the sale of the skins. In 1783 a certain Daniel Brodhead brought goods from Philadelphia and opened what is supposed to have been the first store in the state. Goods sold up to double their Philadelphia price. Some of the merchandise used in Kentucky may have been brought up river from New Orleans, a procedure that had already been found to cost only one-third as much as the Philadelphia freight. In addition to transportation, however, the importer by way of New Orleans had to consider the Spanish duties, which were as high as 25 per cent.[25]

This incipient prosperity was not to develop unhindered. Spain had never favored American independence wholeheartedly and now saw that a free use of the Mississippi would cause a rapid growth of the trans-Appalachian region, which would constitute a threat to her domination in Louisiana and Florida (the latter had been ceded to her by Great Britain after the Revolution). In 1782 Great Britain had agreed to share with the United States her rights to the navigation of the Mississippi, but the Spanish king, claiming that this right could not be ceded, issued a decree on March 12,

1784, forbidding American trade in Spanish territory. There had already been attempts to stop American trade on the Mississippi, and the Indians had been incited against the settlements, but now Spanish vigilance was doubled. Americans were held up at Natchez, and if they were allowed to sell at all it was only on onerous conditions. Sometimes they were held incommunicado; it was said that several members of the crews of some Pittsburgh boats held at Natchez starved to death during an enforced detention of fifty days. Even American immigrants bringing in supplies for themselves might have them seized, as happened to the forty barrels of flour imported by a certain Calvit for his own use. Those who braved the edict and tried to smuggle produce down river had their property confiscated upon capture.

Such actions, of course, could not help but arouse resentment in the West. In June, 1786, Thomas Amis of the Cumberland country arrived at Natchez with a cargo of flour and iron castings. He gave out that he intended to carry his goods on to the mouth of the river, supposedly for transshipment, but the Spaniards heartlessly confiscated them and then sent him home with a passport stating that he had "behaved like a gentleman and a man of the strictest honor." Amis returned home and broadcast his misfortune to the world. Through the orders of the legislature the North Carolina Congressional delegation laid the matter before Congress, which as usual referred it to a committee. Amis, however, had accomplished his purpose, which was to air his grievances in public. During the next ten years the West was a welter of conspiracies and intrigues, most of them having as their object the opening of the Mississippi to the trade of the new settlements.[26] Confronted by what appeared to be the dilemma of leaving the Union or sacrificing its own economic prospects, the West was in no mood to hold out for ideals. Besides, the example of the Revolution was too recent for these rebels against Great Britain to gag at treason. It was the moment for some William Tell to arise and lead the people against the power that was trying to crush them. Instead, there arose James Wilkinson.

Wilkinson had one of the longest and most checkered careers in American history, and for a decade it closely affected the history of western commerce. Laden with stolen laurels, at the close of the Revolution he engaged in business and quickly lost his wife's fortune; thus it was that at the age of twenty-seven he opened a store in Lexington. Two years later he opened a business on the Kentucky River and became the founder of Frankfort. He undoubtedly had talents; he possessed a charm that often blinded those around him to his faults; and above all he was enterprising, even to the point of audacity. On the other side of the ledger, he was ambitious without scruples and an adept at political and business chicanery. The result of this combination of qualities was that James Wilkinson, instead of becoming a leader, became a plotter—in the end a disappointed and ineffectual plotter. Nevertheless, he covered his fires well, so well that though his contemporaries saw the smoke distinctly, the flames were not detected till long after his death.

The West to which Wilkinson came a few years after the close of the Revolution was a land of strange anomalies. With a soil actually able to produce a hundred bushels of corn or thirty bushels of wheat to the acre, the inhabitants were receiving nine pence per bushel for corn and twelve shillings per hundredweight for flour and yet were able to sell only to immigrants who had not hitherto had time to raise crops of their own. Tobacco was bringing two dollars a hundredweight. Whiskey, ginseng, and furs were about the only products light enough and valuable enough to repay the long haul to the eastern seaboard. Land, of course, was cheap. In Kentucky, Louisville was a village with a hundred cabins, building or built, a store, and about three hundred inhabitants; and Lexington, soon to be the metropolis, was of approximately the same size but was already beginning to feel its handicap in the lack of water transportation. Pittsburgh, the gateway to the Ohio, possessed perhaps five hundred inhabitants, and its facilities for manufacture were on the verge of being outclassed by the adjacent interior village of Washington.

It was largely due to Wilkinson that a breach was finally made in the wall of Spanish exclusion. He was aware, no doubt, that there were ways of greasing the hands of Spanish officials so that goods brought down river would slip through them and turn up at the New Orleans market. One of the men who was able to carry on trade was a Colonel Perrie of the Monongahela country, and Robert Williamson of the Cumberland settlements seems also to have discovered the secret, for years later he boasted of having sold flour in New Orleans in 1787 at twenty-two dollars a barrel. Perhaps Wilkinson, whose partnership with Abner Dunn in the salt and hide business was not very flourishing, thought to gain some business by the same means, since he was reported to have been in Natchez in the fall of 1786.[27] However this may have been, he did not succeed in getting the necessary permit, for the next year he resorted to an audacious scheme of which the only justification was its success.

He left Kentucky in April, 1787, with a boatload of tobacco. Upon his arrival at Natchez he escaped arrest either by the connivance of Grandpré, the commandant, whom he may have met the year before, or by the intercession of Cruzat of St. Louis, with whom he had been in correspondence. The boat was allowed to proceed, and Wilkinson followed within a few days. When the produce arrived at New Orleans a guard was at once sent aboard to confiscate it. Wilkinson had foreseen this and had perhaps arranged the next step with one of the several American merchants resident in the city. At any rate, a certain Daniel Clark, who exercised considerable influence with the colonial government officials, pointed out to Governor Miró that it was one thing to confiscate the cargo of an ordinary citizen of the American West, but another thing entirely to confiscate that of a man who had held a general's commission in the American army and was now one of the most popular and influential political leaders in Kentucky. It was also hinted that Wilkinson desired nothing better than to have his cargo seized; it would give him the excuse he wanted to inflame the westerners against Spain and would enable him to lead them in a war of conquest against Louisiana and Florida. The result was that Miró had the guard withdrawn from Wilkinson's boat and released it to Wilkinson's agent, Patterson. Upon his arrival at New Orleans, Wilkinson was escorted to the government house by a corporal of the guard. The story is told that he continued the imposition on the governor and begged him not to deviate from his duty by making any exceptions to the trade laws laid down by Spain. The Spanish officials, constantly on nettles because of the threats of invasion by American frontiersmen, were ready to listen to certain propositions that Wilkinson now proceeded to make.[28]

It would be interesting to have the details of those interviews in that massively furnished room in the government house. On one side was the adroit, polished, prepossessing American, conscious of his advantages and knowing what he wanted; and on the other side were Governor Miró and Intendant Martin Navarro, grave, inscrutable, a little suspicious, and conscious of the weaknesses of their colony but also of the fact that they held the trump card in the control of the navigation of the Mississippi. We can only guess at the preliminary hedging and fencing indulged in by both parties, the cautious broaching of ideas and their cautious examination, the giving way of suspicion to comprehension, though scarcely trust, and the final laying of the cards on the table in Wilkinson's oath of allegiance to Spain and in his memorial. This memorial was a long discussion of the advisability of Spain's encouraging the West to come under her protection by holding out the bait of free navigation of the Mississippi. Wilkinson ended by upholding this policy and urged the erection of a fort opposite the mouth of the Ohio and the offering of inducements to Americans to settle on Spanish soil. The Mississippi would not be opened to American commerce unrestrictedly, but certain "men of real influence" would be given special privileges in order to drive home to the westerners the advantage of courting Spanish good will. Wilkinson agreed to do everything in his power upon his return to Kentucky to influence that district to place itself under Spanish protection. Miró and Navarro replied by letter stating that they would recommend his plans to the home government and meanwhile would give him the right to send to New Orleans a limited quantity of tobacco, Negroes, cattle, swine, and apples. With this by no means negligible concession and the hope of securing greater concessions in the future, Wilkinson began the return journey by sea and finally reached Kentucky in February, 1788.[29]

Wilkinson thus did not completely attain his objective, which was to get the monopoly of Kentucky's trade down the Mississippi, but his memorial bore fruit. The Spanish Council of State empowered Miró to allow the importation of goods from Kentucky with a duty of 15 per cent instead of the customary 25 per cent and also authorized him to accord further reductions to certain favored ones whose good will it was important to gain. We may be sure that Wilkinson was the chief of the elect. By the spring of 1789 he was ready to accompany a consignment to New Orleans. Warehouses that held the crops of the past three or four years were emptied to make up the cargoes of the twenty-five boats in his flotilla. The expedition flew the flag of Kentucky, and to withstand Indian attacks every boat was armed with swivels and some of them with threepounders. Altogether there were about 150 men in the fleet.[30]

This sudden stimulus to business made Wilkinson the hero of the West, and scores of merchants and planters, from the Redstone country down to Kentucky, flocked to him for permits to enable them to transport their goods to New Orleans. Daniel Clark, the younger, wrote of Wilkinson that "for some time all the trade of the Ohio was carried on in his name, a line from him sufficing to insure to the owner of the boat every privilege and protection he could desire."[31]

Wilkinson's shipments continued during the next two years, and he did everything in his power to keep the good will of the Spanish officials. In 1791 he formed a secret partnership with Hugh McIlvain, a merchant of Lexington, in which the latter was to perform the business and the former was to take the risks. Wilkinson's letter of instruction to McIlvain is illuminating. The merchant was to set out with five boats, making it an object to arrive in New Orleans before a certain Mr. Winters. At New Madrid he was to get into a canoe with two hands and, ordering the boats to go on, show his invoice and register to the commandant, make him a present, beg his pardon for hurrying, and push on. At Natchez he was to put on his "best Bib and Tucker" and wait upon the commandant with his papers, explain that he had come to settle, and request the oath of allegiance. This done, he was to make the commandant a present and request a certificate of citizenship and a passport to New Orleans. At that city a sergeant would perhaps lead him to the governor, as this was customary, and he was to inform that official that he had come to Louisiana to settle and that he had brought along some tobacco and would be happy to furnish the royal magazine, if a supply should be wanted. To the governor's inquiries concerning Kentucky he was to say nothing not flattering to Louisiana; he was to say that "the ignorant and low class of people with a very few reputable characters, such as Marshall [,] Scott, & Muter [*pet enemies of Wilkinson*], are hostile to Spain, but that the judicious, Intelligent men of the Country, know the importance of supporting an amicable intercourse;— consider me the head of those Characters, and pay me any other Compliments you may think I deserve."[32]

But Wilkinson's ventures were not uniformly successful, and what profits he did make were eaten up by his outrageously high standard of living. Finally he re-entered the army and withdrew from trade, except perhaps for an occasional venture. He may have been the worst scoundrel of American history, yet this fact should not blind posterity to the importance of his position in the history of western commerce. To him goes the credit for bringing about the loosening of Spanish restrictions on commerce and immigration. This less rigorous policy was never wholly abandoned, even though the American trader sometimes had to depend upon bribery and subterfuge to win his way to New Orleans. From this time on, western trade down river continued to expand, and the West, now that it had an outlet for its products, began to grow faster than ever. Tobacco, for a while at least, brought $9.50 a hundredweight instead of $2.00, and for a time 1,500 to 2,000 hogsheads were exported annually from Kentucky alone. Flour shipments increased to as much as 1,500 barrels a year, and the price rose from about $2.50 a barrel to $7.00 and even higher. Wheat rose to five shillings, corn to two shillings. In western Pennsylvania food prices were said to have risen 60 per cent by the spring of 1790, and dozens of boats were going down river to trade. No doubt with increased prices there was also a proportionate increase in the price of land. Two corollaries of Wilkinson's enterprise might be mentioned here. The Spanish dollar and warehouse receipts began to displace the regime of barter and paved the way for a banking system. Not least important, the partial satisfaction of the western demand for a trade outlet helped to quiet any secession sentiment that may have been aroused in the West. Wilkinson surely must have foreseen this result, but it is not certain that Miró realized for some time the trap into which the perfidious American had led him.[33]

The mainspring that impelled the Spanish to utilize Wilkinson lay in their fear of American aggression. Attempts to hinder it by Indian raids had resulted only in gaining the ill will of the frontiersmen. In Philadelphia, the Spanish minister, Diego de Gardoqui, had proposed the encouragement of American immigration to Spanish territory, perhaps on the principle of using fire to fight fire. Miró and Navarro, spurred on by Wilkinson's first memorial, adopted the same plan; they were apparently blind to what would seem the obvious fact that the oath of allegiance could not turn the lawless, independent American frontiersman into a docile beast of burden.[34] Nevertheless, the Spanish government, evidently as a result of Wilkinson's memorial, decided to try the policy of encouraging immigration at the same time that it allowed Miró to grant special commercial privileges. Free grants of land were given. Slaves, stock, household utensils, and provisions for two years were allowed to be brought in without duty. Immigrants were given the preference in selling tobacco to the royal stores. Freedom of worship in private was to be allowed, though Irish Catholic priests were to be imported to spread their religion among the immigrants. As a result of these actions there was a considerable influx of settlers. George Morgan, reappearing for the third time in western history, founded under Gardoqui's patronage the town of New Madrid opposite the mouth of the Ohio, but he soon abandoned it, perhaps because of the opposition of Miró, whose mind Wilkinson had poisoned against the project. New Madrid, however, remained and soon became the principal commercial town of upper Louisiana and a port of entry.[85]

With the promulgation of the new immigration laws, American traders found new ways of obtaining entrance to Louisiana with their goods. The taking of the oath of allegiance was a common method of gaining admittance and avoiding the payment of duties, though it probably did not fool the Spanish officials. Other methods were to petition the governor for a grant of land or to swear that the cargo belonged to a Spanish citizen. With the growing complaisance of the Spanish government, additional American agents settled in New Orleans and re-established the maritime trade with Philadelphia that had been interrupted after the Revolution. Exportation of specie was forbidden except on certain conditions, but much of it was smuggled out with the connivance of the customs officials. In spite of their growing leniency, Spanish officials did not view with complete equanimity the expansion of the Americans and even went so far as to encourage the erection of native-owned flour mills in Louisiana and to cut by 90 per cent the government purchases of tobacco. Spanish paternalism, moreover, did not agree with the Americans, who regretted the loss of their privileges to speculate in lands and to run their local governments.[86]

An incident indicative of possibilities was claimed, on uncertain authority, to have occurred at Natchez in the winter of 1788–89. A certain Colonel Armstrong of the Cumberland country, with six boats and thirty men, landed there with a quantity of provisions, and the commandant, in need of supplies for the garrison offered to buy them. His price was too low to suit Colonel Armstrong, who would have gone on to New Orleans but was refused a passport. He therefore found purchasers among the settlers in Natchez and was starting homeward with his men when the commandant sent fifty soldiers to arrest him. Natchez, according to American claims, was in United States territory, and Armstrong refused to be arrested by the Spanish. The upshot was a skirmish in which the Americans used rifles and tomahawks freely and drove off the Spanish with the loss of five killed and twelve wounded. Armstrong and his party escaped, but the settlers of Natchez seem to have paid the penalty in subjection to petty persecutions.[37]

American trade, however, continued to increase. In 1791, John Pope made a voyage from Pittsburgh to New Orleans, and in his journal can be read the signs of the times. In spite of hostile Indians on both shores, numbers of boats were passing down river. The one in which he traveled was called the "Smoke House" and had on board one Irishman, one German, one Kentuckian, one man born at sea, one Virginian, and one Welshman. On St. Patrick's Day the Irishman purloined all the brandy, sugar, and eggs on board and made a tub of eggnog, of which he drank so copiously that while at the helm he steered the vessel into an eddy so strong that it took the crew the rest of the day to get it out. Near the Arkansas River the party was hailed by a Pennsylvanian and a boy transporting buffalo meat to a settlement of thirty families, apparently Americans. Boats laden with flour and tobacco passed by, one of which, belonging to a Mr. Craig, had lost its rudder and sprung a leak. The crew implored the aid of the "Smoke House," but it was denied "through prudential motives." On March 21 the party "decried a Keel bottom'd Boat with a square Sail" bound up river for New Madrid and making two and a half miles an hour without the aid of oars. Soon afterward another keelboat passed, and about sunset three more of Mr. Craig's tobacco boats caught up with the "Smoke House." The next day at sunrise the crew hailed a boat of General Wilkinson's, under the command of Captain Swaine. At eight o'clock there were "six Sail of the Line" in view.

Above Natchez, Pope found a Spanish fleet consisting of the governor's barge, an armed schooner laden with military stores, and two provision boats. He went aboard the barge and found Governor Gayoso to be a gentleman of majestic deportment, with "Manners the most engaging and polite," who regaled him with nuts and wine. At Natchez he was entertained by the Spanish officials and their ladies with fruits, wines, and Parmesan cheese, and with such an absence of the characteristic Spanish austerity and reserve that he was fain to dub his hosts true "Castilians." On leaving Natchez, the "Smoke House" discovered the wreck of one of Mr. Craig's tobacco boats. A great quantity of provisions had gone down with the tobacco, but the boatmen "appeared to bear his [*Mr. Craig's*] Loss with great Composure and Christian Fortitude." Between Natchez and New Orleans, Pope passed a number of American settlements, another row galley, boat yards, and clouds of "Musquettoes." The significance of his account lies in the signs he saw of American penetration. It is no wonder that the Spaniards were beginning to see the handwriting on the wall.[38]

Northern traffic grew during the closing years of the century as various Philadelphia merchants began to establish connections with the Ohio and Mississippi commerce. Among these was the Gratz family, which traded extensively with Kentucky and certain members of which settled in that state. The firm of Reed and Forde was at the same time opening up a flour and fur trade between Pittsburgh and the West. Guy Bryan was also stocking Peter Maynard and William Morrison with trade goods, and the latter were bringing an annual cargo of furs from the West. Tarascon, Berthoud and Company came from Philadelphia in 1802 and established a mercantile and shipbuilding business in Pittsburgh. Cargoes were carried in twelve-oared barges employing French crews, and these barges were said to have waited at Pittsburgh during the eight weeks that it took to exchange goods with Philadelphia. James O'Hara of Pittsburgh included a trade with St. Louis among his many ventures. From the other end of the Ohio, the well-known François Vigo was dealing with Pittsburgh, and there is a record of three of his boats ascending to that city at once.[39]

The various expeditions against the Indians during the last decade of the eighteenth century greatly increased the amount of traffic on the Ohio, since the river was the only feasible transportation route. Practically everything brought from the East for the use of the army came through Pittsburgh. From February to June, 1793, Major Isaac Craig, the deputy quartermaster general, forwarded to Wayne's expedition 104 flatboats laden with provisions, horses, and equipment, in addition to goods sent by other craft. It is not without interest that a hospital boat was operated in connection with the army, though nothing beyond the bare mention of it survives. There was also an express boat for carrying dispatches. Wilkinson, who by now was the commander in chief, apparently traveled in state, for about 1795 or 1796 he came up the Ohio in a barge propelled by poles, cordelle, and oars, and with twenty-five or thirty men in the crew. H. M. Brackenridge, a mere lad at the time, remembered the splendor of the furniture, the elegance of the ladies' dresses, and the general's band of musicians.[40]

Pinckney's negotiations with Spain obtained for the Americans by treaty a right they had so far enjoyed only by sufferance. The navigation of the river was to be free, and for three years New Orleans was to be a "place of deposit" from which Americans could transship their goods free of duty. The treaty of 1795 was granted, however, only because Spain, busy in Europe, feared to rouse the fiery frontiersmen. The disillusioned Governor Carondelet had foreseen that such an agreement would be fatal; a year earlier he had prophesied a revolution in Spanish-America unless "this prestigious and restless population" was prevented from reaching the Mississippi. Already it was too late to prevent this revolution. Immigrants were pouring over the mountains and making their way down the Ohio and Tennessee in spite of hordes of opposing savages. Blockhouses were giving way to villages, and villages were becoming towns. A feeling of hopelessness began to pervade Spanish officialdom as it saw the relentless advance of the American frontier.

Though the treaty had opened the Mississippi, hatred and jealousy still led to various petty persecutions of American navigators. A Spanish commander could and sometimes did seize a cargo of provisions and deliberately set his own price. This happened to a western Pennsylvanian named McCluny, who had three hundred or more barrels of flour seized at Walnut Hills, now Vicksburg, and was paid about three dollars a barrel below the market price. Soon afterward an Englishman named Francis Baily sold some of his surplus goods to a Spanish officer and was tendered certificates that passed at 12 per cent discount. An appeal to Gayoso was fruitless—

that dignitary insisted that Baily must accept the certificates. Needless to say, Baily's description of Gayoso is not as flattering as Pope's. The Englishman braved the Spaniard's anger and appealed his case to Carondelet at New Orleans, but the delay was so lengthy that he finally gave up and proceeded on his travels.[41]

The American menace was not the only one that filled the nights of conscientious Spanish officials with bad dreams. In 1796, General Collot, the French governor of Guadeloupe, who had been captured by the British and released on parole in Philadelphia, was sent by the French minister on a secret mission to report on the defense of Louisiana. While he was at St. Louis some hotheads took it for granted that because he was a Frenchman he was a revolutionary agent, and they developed an acute case of sympathetic sans-culottism. When Collot came down river, Governor Carondelet had him arrested. The governor then proceeded to organize the expedition that, in the annals of the West, has made 1796 *l'année des galères*. Don Carlos Howard, an Irishman in the service of Spain, was sent with two galleys, two galiots, and a gunboat to overcome the St. Louis malcontents and jail their leaders. At the same time he was to prepare to resist a threatened British invasion from the north and to clear the British traders from the upper Mississippi.[42] This fear of British invasion was the result of rumor, but it was accentuated by Britain's tendency to follow trade with troops. The Scotch merchants of Canada had pushed their trade out to the Mississippi and were encroaching upon the Missouri in spite of the fact that the transportation of Indian goods from Quebec cost about three times that from New Orleans. At that time the annual value of furs and peltries drawn from the region of the upper Mississippi was around two hundred thousand dollars, of which about 27 per cent was profit. Howard's expedition could not and did not have any decisive results. The British remained in the business and became competitors of the Americans when the latter entered the region.[43]

In 1798, after years of dawdling upon one pretext and another, the Spanish evacuated the country above Baton Rouge, and Natchez came under the American flag. A customs post was established at Loftus' Heights and several armed vessels were stationed there. The closing years of Spanish control in Louisiana brought no moderation in the kaleidoscope of annoyances to which Americans had submitted for years, but in spite of the hindrances and prohibitions, American trade increased by leaps and bounds—threefold in 1801, according to one observer. An American consular agent in New Orleans reported in August, 1801, that between 350 and 400 boats had come down river within the last year. It is stated that in 1801 produce to the value of $3,649,322 arrived at New Orleans. Suddenly, late in 1802, the country was startled by the news that the Spanish governor had withdrawn the right of deposit. A wave of indignation swept the country, and the westerners were in favor of settling the problem for all time by marching on New Orleans. James Madison showed sympathy for their plight when he wrote that the Mississippi was "to them everything. It is the Hudson, the Delaware, the Potomac, and all the navigable rivers of the Atlantic States, formed into one stream."[44] Fortunately the order was rescinded and the right of deposit restored. The incident, however, had brought home to the administration the importance of a free outlet for western commerce.

By the secret Treaty of San Ildefonso in 1800, Napoleon had forced Spain to cede Louisiana to him. He had hoped to make it the nucleus of a new colonial empire, but the defeat of his armies in Haiti, as well as approaching European complications, caused him to abandon the project. Though France had not assumed control of Louisiana, the terms of the Treaty of San Ildefonso had become known, and the United States now attempted to purchase New Orleans as an outlet for American commerce. Napoleon casually offered to sell the entire territory, and the United States eagerly snatched at the opportunity. The Louisiana Purchase definitely removed the last hindrance from the westerners' free use of the Mississippi. With that happy condition assured, the great day of the boatman dawned.

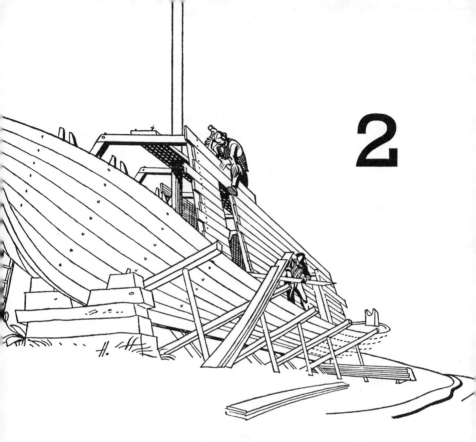

2

Boats
& Boat Building

WHEN Thomas Hart Benton and Governor William Clark
of the Missouri Territory undertook about 1820 to estimate
the extent of the "boatable waters" in the Mississippi Valley
they arrived at a grand total of fifty thousand miles. "Of
course," admitted Benton in later years, "we counted all the
infant streams on which a flat, a keel, or a bateau could be
floated."[1] However exaggerated this interpretation of navigable waters might seem to the modern steamboatman with

his clamor for a nine-foot level, it certainly was valid in the reckoning of his great-grandfather, who boasted that he could float his steamboat on a heavy dew and who had served his apprenticeship by pushing a keel against a stubborn western current. There is scarcely a willow-fringed stream flowing through the quiet meadows or sleepy inland towns of the present but might, if one could translate its murmur, relate tales of the days when the fall and spring rains made it a byway of commerce.

The necessity of providing transportation on shallow water led to the development in the West of an amazing variety of watercraft, most of them modeled in whole or in part upon those boats already in use in Europe and eastern America. The most primitive craft was the bullboat, used most commonly on the Missouri and on the other plains rivers where timber was scarce or unsuitable, and found to some extent on the Ohio and its tributaries. A framework of red willow withes was made in the shape of either a canoe or a bowl about seven feet in diameter; over this was stretched wet buffalo hide, with the hair inside, and the edges were lashed to the gunwales. The hide was pitched with a mixture of tallow and ashes—an operation that had to be repeated daily. The boat was propelled by poles or paddles constructed of a stick and a buffalo's shoulder blade, if no suitable wood was handy. A water-logged bullboat leaked rapidly and sat so low in the water that its carrying capacity was much reduced, so that it became the custom for voyagers to prop their boat over them at night like a tent to allow the wind to dry it or if that system was not efficacious they dried it by a fire. The awkward, circular type of bullboat was capable of carrying a heavy load, a third of a ton or more, though it might drift downstream as much as a mile in crossing a river; and the canoe-like boat, perhaps thirty feet long by twelve feet wide and with a two-foot draft, carried about three tons of furs or trade goods. The use of bullboats persisted among the pioneers, and, clumsy and frail as they were, these craft sometimes performed voyages of thousands of miles and not infrequently appeared in St. Louis after floating from the foot of the Rocky Mountains.[2]

In the North the necessity of frequent portages kept the birch-bark canoe in common use for at least two centuries after the coming of the white man. It was occasionally portaged from Lake Erie or the Genesee River to the headwaters of the Ohio, and on the latter river the Indians sometimes constructed canoes of elm bark. On the Ohio and Mississippi rivers the dugout canoe, or pirogue,[3] was more familiar. It was hollowed by fire or adz, usually from the sycamore, cypress, or cottonwood tree, and had one or both ends squared. Sometimes it was made from two logs, each formed to serve as a side. Its capacity could be increased by inserting planks between the two halves and spiking them in place, or by binding the planks with thongs and filling the interstices with clay or rosin. Another variation was a catamaran-like structure with a platform laid upon two pirogues, thus providing two covered cargo boxes in addition to the platform space. These dugouts were of all sizes. Some of the larger adaptations were fifty or more feet long and five feet in beam, and were able to hold thirty men and forty or fifty tons of freight. They were steered by a stern oar and propelled by poles, oars, or sails. Since portages were less frequent in the South than in the North, the weight of the pirogue was no great drawback so long as there was not a swift current to stem.[4]

Rafting was one of the important industries of the West; rafts of timber were being floated from the lower Mississippi to New Orleans before the Revolution. After the settlement of the West began, it became profitable to float logs down from the upper Monongahela and Allegheny rivers to be cut into boards, staves, or shingles at the end of the voyage. The rafts were often an acre in extent and were loaded with lumber, shingles, and laths.[5] Sometimes an immigrant family would buy a raft on which to float themselves and their goods down river, and then sell it at a profit at their destination.

Bateau was a word often applied indiscriminately to many sorts of floating craft, so that it is sometimes difficult to distinguish just what type of boat a writer had in mind. In general, however, the bateau seems to have been a keelless, flat-bottomed boat with ends tapering to points, built of plank, and usually lighter and more mobile than a pirogue. The smaller bateaux were sometimes called skiffs, and this name was also applied occasionally to the larger bateaux, usually with the prefix "Allegheny" or "Mackinaw," which probably had little to do with the origin of the particular boat named. Bateaux were propelled by oars, setting poles, or square sails, and were steered with an oar or a rudder. This type of boat could carry burdens up to about forty tons and sometimes employed eighteen or twenty rowers. It was often equipped with an awning or a wooden shelter cabin built in the rear for the accommodation of the crew or the stowage of goods. The great day of the bateau was between the French and Indian War and approximately 1790. The boats that were built by the firm of Baynton, Wharton, and Morgan in 1767 were probably all of this type. In 1784 Crèvecœur described the boats built in Pittsburgh as carrying fifty to seventy tons and having bottoms a little rounded, but without keels. Thirty bateaux built during the Revolution were described as being forty feet long, nine feet wide, and thirty-two inches deep.[6]

Some person unknown, at an indeterminate time before 1800, nailed a long beam about four inches square lengthwise to the bottom of a bateau to hold the boat on its course when

River scene showing flatboats and two keelboats.

it was being towed and to absorb the shock of contact with rocks and logs. The craft resulting from this experiment were obviously handicapped by greater weight and draft, but they remained in use for years. Unfortunately for the sake of clarity, these craft and all their mongrel derivatives were called keelboats. This fact has made it impossible to know whether the word, when used, referred to boats with an external keel or a built-in keel, unless the writer was kind enough to specify; when he did, it is interesting to note that with very few exceptions the keelboats mentioned were those with built-in keels. Because of this confusion, the opinion has persisted in some quarters that the western keelboat was a heavy, almost unmanageable vessel, with flat bottom bearing one or two skids, or "keels," and with vertical sides, square stern, rounded bow, and no sign of rake at any place. Obviously, such a craft would be little better than a flatboat for upstream work; and if there ever were such monstrosities—and there may have been—they never could have been very common. On the other hand, there is abundant proof that the keelboat was a light, well-modeled craft.

It was probably soon after the Revolution that keelboats came into general use on the Ohio. They were divided into two classes—keelboats proper, and barges—and the distinction was often blurred by the indiscriminate use of the names for either or both classes. The distinguishing and common characteristic was that they were built on keels with ribs and covered with plank. It would be futile to draw an exact line between the two types, but in general one can accept the keelboat as a long, narrow boat of light draft intended for shallow waters, and the barge as much wider and heavier, drawing more water, and therefore intended for the deep waters of the Mississippi and the lower Ohio.

The ordinary keelboat was forty to eighty feet long and

from seven to ten feet in beam, had a shallow keel, and was sharp at both ends. It drew about two feet of water when loaded. The middle part of the boat might be left open, but usually it was covered in whole or in part by a cabin or a cargo box that had an inside clearance of about six feet. Here the goods were stored and here the passengers found shelter. All around the gunwales ran a cleated footway, twelve to eighteen inches wide, where the crew walked when poling the boat. At the bow were seats for the rowers, four to twelve in number, who sometimes received assistance from a square sail. The sail, however, was useless except on comparatively broad waters, so that many keelboats carried none. Steering was done by means of a long oar pivoted at the stern and extending ten or twelve feet beyond the boat. The steersman, who was usually the boat's captain, or patroon, as he was called in the West, stood upon the roof of the cabin or upon a block made of a length of log upended and with notches cut in the side to enable him to mount. The keelboat's burden ranged between fifteen and fifty tons, but was usually less than thirty. The burden was not always rated by tons, and on the upper Allegheny, keels were sometimes spoken of as carrying sixty or one hundred barrels of salt.[7]

Barges were a great deal wider than keelboats, probably varying between twelve and twenty feet. Their length ordinarily did not greatly exceed that of the smaller craft, but in the later years certain river giants approached one hundred and twenty feet. Their draft was about three or four feet. There was always a mast, often two, and the barges were fitted with square sails or rigged as schooners or hermaphrodite brigs. Steering was done by means of a rudder. A barge always had a cabin though it might be only a small one in the stern, and like the cabin of an ocean vessel it was fitted with portholes and casements with sliding shutters.

Sometimes there was a deck in the prow with a sort of fore-castle under it to shelter the crew at night. With this size and equipment, barges were not inferior to many of the ships then engaged in ocean trade. When the cabin did not occupy the waist, the goods disposed there were protected from the elements by "tarpaulin or painted sail cloth stretched on stanchions." Here the rowers had their seats unless the waist was taken up by the cabin, in which case they sat in the prow. Here also was the iron grate for cooking, and here the game shot during the voyage was hung. As on the keelboat, a cleated footway ran around the gunwales. The boat was directed by the captain or by the helmsman, who, being stationed on the roof of the cabin, could see far ahead. A barge employed from fifteen to fifty men, depending on its size, and it could be brought downstream with less than half the men necessary to take it up. Probably a great majority of the barges were small, with a burden of around forty tons, but there were in use, especially during the later years, a number with capacities ranging up to one hundred and seventy tons, and even larger. In New Orleans capacity was oftener than not figured in barrels, and a number of advertisements mention boats capable of holding from two hundred and fifty to five hundred barrels. On the basis of two hundred pounds of flour to the barrel, these boats would have held twenty-five to fifty tons.[8]

The barges in use on the Missouri had to contend with more mud and sand than those on the Ohio and the Mississippi and so were narrower and had lower gunwales and flatter bottoms. The oars were short so that the boats could run close to shore and take advantage of the countercurrents on their way upstream. These barges were armed with swivels for defense against the Indians, just as the Mississippi and Ohio boats were armed previous to 1795.[9] They were usually called keel-boats, but there is little doubt that they were, save in draft, more like the Mississippi barges than the keelboats used on the Ohio and its tributaries.

By far the greater part of the downstream transportation in the West was in flatboats. These craft, though they might vary slightly in construction, were essentially alike whether they were called Kentucky or New Orleans boats for their intended destination; broadhorns for their wide-bladed sweeps; or arks for a fancied resemblance to the craft of the first mariner.[10]

Zadok Cramer described the boats intended for the Mississippi as being necessarily "much stronger in their timbers, and more firmly built than those for the Ohio only.—They ought also to be caulked better, and much higher all around, better roofed, and have a longer and stronger cable." Major Isaac Craig's contracts provided that Kentucky boats should be covered from twelve feet to one-third of their length; Orleans boats were covered for the full length. The flatboat was certainly in use on the Ohio by 1780 and no doubt much sooner, and as a means of transportation it retained its importance until it reached its peak in 1846–47. Thereafter it steadily declined until the War between the States practically put an end to its use.

Flatboats varied in length between twenty and one hundred feet and in width between twelve and twenty feet. Government flatboats in the 1790's were, on the average, twelve or fourteen feet wide and forty-five or fifty feet in length. These figures seem to have held good in later years for the general run of flatboats. Boats fifteen feet wide were used for the transportation of horses, since the horses could be tethered in two rows across the width. Burden, of course, varied with size, and was often expressed in barrels rather than tons. The average flat probably held between four and five hundred barrels, or forty to fifty tons.[11]

THE KEELBOAT AGE

The best building material was oak, but cheaper boats were built of other woods, especially pine. The wood was seldom seasoned, both because of the expense and because the short life of the boats hardly made such treatment worth while. Boats were constructed without iron; wooden pins or tree nails, preferably of white oak, held them together. This practice was cheaper, but it made the boats likelier to collapse under shock. The flatboat was built on sills or gunwales of heavy timbers about six inches thick and was strengthened by sleepers. The gunwales were a foot or two high, and on top of them were mortised studs, perhaps three inches thick and four to six inches wide. At the top of these studs were fastened the rafters that were to bear the roof. The planks of the floor were about two inches thick, but the siding boards were of ordinary thickness. The bow was raked forward so that it would offer less resistance to the water. The roof, the eaves of which were about six feet above the bottom of the boat, might be gable-shaped or rounded and might cover all the boat or only the rear portion, according to the fancy of the owner. The calking was tow or any other substance that would answer the purpose.[12]

Steering was done by means of a thirty or forty-foot oar, made by fastening a board to the end of a long pole. The oar was pivoted in a forked stick fastened to the roof or to a porthole in the rear. Two or more sweeps, or broadhorns, similarly pivoted on the sides, were used to keep the boat in the current. The crew of an average flatboat consisted of two men for each broadhorn, and a steersman. Curiously enough, though travelers rarely speak of the use of sails, a number of illustrations drawn by artists of the day show flatboats equipped with sails. A pump was a necessity for the careful boatman, so that in case of leakage he could prevent the hold flooding until there was an opportunity to make repairs or to beach his craft. Some flats were equipped with brick fire-places and chimneys. Others used boxes filled with sand or kettles as "cabouses" in which to keep their fires. On November 2, 1800, William Henry Harrison gave Major Isaac Craig at Pittsburgh a receipt for "one Kentucky boat forty five feet long, fitted up with three rooms, two chimneys, two windows (of six lights each) a Necessary, a tarred cloth over the cover of two rooms, being old tents, together with Oars, Pump, and Cable 20 lb., also one Batteau and one Tent."[13]

Since a flatboat could not be brought back up river it had to be disposed of at the journey's end. As long as it was above New Orleans there was always a chance that it might be sold to someone with a cargo to transport. If no buyer was found, it might be cast adrift, or taken apart by the immigrant and used to build a shelter or saved up for fuel. It is claimed that forty or fifty flatboats were used in the construction of Fort Washington at Cincinnati. The demand for sawed timber in the growing towns of the North was matched by that in New Orleans. Houses in that city were built of flatboat sills and planks, and some of these were exhibited there until quite recent times. In the suburb of Marigny, flatboat planks were used to make sidewalks. The custom of breaking up flats opposite the more thickly inhabited parts of the city caused considerable complaint because of "the disagreeable smells" and because the water carriers had to get their water from places contaminated by these smells. In 1807 the council decreed that the breaking up must be done at certain places farther up or down the river. At some times there were so many flatboats available that they could not be sold, and so were cast loose and allowed to drift down the river. But Emerson Gould mentions that in 1861 the cutting off of commerce with the North raised the price of second-hand flatboats to two hundred dollars.[14]

The Mackinaw boat in use on the Missouri was an adaptation of the flatboat and of the Mackinaw skiff, and was made of cottonwood planks about two inches thick. It was fifty or sixty feet in length and twelve in beam, was pointed and raked at the ends, and had a flat bottom. The gunwales were three feet high amidship and somewhat higher at the ends and were supported by knees. A roofless cargo box was built in the middle, and after the furs were loaded, the whole was covered with tightly stretched buffalo hides. The crew usually consisted of five men, and since the boat was only a downstream craft there was nothing to do but keep it in the current. Mackinaw boats usually traveled in companies for mutual protection, but single boats sometimes plied the river.[15]

English boatbuilding on the western waters must have begun some time before the French and Indian War, for George Croghan possessed a fleet of bateaux in 1754. In May, 1760, Jehu Eyre, a shipwright of Philadelphia, was sent west by the government with sixteen helpers and spent some months building bateaux at Pittsburgh and on Lake Erie. In the winter of 1762–63, when General Amherst planned to send four hundred men to seize the French forts in the West, three shipwrights were sent to Fort Pitt to build twenty bateaux. In addition they repaired some old boats found there, so that, though the projected expedition was abandoned, the English had twenty-three bateaux at their disposal.

When Baynton, Wharton, and Morgan entered the Illinois trade, their agent, John Jennings, arrived at Fort Pitt in January, 1766, to arrange for boats. The ones that he used may have been bought from the army or from local craftsmen, for on the day of Jennings' departure for the Illinois, another agent, Joseph Dobson, wrote the firm that "your Carpenters are hear Butt has not done much yett they have one on the Stocks and are making Ready for a Nother two I believe will Be Done in about two Weeks." Contracts made with boatwrights and sawyers in April and June provided eleven pounds (Pennsylvania currency) a month for the first type of workman, and eight pounds for the latter. In August the firm wrote its Pittsburgh representative that it planned to send the boats to Illinois later than announced, but this was to be kept secret from the carpenters, for "if once the Carpenters had Knowledge thereof, they would Slacken their work immediately . . . . Don't spare a few gallons rum extraordinary at proper times, to effect this great work for us." The boats finally developed by the company's builders were about forty feet long, five deep, and twelve in beam, and were built of "Seasoned Stuff with Square Sterns & no lap or clinch Work but close square Seams." Sailcloth covers were also provided. It was no easy task to undertake the building of bateaux on the western waters. Not only the carpenters, but also the tools and any iron parts used in the construction, had to be sent from the East. Then, too, distance from headquarters encouraged carelessness in the workmen. George Morgan complained from the Illinois country that "Meldrum, the carpenter, has done great Injustice to Every Boat he has built." Disputes between workmen and quarrels over jurisdiction further complicated business.

The various expeditions sent out and projected during the Revolution and the necessity of provisioning and garrisoning the river forts stimulated boatbuilding. When in May, 1776, Morgan arrived in Pittsburgh as Indian agent, the boat yards began to increase their activities. In February of the following year, fourteen boat carpenters and sawyers arrived from Philadelphia and were employed at a sawmill fourteen miles up the Monongahela. Their efforts resulted in the construction of thirty bateaux. During the next spring, six more bateaux, to serve as gunboats, were begun. The builders were provisioned from the army stores and boarded in the home of a local trader. Before the end of the Revolution, boatbuilding activities had extended up the Monongahela, and it is probable that some of Clark's boats for his Kaskaskia expedition were built at Redstone.[16]

During the flatboat period that succeeded the Revolution, there was scarcely a creek in the Ohio Valley that could be made boatable by the rains that did not at one time or another have some sort of boat built on its banks. Fugitive glimpses remain to us of the neighborhood gatherings at the loadings, of the merrymaking, and of the jokes on the green hands. There were, however, certain recognized boatbuilding centers. On the upper waters, Brownsville (Redstone) and Pittsburgh were the most important. The *Pittsburgh Gazette* from the time of its establishment bore advertisements of boat yards scattered along the Monongahela as far as Brownsville; there were several at Pittsburgh itself, or across the river from it; another was at the mouth of Turtle Creek; and the Youghiogheny River had a number of them. Colonel John May on May 4, 1788, recorded the raising at Elizabeth of a large shed for building boats. The business thus begun by Stephen Bayard, a Revolutionary officer, formed the nucleus of a town that was destined to become a great boatbuilding center in the steamboat era and one of the chief rivals of Jeffersonville, Indiana. By the turn of the century, Brownsville was making one hundred boats annually for the immigrant business. It is said that at Pittsburgh in the early 1800's there were boats built each year to the total value of twelve thousand dollars. At the same time the Allegheny River began to furnish boats, which, coming laden to Pittsburgh, could be sold to immigrants at reduced prices. References to boat yards farther down river are numerous. Beaver Creek, Wheeling, Gallipolis, Marietta, Charleston, Maysville, Cincinnati, and Louisville were important centers. Wilkinson's activities stimulated boatbuilding along the Kentucky River, and there survives an interesting contract by which William Pope and Hugh Ross agreed to build for him a number of boats.[17]

In the 1790's Major Isaac Craig was paying $3.00 apiece for canoes to be used as tenders, and proportionately higher prices according to the size of the boats. Bateaux cost $1.00 a foot. Flatboats twelve feet wide cost about $1.00 a foot, and those fourteen feet wide, up to $1.50 a foot. These prices nearly always included one steering and four rowing oars, and the prices for boats that were covered the full length ran slightly higher than those for boats covered one-third of the length. Sometimes interior fittings for granaries were included, as well as pump and cable; separately, pumps cost $1.00 to $1.50. At the same time, Craig was paying $2.66⅔ a foot in Pittsburgh for most of the keelboats and barges he bought. General Collot in 1796 found these boats selling farther up the Monongahela at $1.50 a foot, and he warned that boats should be bought there, as the Pittsburgh prices were exorbitant. Christian Schultz, about 1808, found canoes selling at $1.00 to $3.00 each, pirogues at $5.00 to $20, skiffs at $5.00 to $10, and bateaux at $20 to $50. Barges he listed at $4.00 to $5.00 per foot and keelboats at $2.50 to $3.00 per foot. John Melish, another accurate observer, recorded that in 1811 keelboats cost $2.50 to $3.00 a foot. The foregoing estimates probably did not include equipment or cargo boxes and must have applied to small craft intended chiefly for the upper waters. At the other extreme is the statement of a writer in the *Palladium* (Frankfort, Kentucky) of September 29, 1804, who estimated that a thirty-ton barge would cost $3,000 and would take $200 a year to keep in repair. The price was probably absurdly high, as Schultz stated that the rigged boats of Marietta cost $50 per ton.

THE KEELBOAT AGE

The price of flatboats all during the keelboat age can be placed definitely as between $1.00 and $1.50 a foot, depending somewhat upon the width desired and upon the equipment. This price would make an average flatboat of fourteen by fifty feet cost about $75. The cable, pump, and fireplace would come to about $10 more. In general, the price was lower at the beginning of the period and higher toward the end. Ship carpenters' wages were usually between $20 and $26 a month for the men working under Craig for the government in the 1790's, but the men working on the gunboats, "President Adams" and "Senator Ross," in 1798 received $1.50 a day. The principal shipwright was paid $50 a month, plus $12 for superintending the workmen.[18]

Boatbuilders were not always honest and careful in constructing and calking their boats. Cramer in his *Navigator* warned immigrants and traders that they must exercise the greatest care in purchasing; if possible, they should be accompanied by persons familiar with boats, who could detect rotten planks and defective calking. Three-quarters of the accidents, he said, were the result of building with knotty, rotten plank and of using tender wood just above the gunwales. The custom of calking only as high as the gunwale joint was dangerous, and Cramer advised travelers to take along a few pounds of oakum, a mallet, and a calking iron. Cramer himself gave an instance of defective workmanship, and the tale was amusingly paraphrased by a St. Louis newspaper:

In the fall of 1807 a certain Mr. Winchester's boat struck a rock a few miles below Pittsburgh and sank, and several thousand dollars' worth of merchandise was ruined or damaged. The proprietor, blaming the patroon for carelessness, brought suit before Justice Richardson of Pittsburgh, who incidentally had gained through sad experience considerable knowledge about Kentucky boats. The defendant, with two witnesses, went to the scene of the accident and after a great deal of trouble procured a section of the plank that had broken on the rock and let the water into the boat. On the day of the trial he presented the plank as evidence, at the same time observing, "Your Honor will see that it was my misfortune to have been placed in charge of one of these damned Kentucky boats." His honor received the plank and found that it was thoroughly rotten and defective. After being satisfied that it was really from the part of the boat that had failed to withstand the shock of collision, Justice Richardson delivered his opinion: "This court had the misfortune once to place a valuable cargo on a Kentucky boat, not knowing it to be such; which sank and went down in seventeen feet of water, this court verily believed, by coming in contact with the head of a yellow-bellied catfish, there being no snag, rock, or other obstruction near her at the time; and this court, being satisfied of the premises in this cause, doth order that the same be dismissed at plaintiff's costs, to have included therein the expenses of the defendant in going to and returning from the wreck, for the purpose of obtaining such damnable and irrefutable evidence as this bottom plank has furnished."[19]

3

The
Art of Navigation

JOHN RANDOLPH once described the Ohio River as frozen up during one half of the year and dried up during the other half. The gentleman exaggerated, we must hasten to add; nonetheless, his epigram epitomized the difficulties of navigation. The Mississippi presented many of the same dangers as the Ohio, only that they were heightened by the more rapid current and greater volume of water. For the convenience of immigrants and traders, the printers of the Ohio Valley early began the publication of guides to the rivers. The first one of which there is any record was the *Ohio Navigator,* by author or authors unknown, but published by Hunter and Beaumont at Frankfort, Kentucky. The date of publication was March 26, 1798, as shown by an advertisement of the book in the *Washington* (Kentucky) *Mirror* of March 31. A second edition was advertised in the initial number of the *Palladium* on August 9, 1798. This pilot book could not have been very large, for it sold for only twenty-five cents, but it endeavored to give a description of the Ohio in low water and in flood, with directions for its navigation. It claimed that the information given was drawn from "the Journals of Gentlemen of Observation who have frequently navigated it."[1]

The "Blunt" of the western waters, as Christian Schultz put it, was the *Navigator,* colloquially called the "Pittsburgh Navigator," first published in Pittsburgh in 1801 by Zadok Cramer. Cramer was a New Jersey Quaker by birth and was reared in Washington County, Pennsylvania. In 1800, at the age of twenty-seven, he set up in Pittsburgh as a bookbinder and publisher at the "Sign of the Franklin Head." His interests were diverse. He ran a bookstore, a circulating library, and a paper mill; he collected rags for paper and skins for binding; and he published almanacs as well as other books. In 1811 Cramer was in Natchez seeking to cure his consumption and was talking of establishing a warehouse and commission store. There he issued the *Louisiana and Mississippi Almanack for 1813,* another edition of which was issued a year later from New Orleans. He died at Pensacola on August 1, 1813, but his publishing interests were continued in Pittsburgh by his partners and his wife.[2]

The earliest surviving edition of Cramer's pilot book is that of 1802, a small octavo pamphlet bound in coarse paper covers and containing about forty pages; it retailed for twenty-five cents and was called the *Ohio and Mississippi Navigator*. (According to an advertisement in the *Tree of Liberty*, the *Navigation of the Mississippi* was to follow in a few days and was to sell for fifty cents.) The preface, dated in February, states that there had been two previous editions, both confined to the navigation of the Ohio and both sold in very short order. It is a question whether Cramer had any first-hand knowledge of the river at that time; the title page states plainly that the directions were taken "from the Journals of Gentlemen of observation, and now minutely corrected by several persons who have navigated those rivers for fifteen and twenty years." By the time of the issuance of the fifth edition in 1806, the title was established as the *Navigator*, and maps and miscellaneous advice and information were being added. The selling price was one dollar. The *Navigator* ran through twelve editions, the last appearing in 1824. Successive editions of the work contained additional material until by 1814 it had become an olla-podrida not only of navigating directions but also of information and accounts of explorations.[3]

The *Navigator* in its later editions was complete in its advice to the immigrant and trader, even giving them directions as to their purchase of a boat lest they have a defective one foisted on them. The best seasons for descending the Ohio were stated to be in the spring, from the breaking up of the ice about the middle of February to some time in May or June, and in the autumn through October and November. The best places for embarkation were named as Brownsville, Pittsburgh, and Wheeling, depending upon the stages of the rivers. The voyager was warned to load his boat evenly so that it would draw an equal depth of water all around, for when one corner was lower than the rest, that corner in case

THE

NAVIGATOR:

CONTAINING DIRECTIONS FOR NAVIGATING

THE

| MONONGAHELA, | OHIO, AND |
| ALLEGHANY, | MISSISSIPPI |

RIVERS;

WITH AN AMPLE ACCOUNT
OF THESE MUCH ADMIRED WATERS,

FROM THE

HEAD OF THE FORMER TO THE MOUTH OF THE LATTER;

AND A CONCISE DESCRIPTION

OF THEIR

TOWNS, VILLAGES, HARBOURS, SETTLEMENTS, &c.

———•◦•———

WITH ACCURATE MAPS OF THE OHIO AND MISSISSIPPI.

———•✧•———

TO WHICH IS ADDED

An Appendix,

CONTAINING

AN ACCOUNT OF LOUISIANA,

AND OF

THE MISSOURI AND COLUMBIA RIVERS,

AS DISCOVERED BY THE VOYAGE UNDER
CAPTAINS LEWIS AND CLARK.

———•◦•———

SIXTH EDITION—IMPROVED AND ENLARGED,

PITTSBURGH,

PUBLISHED BY ZADOK CRAMER AND SOLD AT HIS
BOOKSTORE, MARKET-STREET.

[PRICE ONE DOLLAR.]

———•◦•———

FROM THE PRESS OF CRAMER & SPEAR......1808.

Title page of *The Navigator*. From a copy in the
Darlington Memorial Library, University of Pittsburgh.

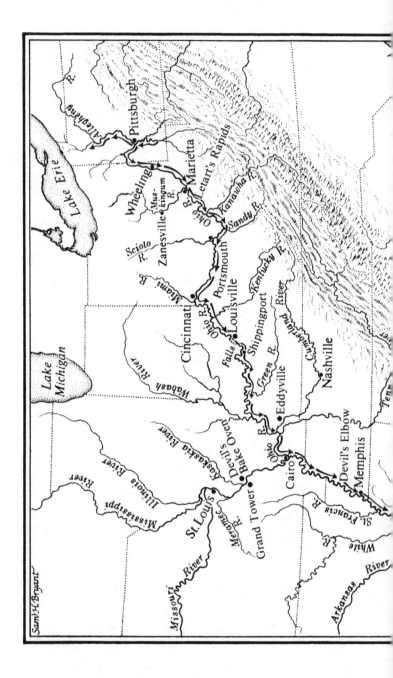

MAP OF WESTERN RIVERS

0 25 50   100   200 Miles

0   50 100   200 Kilometers

Gulf of Mexico

Mississippi River

Red R.

Natchez

New Orleans

THE JUNCTION OF THE OHIO AND MISSISIPI.

MAP I.

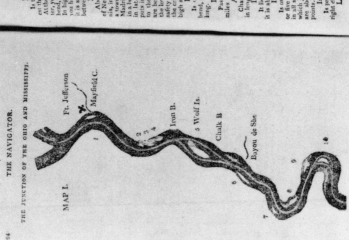

Ft. Jefferson
Mayfield C.
Iron B.
5 Wolf Is.
Chalk B
Bayou de She

Island No. 10, three miles below No. 9,
Is tolerably large, about one mile long, and lies nearer the left shore, the river turns short to the right.
At the head of No. 10, is an ugly sand bar in this water, you must hug the left shore pretty close around the
bend, keeping both the bar and the island to your right.
In high water, the right pass may be gone, providing
you hug the right hand shore, keeping off the island;
it is something nearer than the left channel. The pass
between the bar and the island is extremely dangerous.

NEW MADRID, 12 miles below No. 10,
About 20 years ago Col. George Morgan, formerly
of New Jersey, now of Washington county, Pennsylvania, in company with several other gentlemen, laid out
a town here on a large scale, which they called New
Madrid. It contains but a few houses, and is situated
in a beautiful tract of land on the right bank of the river,
in lat. 36° 30' N. Just above New Madrid a creek
puts in, and to effect a landing here, you must keep
to the outer edge of the counter current until you
are below the mouth of the eddy you can make a landing with
safety and ease, and the nearer you land to the mouth of
the creek the better, for opposite the town the bank is
high and continually falling in.

Island No. 11,
Is on the right side, and close to the upper end of a
bend, channel is on the left shore, it is about 2 miles
long.

Island No. 12, about 2 miles below No. 11,
Pass this island on the right side, it is about two
miles long.

A sand bar below No. 12, about three miles,
Channel good on both sides, this bar is nearly a mile
in length.

Island No. 13, about 3 miles below the bar,
It lies near the left shore, channel on the right shore,
it is about three miles long.

Island No. 14, nearly one mile below No. 13,
Is on the right side, and on the left side of it are four
or five willow islands, take the left side of these islands
in all stages of the water; in very low water a sand-bar
which joins them makes its appearance; these islands
are about three miles long, with drift wood on their
points.

Island No. 15, better than 2 miles below 14,
Is pretty large, lies close to the left side, take the
right channel at all times; it is about three miles long.
Little Prairie, about 3 miles below No. 15,

6	57
	70
13	
	75
5	79
4	84
5	88
4	93
4	97
5	103
6	

of accident would fill quickly and the boat sink the sooner. When tying up for the night it was well to see that the entire boat was left afloat; otherwise a sudden fall in the river might ground one end and fill the boat with water. For the convenience of those who started on the headwaters, the *Navigator* opened with brief guides to the Monongahela River below Clarksburg and to the Allegheny River and French Creek below Waterford. Pittsburgh, of course, was given the most elaborate and laudatory description of any town, though the rest were by no means neglected.

Distances from place to place were taken from the head of one island or bar to the head of the next, "principally by the eye and running of the boat," and were not guaranteed to be correct. In the 1814 edition, Cramer gave the distance from Pittsburgh to the mouth of the Ohio as 1,132½ miles, though present-day government figures show 979 miles. From the mouth of the Ohio to New Orleans, he gave 1,009 miles, as against the present 973. If one were seeking an explanation of the discrepancy, it could be found in the frequent crossings necessary in following the channel in the days before dams, and to some extent in actual changes in the course of the river. The navigating directions were intended for low water. The channels were carefully pointed out with reference to local features. Ripples (or riffles), sand bars, snags, and rafts were located, and directions were given for avoiding them. Maps accompanied the text, with the channels, islands, tributaries, and towns appearing upon them. To make the directions clearer, Cramer numbered the islands; there were 98 in the Ohio, 68 from the mouth of the Illinois to the mouth of the Ohio, and 126 from the Ohio to New Orleans. As Melish remarked, the prosperity of the western waters seemed "to be an object of peculiar solicitude with the editors," who began early to branch out from the subject of navigation.

Here and there through the text were anecdotes of men and events, moral and religious observations, and descriptions of flora and fauna peculiar to the lower Mississippi; at the end, in all editions after the first few, were extracts from explorers' or travelers' accounts of Louisiana and the West.

It is apparent today that the *Navigator* was by no means omniscient, but its directions were universally recognized as more accurate than those of any other pilot books of that period, and in time of danger the traveler, instead of running to the oar, ran to the *Navigator*. Cramer earnestly endeavored to keep his information up-to-date—no mean task when one considers the penchant of the Mississippi and lower Ohio rivers to cut and build on their banks, to alter or remove islands, and even to change their channels. When the New Madrid earthquake of 1811 radically altered the configuration of the Mississippi, Cramer lost no time in publishing a report on the subject sent to him by a James Smith. Fortescue Cuming in 1807 speaks of proving Mr. Cramer's *Navigator* and of correcting it in a few places, but it must be remembered that this was one of the early editions. Twelve years later, however, Thomas Nuttall, just below the Canadian Reach of the Mississippi, was peering vainly through the fog for the dangers listed in the pilot book, the position of which he could not ascertain "by the vague trifling of the Navigator."[4]

There were a number of other pilot books, some of which ran through numerous editions. James M. Bradford's *Notes on the Navigation of the Mississippi* may have been an independent work and appears to have had only one edition.[5] Next to Cramer's book the *Western Pilot* of Samuel Cumings was the most important, and in some respects was more accurate; it was first published in Cincinnati in 1822 and ran through at least ten editions by 1854. Indeed, it might be suggested that Cumings' superior maps and greater accuracy were factors in the discontinuance of the *Navigator* just two years after the initiation of the *Pilot*. Cumings' text was far briefer and contained few of the interesting observations and descriptions that no doubt intrigued public interest in the *Navigator*. It did, however, give some information on marine insurance and barratry and even reprinted Morgan Neville's *The Last of the Boatmen*.

In the days of the French control of the western waters, upstream craft seem to have been propelled by oars and sails, though the boatmen must have used the towline at Grand Chain of the Mississippi and at the Falls of the Ohio. In later days, even the Americans admitted that the Creoles were the best oarsmen, though they considered a "Kentuck" best at the setting poles. Henry Ker described the typical western manner of rowing: the oars were drawn back "with such agility that they were scarcely perceptible, just admitting them to skim the surface, then sinking them deep in the water and raising themselves the boatmen bend the stubborn ash while the sweat streams down their cheeks. The exact time they keep in rowing is pleasing to a stranger."[6] Cramer did not rate bargemen very highly as sailors; he tells of a fine barge being upset during a gale at Natchez in 1813 because of improper management of the sails. Four men were drowned, and a valuable cargo was almost wholly lost. Ker stated that one or two sailors were usually taken in a crew to manage the sails, as the Kentuckians were awkward with them.

The hundreds of bends in the rivers made prolonged sailing difficult, but advantage was taken of every opportunity. On the Ohio, though the winds were variable, they blew most commonly from the south and southwest during the daytime, and by their aid a boat could ascend at the rate of two to five miles an hour. Sails also gave considerable help on the Mississippi. H. M. Brackenridge wrote that the voyage was rare during which there were not six or eight days of sailing, and on some of these the boat might make as many as thirty miles without any assistance from the crew.[7] In order to avoid the full force of the current, ascending boats kept close to shore in the shallower water. Below points of land, there was usually a returning current or eddy of which boatmen could take advantage and by means of which they could allow their boats to drift up the river without any effort other than keeping a sharp lookout for snags.

The usual method of propulsion "fernenst" the stream, as the boatmen called it, was by setting poles. They were used most frequently on the upper rivers, for the Mississippi was generally too deep, or its bottom too soft, for their effective operation. Setting poles were about twenty feet long, shod with iron at one end, and equipped with a button at the other. They were apparently introduced by Americans from the East, for there is no record of their previous use by the French. They were being used on the Ohio as early as 1755. In order to bring his whole weight upon the pole when pushing a heavy load, the boatman placed the button against a thick pad on his shoulder, then leaned forward and crept aft on his hands and toes the length of the gangway. As Schultz remarked when he first saw a keelboat on the Mohawk, the "sight of four men on each side of a boat creeping along on their hands and toes, apparently transfixed by a huge pole, is no small curiosity."[8]

There were several methods of using poles. One way, which was probably preferred, was for the men at a given order ("Stand to your poles!"), to range themselves in two files, one on each runway, facing the stern, with poles "tossed" ready for action. The captain or patroon was steersman if the boat was small, and he stood straddling the oar while he gave his orders. If the boat was a large barge, there was probably a special helmsman. One or two men called bowsmen or "bossemen" were stationed in the prow with poles, to look out for snags and other obstacles and to keep the boat off the shore. At the patroon's call of "Set poles!" the men would sink their poles to the bottom of the river, and at the call "Down on her!" would place the buttons against their shoulders, bend her down, and walk aft, pushing the boat upstream under them. When the front man reached the stern, the patroon called "Lift poles!" and the men turned and walked forward, trailing their poles in the water.

If the current was sluggish it was possible for the men to push the boat by setting and lifting their poles without moving from their places. Sometimes a file of men on the shore side used the setting poles while the rest of the crew rowed on the outside. Again, the whole crew might push on the same side, each man as he came aft lifting his pole and running around the cargo box to take his place forward at the rear of the line. Hence the term "running boards," or *passé avant*. At other times the men on one side pushed while those on the opposite side changed positions for a new "set." If the bank became steep and the bottom fell away, the men "tossed poles" and laid them aside, shipped the oars, and rowed across the river to find suitable bottom.

When a log lay in their course, the men plunged the spike ends of their poles into it and pushed the boat around it; this was called a "reverend set." The order to sheer off from such an obstacle was apparently "Throw your poles wide and brace off." In backing away, the steersman called "Set poles! Back her!" and the crew responded with a mighty heave. Ascending rapids by poling was a delicate operation. While the men in the stern held the boat steady, the two men toward the bow end at the command "Head two!" ran forward, set their poles, and held the boat; then at the command "Up behind!"

the others changed positions. The change of set might have to be made by pairs; thus never more than two men were absent at one time from their stations. In this way the boat was able to make headway slowly, a length at a time. A single man pushing at an angle to the current might swing the head of the boat across the stream and drive it upon a rock or a snag and perhaps sink it. Even if the vessel escaped destruction, the man who was responsible for such a mishap lost caste and was never trusted with the head pole, the place of honor. If the rapids were not very swift or dangerous, half the crew might be shifted at once.[9]

If the river was too deep on both sides for setting poles, the cordelle, or towline, was used, provided the shore was suitable. The cordelle was several hundred feet long, sometimes as much as a thousand. One end was fastened to the top of the mast and the other passed to the crew on shore. The bridle, a short rope lashed at one end to the bow and at the other end to a ring through which the cordelle passed, was used to keep the boat from swinging. The crew was expected to wade ashore, or, if the water was too deep, to swim, and one of them carried the end of the cordelle in his teeth. A suitable shore does not mean that the bargemen expected to find a smooth towpath. On the contrary, they were used to fighting their way through the brush and wading or swimming the estuaries that came in their way. Sometimes when the growth was insurmountable they would send a party ahead to clear the way with axes. When there was danger of Indian attacks they carried their guns strapped to their backs. Often the cordelle had to be extricated from snags or thrown over trees, and at the Cornice Rocks at the Grand Chain of the Mississippi between St. Louis and the Ohio, the men walked along the edge of a cliff a hundred feet or more above the water. On warm days this cliff was infested with snakes, and the

Reverend Timothy Flint tells of the cordelle men teasing their parson boss by kicking the snakes down upon the deck of his keelboat. An Irishman who had agreed to work his passage from New Orleans to St. Louis expressed his sentiments after a few miles at the cordelle in the words, "Faith, if it wasn't for the name of riding I'd about as soon walk."[10]

When the bottom of the river was too soft for poling and the shores on both sides were unsuitable for cordelling, resort was made to warping. Essentially this was cordelling reversed. Two skiffs were used in this operation, though it could be accomplished with one. A skiff would carry a cordelle upstream and fasten the end to a snag or a tree, and the men in the bow of the boat would draw the boat up by means of a capstan or windlass, or perhaps hand over hand, and thus haul the vessel forward. Meanwhile the second skiff was carrying another cordelle upstream. This was the most laborious of all the methods of propulsion used, and six miles of progress in a day was considered good.

The final method of propulsion was called bushwhacking and was most easily practiced when the river was high and the water flowing among the trees at the sides. Each man in turn, commencing at the bow, seized a branch and, holding to it, walked aft. When he reached the stern he loosed the branch, walked to the bow, and repeated the operation. A couple of oars or some poles were commonly kept plying on the river side.[11]

With the labor so great it is no wonder that keelboatmen were entitled to a rest every hour. In spite of the fact that keelboats often traveled in pairs in order to assist each other, progress was very slow. At no time was it so great but that a man might, under reasonable walking conditions, keep abreast on the shore. A day of warping, as we have seen, might result in a gain of six miles, and a day of sailing, in a gain of thirty. Fifteen miles was probably a fairly dependable average. It is perhaps better to calculate the speed of barges and keels by the time consumed in a complete voyage. The 1,950-mile voyage from New Orleans to Pittsburgh took four months or more, and the return took four to six weeks, depending on luck, skill, and the stages of the rivers. At that rate it was practically impossible for a barge to make two round trips a year, even when the winter was mild. The more usual voyage was between New Orleans and Louisville, about 1,350 miles. Six months were allowed for this round trip—three to four months upstream and four weeks downstream.[12]

The shortest time of which there is any record for the 1,500 miles between New Orleans and Cincinnati was that made by the barge "Cincinnati" in 1811: seventy-eight days. In 1815 another boat of that name ascended to Cincinnati in eighty-seven days. By 1816 barges were making two round trips a year from New Orleans to Cincinnati. In the summer of 1809 a barge of fifty tons ascended from New Orleans to Nashville, about 1,150 miles, in eighty-seven days.[13] From St. Louis to New Orleans, a little under 1,200 miles, it was claimed that the descent in time of flood had been made in ten days, though the same journey often took four to six weeks in low water. The difference came in the freedom from obstructions and the opportunity to use short cuts that flood time offered. The upward voyage was likely to take three or four months. Boat crews and owners probably took as much pride in the speed of their craft as did the men of the steamboat era. In 1813, according to the *Navigator,* a barge, by going day and night, descended the 1,100 miles from the falls to Natchez in fourteen days and five hours. "Nothing," the authority comments, "ought to induce such running but a case of life and death." The boat was the keel "Susan Amelia," and her trip was a standard of swiftness for many years.[14]

THE ART OF NAVIGATION

The flatboats, being solely downstream craft, did not have as many problems to meet as the keelboats and barges, and they often traveled at night. They commonly floated with the current, and the crews merely kept a sharp lookout for snags and bars; now and then a pull at the oars was taken to keep the boat in the current. If, however, a strong wind, carelessness, or inefficiency allowed a flat to drift into an eddy or toward an obstacle, the crew might have to labor for hours to escape the danger. Lashing two or more boats together was supposed to quicken their progress by offering a broader surface to the current, but the best explanation of the custom is probably found in the desire for protection against Indians and pirates and for companionship. Visiting and bargaining among crews could be carried on conveniently, and frolics and dances were held. Timothy Flint tells of traversing a fleet of eight boats at one time. On one the men were killing hogs; another was laden with apples, cider, nuts, and fruits; and a third was a dram shop.[15]

The speed of the flatboat was of course governed by that of the current, which depended upon the stage of the water. Floods on the Ohio sometimes reached the astonishing height of sixty feet, and rises of ten feet in a night were not uncommon. On the Ohio in low water, a boat's speed might be as little as a mile an hour, and in flood, perhaps five miles. Nuttall traveled eighty miles in twenty-four hours without labor in the December flood of 1818, and a John Bower spoke of going a hundred miles in the same time as nothing unusual. On the Mississippi the flood generally came in the first six months of the year; its height depended on the nature of the channel and the angle of descent. The current was ordinarily faster than that of the Ohio and varied with the stages of the water between April and July. According to the *Navigator,* the average length of time it took a flatboat to travel from Pittsburgh to New Orleans, a distance of 1,950 miles, was five or six weeks. From Louisville to New Orleans the journey took about a month.[16]

There are on record a number of instances of horses being used to turn paddle wheels to propel boats, and, if we can believe Timothy Flint, these contraptions were fairly common. Around 1819, General Henry Atkinson tried a paddle-wheel boat operated by man power and claimed to make eighteen to twenty-two miles a day as against eight to ten miles by the old methods. Some time later he had ten such boats in service or being equipped.[17]

It was the hardship of the riverman that he could rely on very few of his difficulties to remain constant. Those difficulties that came the nearest to proving exceptions to this rule were the chains and rapids formed at places where the rivers had broken across tiptilted strata of rock. There were such falls on nearly every navigable tributary of the Ohio, and the unskilled boatman who attempted them was likely to have the seams in his boat opened, if it escaped breaking in two. The best known on the upper Ohio was Letart's Rapids, and a permanent warping equipment was kept there to aid ascending boats. The Falls of the'Ohio at Louisville were occasioned by a great ledge of limestone extending across the river. Rapids would perhaps have been a better appellation than falls, since the fall of the water was about twenty-two feet in two miles, and the falls were therefore dangerous only in low water. There are records of voyagers having gone over them without realizing it. There were three channels or chutes. The main one, on the Indiana side, was called the Indian Chute and, though rapid, was smooth most of the way, but the rocks on either side were perilously close. The Middle Chute was passable at times; and the Kentucky Chute, on the southern side, was almost dry during part of the year. The latter two were sometimes used in high water.

In "taking the chute" in low water, it was best partially or wholly to unload a boat, and the pilot needed to exercise the utmost care and skill. In 1797 the Kentucky assembly provided for the appointment of a falls pilot, whose regular fee was two dollars and who was instructed to keep a record of the boats and cargoes that he took through the chute. Other pilots took up residence at Jeffersonville, Indiana, and drove a thriving business. From the first, however, the southern shore was favored for this purpose, in spite of the fact that flatboats that had anchored in Bear Grass Creek, on the southern side, had laboriously to cross the river and row half a mile upstream in order to enter the main chute. It is possible that the danger of Indian attacks started the custom of using Bear Grass Creek in preference to the better anchorages on the Indiana shore. At any rate, Louisville profited, and has ever since maintained its lead over New Albany and Jeffersonville.

In the low water the falls were at their grandest. The roar of the water among the rocks carried several hundred yards from the shore. James Hall, who as a young man traveled down the Ohio by keelboat, has left the record of his passage over the falls:

As you approach the head of the rapids, the mighty stream rolls on in a smooth unbroken sheet, increasing in velocity as you advance. The business of preparation creates a sense of impending danger; the pilot, stationed on the deck, assumes command; a firm and skillful helmsman guides the boat; the oars, strongly manned, are vigorously plied to give the vessel a momentum greater than that of the current, without which the helm would be inefficient. The utmost silence prevails among the crew; but the ear is stunned with the sound of rushing waters; and the sight of waves dashing and foaming and whirling among the rocks and eddies below is grand and fearful. The boat advances with inconceivable rapidity to the head of the channel—'takes the Chute'—and seems no longer manageable among the angry currents, whose foam dashes upon her deck, but in a few moments she emerges from their power, and rides again in serene waters.

The falls were by no means closed to vessels going upstream. Ever since the French days, it had been common to see bateaux, keels, and barges being hauled up by means of cables and the sheer strength of hardy crews of boatmen. It was even claimed that in high water boats had ascended under no other power than that of their sails. Nevertheless, there was danger in the process. In 1821, while the two-hundred-ton steamboat "Maysville" was being hauled up, its cable broke, and the boat swung around on the rocks and remained there until the next rise. The project of digging a canal was proposed in the very early days, and in 1804 a company was incorporated; but the work did not begin until 1826.[18]

The Grand Chain of the Mississippi was about thirty miles above the mouth of the Ohio and formed the first of a series of difficulties extending for thirty miles up the river. Here the river boiled against a rock jutting boldly from the Illinois shore and known from its shape as the Devil's Bake Oven; failing in its attack against this rock, the current flowed around its base and threw itself against another rock, the Grand Tower, on the opposite side. In this neighborhood were the Cornice Rocks, the Devil's Anvil, the Devil's Backbone, and the Devil's Tea Table, names that indicated, as one traveler suggested, "the divinity most religiously propitiated in these dangerous passes." Here the boatmen were obliged to land in order to cordelle their boats through the rapids, and in the early period the Indians lay in wait to massacre and rob them.[19]

"A Farmer," writing in the *Tree of Liberty* of Pittsburgh

on June 26, 1802, described some of the perils encountered by boatmen on the lesser streams. There had been an endeavor to improve channels by extending two ranges of stones downstream so that the current was forced through the middle. This was of some service to small craft in low water, but dangerous to large boats in flood times, as the ranges were con-

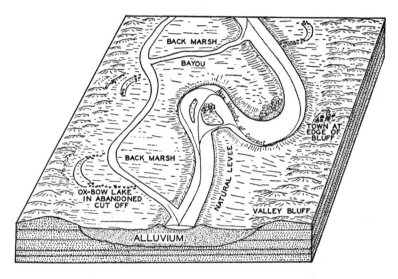

PHYSIOGRAPHY OF THE LOWER MISSISSIPPI

cealed. Wing dams inclining upstream to carry water to mills were even more dangerous. The law allowed them to extend only one-third of the way across, but they soon tended to reach the opposite shore.

The features of the rivers most continually shifting were the sand bars and islands—really the same thing in different stages of development. The breaking of the water over the bars and chains was known to the boatmen as ripples, or riffles, and the first hundred miles of the course of the Ohio were so full of them that immigrants and traders often preferred to trek across to Wheeling to begin their downward voyages. Barges of two hundred tons could make their way north only as far as Wheeling during low stages, and the rest of the journey to Pittsburgh had to be performed in keelboats, and then only with difficulty. If a bar was made up of sand alone, a rise in the water might disintegrate it, and the unwary traveler camping thereon might awaken to find his bed dissolving under him. Quicksand could be recognized by its luster and humidity under the hottest sun. The more permanent bar was formed by sand, gravel, clay, and driftwood collecting against an obstruction, such as a log or a ledge of rocks, and continuing to grow through the years. When the river was low, sand bars were a serious hindrance to navigation, and the guidebooks gave minute directions for avoiding them. Few voyagers, however, escaped the common fate of grounding, and the records of western travelers are full of these heartbreaking experiences. It was nothing unusual to ground several times a day and have to spend hours in working the boat off.

When a boat grounded, the rule was that all hands must jump overboard and help to push it off. No one was excepted. Captain Thomas Carter, who commanded the keelboat on which Louis Philippe and his brothers traveled, wrote that when the boat grounded on a bar a boatman would call to the royalty in the cabin, "You kings down there! Show yourselves, and help us three-spots pull off this bar"; and the "kings," be it said to their credit, responded without complaint.[20]

If pushing failed to dislodge a boat, the crew resorted to handspikes and tried to lever it gradually one way or the other. Sometimes it was possible to dig a channel and float the boat out, but this was often impracticable because of the driftwood and clay mixed with the sand and gravel. When all these efforts proved fruitless, the farmer whose services as a pilot might have been secured for fifty cents reaped a richer harvest by charging a dollar or two for dragging the boat off the bar with his horses or oxen. In case no team was to be found, the luckless voyagers might have to unload their boat on shore or into a lighter craft. Boatmen did not always escape with a delay of a few hours or even of two or three days. In December, 1790, a flour boat bound from Pittsburgh to the Illinois grounded in the Mississippi above the mouth of the Ohio, and before the crew could get it off, the water fell eighteen inches. A canoe was sent to New Madrid for helpers, who took over six days to traverse the forty miles to the boat, because of the ice and driftwood. Rollers were cut, and an unsuccessful attempt was made to roll the boat off the bar. Next, the crew tried slippery-elm poles, and after these were finally placed under the vessel, seven or eight hours of labor succeeded in getting it to the water. Eleven days had been lost, and in addition, nine extra men had been hired and boarded, and a pirogue rented, at a cost of more than ninety-nine pounds, Pennsylvania currency.[21]

In time, if the proper combination of circumstances ensued, a bar might become an island by the continued accumulation of sand, gravel, mud, and driftwood. Trees, usually willows, but sometimes sycamores and cottonwoods, would also spring up and give the ground some power of resisting current and flood. As the island continued to build upstream, its foot was being cut away, since the current, split above, united with considerable force below and gradually wore away the lower end. In this way an island would move upstream a considerable distance in a century, provided it was not swept away entirely by some freak of the river.[22]

It was common for the current to hollow out the bed of the river below the islands and form whirlpools or eddies, which offered difficult problems for the navigator. In fact, the luckless boatmen might spend several hours in making their way out of these eddies, which sometimes were as much as two miles in circumference. At the mouth of the Ohio the impact of the two currents rushing together made irregularities in the bottom and caused what were known as boils. Zadok Cramer spoke of having seen a boat shoot across the current before the surprised owner could call his men to the oars. Eddies sometimes proved disastrous. Timothy Flint told of his boat being caught in a basin-shaped eddy near one of the Chickasaw bluffs and whirled around so rapidly that the passengers became dizzy. A short time before, a barge had been broken in two by the strain, and his boat seemed about to share the same fate until a filling of the basin enabled the crew to get a rope ashore and pull themselves out of the suction. The best-known eddy on the Mississippi was at Grand Gulf. There the river threw itself upon a rocky bluff and, being repulsed, formed two whirlpools before it resumed its course at an acute angle to its former direction. If a boat missed the path between the two eddies and was drawn into one of them, it risked being thrust toward the rock at one side or toward the bank at the other side. If by hard work the craft won free of the vortex but came out on the upstream side, it would have the gantlet to run once more.[23]

To the boatmen the terrors of the whirlpools were not without their humorous side. The story was told of a Kentucky flatboatman who, drifting down the river at night, passed a house brilliantly illuminated, where a gay throng was dancing to the lilt of a plantation orchestra. Half an hour or so later, he passed another house where a similar scene was being enacted, and a while later another, and so on through the night. "Well," marveled the Kentuckian, "this is the beatenest country for frolicking I ever seed. The whole river is one universal jubilee." Came the dawn, and with it the flatboatman found that he had got into an eddy, had traveled around and around, and every half-hour had seen the same house.[24]

Bends were usually hard to negotiate either ascending or descending. The current as it reached the bend naturally endeavored to continue a straight course and struck the concave bank with a force sufficient to undermine it gradually, and this action caused the precipitation of masses of earth and groves of trees into the river. Deflected from the straight course, the current carried its sediment downstream and diagonally across the channel of the river, where side currents formed eddies and built up a point, first into a bar and then into rich bottom land. In these places the eddy had its uses. When not too violent, it was useful to the ascending boat, as has been shown. Furthermore, at some river towns, of which New Orleans and Natchez are examples, these countercurrents made attainment of the shore possible without danger of being carried too far downstream. In fact, some work and skill were necessary to keep a boat from being carried back up the river. Schultz was witness one evening to the attempt of a fleet of eleven flatboats to land in the eddy at Natchez. It proved too strong, and most of the boats were carried on up river, where they had to get into the channel and attempt the landing again. Soon afterward a long raft of lumber loaded with shingles attempted the landing but could not even get into the eddy. Ropes carried ashore by boats snapped like packthreads as soon as they were fastened. The raft was landed with great difficulty five miles below the city.[25]

When stopping for the night, it was best to choose the quiet stretches below points, because of their freedom from snags and falling banks. The boatmen's custom was to run their craft directly into the willows that lined the banks and, while clambering ashore, to hold the boat in place by seizing the branches. The wise boatman took care to push the boat well out into the water at night, for a sudden fall might leave one end ashore and so open the seams. At best, the boat would be stuck in the mud or, in cold weather, frozen in. The danger then was that a sudden rise would fail to dislodge it, and boat and cargo would be lost.

The boat bound downstream kept to the current in rounding a bend so that it might avoid both the bar and the snags on the point and the snags and falling banks in the curve. A traveler tells of having been driven against the logs and snags on the outside of a curve; one of the crew jumped out on the logs, put his shoulder to the boat, and pushed so hard that the blood flowed from his nose. Hardly were the boatmen out of this difficulty before they were caught in an eddy and swept around until they finally succeeded in getting into the main current and proceeding. For the ascending boat the rule was to stick as close as possible to the point, since the current was least strong there, and the bank on the farther side of the bend might be dangerous. The force of the current at the point, however, was far from negligible, and unless the bow was kept in the course, the boat would be swung about in spite of the oars. The point was also likely to offer a suitable cordelling path for the crew, or a firm bottom for the poles. Yet it was not unusual for the strength of the current to necessitate warping. Frequent crossings were made in order to take advantage of the most favorable current, bottom, or shore; and it was claimed that a barge would make as many as 390 crossings between New Orleans and St. Louis. This procedure, though necessary, was wasteful of distance gained, and a quarter of a mile might be lost each time.[26]

Since the current was constantly washing out the hollows of a bend, it was inevitable that sooner or later the neck of land would be washed away and the river would send a chute through by the short route. Sometimes this chute became a cutoff, and the main body of water flowed across there, leaving the point as an island; or perhaps the old bed of the river was forsaken entirely. These cutoffs were a source of danger while they were in process of formation, since no boat could be expected to obey the helm in the rushing waters. A similar danger was the crevasse, formed in time of high water when the river broke through a levee. The current rushing into bayous was also dangerous, and the *Navigator* warned boatmen that once in them they could scarcely hope to extricate themselves and therefore should endeavor to keep out in the river when near the entrance of a bayou. One of the phenomena connected with floods was the backing up of a tributary when it struck the swollen waters of the main river. It was said as well that a small river in freshet could drive back the waters of a larger confluent. The *Navigator* stated that in 1810, when the Ohio backed the water up the Muskingum, several New Orleans boats were drawn into it, and their pilots, being enveloped in a fog, did not learn their mistake until they were apprised of the fact by someone on shore.[27]

The caving in of banks and the precipitation of thousands of trees into the rivers led to the formation of several very serious obstacles. Floating logs and the loose, floating masses of debris known as "wooden islands" were dangerous, of course, but not as dangerous as the logs that became fixed in the river bottoms. The root end of a log, being the least buoyant, usually became fixed, and the free end, because of the action of the current, normally pointed a little downstream and lay in wait like a couched spear to impale the boat of the unwary voyager. These logs were known as planters. Sawyers were planters whose free ends were bobbed up and down by the force of the current. They usually made their sawlike motions at regular intervals. Some sawyers sprang up far enough so that they could be seen breaking the water, but the most dangerous, the so-called sleeping sawyers, never broke surface but might come up unexpectedly and stave in the bottom of a boat as it passed over. "Snag" was a term applied to both planters and sawyers, though by some travelers, snags seem to have been defined as planters infesting shoal water. They were called *chicots* by the French. There were stretches of the rivers that had especially bad reputations because of these obstructions. Nuttall tells of counting a hundred of them in the space of a minute and of hearing the water break upon them with a noise that could be heard distinctly for two miles. He mentions that not far from the same place a member of the crew was thrown into the river when a sawyer struck the boat. Fortunately the man was rescued, but the boat was left without the steering oar, which had remained entangled in the sawyer. Nuttall, as well as other travelers, speaks of the number of wrecked boats he saw every day, which, like the victims of the fabled vampire, became destroyers in turn.[28]

A traveler has left an account of what happened one dark rainy night when a keelboat struck a snag up river from New Orleans. There were twelve or fifteen passengers, one of them a woman. As soon as the boat struck, the passengers rushed on deck and ran about like mad people in the murky light of two or three lanterns. Five men from St. Louis dragged up their trunks and carpetbags and, seizing one of the yawls, leaped in with their baggage and pulled for the shore, which, by the flashes of lightning, could be seen thirty yards away. As they landed, the keelboat began to swing with a peculiar rocking motion. "You are all safe," cried the captain. "The boat is on a sand bar and can't sink." The boat had drifted to the bar after it had struck the snag. There the party remained that night in the cold rain, but the lot of the cowards who had abandoned them was even worse. Their boat had drifted away, and in spite of their pleas the captain refused to send for them until morning.[29]

The wooden islands, or rafts, often collected in the hollow sides of bends, where they were a continual peril to the clumsy flatboat and the unskillfully managed keel. N. M. Ludlow tells of his theatrical troupe drifting onto one of them in their keelboat and of the men having to perch the women and a baby on a log while they picked the raft apart. When they finally got loose, the men drifted two miles before they could get ashore and then discovered that they had left the oars of the skiff on the raft, so that they had to improvise new ones before they could ascend the river and rescue the women. In another episode, an Indiana flatboat had struck a log and was sinking; the patroon, struck by a happy thought, threw overboard an armful of quilts. The suction of the water drew them into the hole and closed it sufficiently to enable the crew to lighten the boat and fit in a new plank.[30]

One of the adventures of Davy Crockett had to do with the sinking of two flatboats that he had loaded with staves and with which he had started for New Orleans. The men of the crew, from Crockett down, were absolutely green and could not land their boats the first night out, and so decided to run on. Crockett was sitting in his cabin thinking how much better was bear hunting on hard land when, suddenly, somewhere near the Devil's Elbow—to tell the story in his inimitable way—

The hatchway into the cabin came slap down, right through the top of the boat; and it was the only way out except a small hole in the side, which we had used for putting our arms through to dip up water before we lashed the boats together. We were now floating sideways, and the boat I was in was the hindmost as we went. All at once I heard the hands begin to run over the top of the boat in great confusion, and pull with all their might; and the first thing I know'd after this we went broadside full tilt against the head of an island, where a large raft of drift timber had lodged. The nature of such a place would be, as everybody knows, to suck the boats down, and turn them right under this raft; and the uppermost boat would, of course, be sucked down and go under first. As soon as we struck, I bulged for my hatchway, as the boat was turning under sure enough. But when I got to it, the water was pouring through in a current as large as the hole would let it, and as strong as the weight of the river would force it. I found I couldn't get out here, for the boat was now turned down in such a way that it was steeper than a house-top. I now thought of the hole in the side, and made my way in a hurry for that. With difficulty I got to it, and when I got there, I found it was too small for me to get out by my own power, and I began to think I was in a worse box than ever. But I put my arms through and hollered as loud as I could roar, as the boat I was in hadn't yet quite filled with water up to my head, and the hands who were next to the raft, seeing my arms out, and hearing me holler, seized them, and began to pull. I told them I was sinking, and to pull my arms off, or force me through, for now I know'd well enough it was neck or nothing, come out or sink. By a violent effort they jerked me through; but I was in a pretty pickle when I got through. I had been sitting without any clothing over my shirt; this was torn off, and I was literally skin'd like a rabbit. . . . We all escaped on the raft, where we were compelled to set all night about a mile from land on either side.[31]

Rafts were numerous, and many small rivers at one time or another had their courses choked by them; but the greatest one in history was the Great Raft on the Red River. It was supposed to have begun to form about 1530, and in 1833 it was more than 150 miles in length and so solid in places that plants were flourishing on it and horsemen were using it for a bridge. Navigation, except by certain cutoffs, was almost impossible, and the raft delayed the settlement of the valley for years. It was finally dislodged by Captain Shreve, the pioneer steamboatman, who began the task in 1833.[32]

THE ART OF NAVIGATION

One of the most dreaded perils that confronted the boatman was storms. For days at a time the swell in the river set up by the wind compelled him to seek the protection of a sheltered shore line, where perhaps for hours he frantically bailed with one hand and held to the branch of a tree with the other. If he was caught in the path of a hurricane, as was Collot, and was torn loose from his moorings and driven across the river upon a sand bar, he could be thankful that his fate was no worse. Timothy Flint records that once during a storm he had to let his vessel be driven along as he helplessly watched two boats wreck and their hands go down and saw hundreds of barrels of flour and whiskey being swept into the water. The newspapers and correspondence of the West abound with accounts of storms and the damage they inflicted on shipping. A storm at New Orleans in June, 1805, destroyed and sank several flatboats in port, so that their cargoes floated out. The *Western Spy* saw in this incident "a solemn lesson to adventurers to store up their cargoes immediately on landing, and not trust them to the mercy of the river and weather." A year later four barges were sunk at the levee, including the important "Natchez Packet," which was crushed by a collision with a ship. In the great storm of August, 1812, half of the seventy sailing vessels in the harbor at New Orleans were completely destroyed, and all the flats, barges, and canoes were broken up or sunk. Dwellings, warehouses, and the market house were blown down in the general ruin. To make the confusion worse, that night had been chosen for a slave revolt, which happily proved abortive.[33]

The South may have had its hurricanes, but the North had its ice. The navigation of the Ohio was usually blocked for eight or ten weeks during the winter, and upon the breakup, the floating ice might reach as far as the Mississippi. The ever careful *Navigator* admitted that "of all the enemies we meet with on the Ohio, the ice is the most formidable and dangerous," but advised that the voyager could venture out "with some propriety," provided that the water was high, that there was an appearance of open weather, and that the cakes of ice were not heavy enough to impede or injure the boat. When bringing to for the night, the boatman should choose a sheltered place below a point—a better precaution than felling a tree above the boat, since the weight of the ice might bring the tree down upon the boat and crush it. John Heckewelder told of five boats with fifteen hundred bushels of corn that were crushed in the ice in December, 1792; and eleven years later, there were said to have been two hundred boats that passed the mouth of the Kentucky in the floating ice, some of them containing frozen corpses.[34]

The New Madrid earthquakes, so called because they centered around that town, though the shocks were felt as far away as Pennsylvania and South Carolina, were for months the terror of the boatmen. The first one occurred on the night of December 15, 1811. The bed of the Mississippi was shaken, and temporary rapids formed. Banks and trees were precipitated into the water. The bottoms of lakes were elevated, and lakes were created where there had been dry land. Two or three islands disappeared from the river. The bank on which New Madrid was built sank so low that the next flood covered it, and the town was practically abandoned. The shocks continued with varying intensity during the remainder of the winter and occurred at intervals for a number of years afterward. The number of boats lost can never be known, though an estimate made the following March placed it at forty or fifty. For some time the snags thrown up by the earthquakes were a serious peril, but in the end, the disturbance was supposed to have made navigation safer by loosening and removing those obstacles.[35]

THE ART OF NAVIGATION

The perils of navigation have been quaintly summarized in a quotation from a letter written by an old flatboat captain to his wife:

I think Jonas will have a second time to go down this river Before he learns not to scratch the Shore fifteen or twenty miles before he can get the boat Stopped and then to run night and day in the most eminent danger and the weather most excessive Cold—when the Boats will run above 100 miles in 24 hours and the nights so dark that the Shores Cannot be known from the water any other way than by throwing Stone or Coal out from the sides and hearing where they light—when his rest cannot exceed 4 hours out of 24, and all the rest be watching and fatigue—when running on an Island how to Carry his boat in the river again—when thrown on land by the ice his Oars run in the earth almost to the handle how to get her afloat again and how to run into a harbour for Safety and live in the boat when it is cold enough to freeze a dog to death—such with but few exceptions has been our Case since we embarked.[36]

In view of the almost negligible interest taken in improving the rivers during the keelboat era, it is no wonder that there were many losses. Estimates placed flatboat losses at one-fifth to one-fourth of the total built, though the risk implied in these figures seems great enough to preclude ventures. Insurance rates, as a matter of fact, usually ranged between 5 per cent and 10 per cent. Nevertheless, wrecks were numerous. A traveler arriving in Lexington in the early spring of 1802 stated that sixteen boats were lost between the mouth of the Ohio and New Orleans previous to his leaving Natchez on March 12. It will be remembered that this was at a time when Spanish pettiness was still hindering commerce, so that it had not yet reached a great volume. Nuttall recorded having seen every day the wrecks of flatboats drifted upon the shore. Timothy Flint, an indefatigable traveler, said that he did not remember having traversed the Mississippi on any considerable trip without having heard of some fatal disaster to a boat or having seen the red-shirted body of some boat-man floating in the muddy waters of what that hardy class of men called the "wicked river."[37]

4

The Boatmen

THERE were three classes of boatmen on the western waters: the regular bargemen and keelboatmen, whose only occupation was boating; the flatboatmen, who between voyages were farmers, merchants, or boatbuilders; and the men of the plains and mountains who divided their time between boating and trapping. Fine distinctions among them are impossible since the men often transferred their activities from one class to another. For example, when patroons were ready for the upriver voyage they sometimes filled out their crews with men who had come down on flatboats. Mike Fink, the most famous of the rivermen, began as an Indian fighter, spent his middle life as a keelboatmen, and died a trapper. Manuel Lisa and many others were merchants and traders as well as boatmen.

The group that came nearest to forming a distinct and continuous class was that of the bargemen and keelboatmen, or bargers and keelers, as they called themselves. Barges, since they were used mostly on the Mississippi, were usually manned by Creoles, or in the parlance of the frontier, Canadians or *engagés*. The keelboats of the Ohio generally had American crews; those of the Missouri were mixed, perhaps with Canadians most numerous. The Creole boatmen were natives of the river villages or of Canada, and most of them probably had an admixture of Indian or Negro blood. Inured to labor from infancy, they were an extremely hardy race; in spite of the almost superhuman exertions of their calling, they were happy, obedient, and contented, and seldom complained or deserted. Their Gallic light-heartedness and their faculty for making the best of a bad situation made them the usual choice of the trading companies, by whom they were listed under the general term of *engagés*. The older hands in continuous employment were known as winterers. Those employed in summer transportation between Montreal and the West were dubbed *mangeurs de lard,* or pork-eaters, by the others; their food consisted of salt pork, game, and corn meal or hominy boiled with a little tallow. When on the boats they often worked stripped to the waist, but at other times they wore fringed buckskin trousers, bright red shirts, and blue surtouts reaching almost to the knees. Rough caps, moccasins, and red woolen sashes completed the costumes.[1]

The American keelboatmen appeared as a distinct class

around the close of the Indian wars on the Ohio, and they retained their identity until improved roads and the railroads displaced the keelboat from its role as the means of transportation on the smaller streams. This period might be placed roughly at from 1795 to 1840. Keelboatmen were recruited from the wildest and toughest men on the frontier, at first largely Indian fighters. They were usually tall, gaunt, and big boned, like the western type, and walked with a long stride. More daring and restless than the Creole boatmen, they were also more vicious and bellicose. Like the Creoles, they often went shirtless in the summer and consequently were brown as Indians from head to waist. In cold weather and when in town, they dressed in buckskin or linsey-woolsey, and red shirts. Their coats were of heavy strouding or blanket cloth.[2]

The boatman's food was of the coarsest and plainest, based on the usual western staples of corn, potatoes, hardtack, and meat. The cooking was a matter of indifference. On the keelboat in which James Hall went down the Ohio, the cook was a slovenly Irish lad who was "a cobbler by trade, and a republican by profession" and whose culinary and hygienic shortcomings were balanced by a willing disposition. John Palmer observes that "luckily we found ourselves cooking by turns." When there was a cook on board, he was left in charge of the boat while the crew went on shore in search of diversion. No boat was considered fully equipped without a keg of whiskey on deck, and a drink of whiskey, or a "fillee," as it was called, was the reward of the crew after each arduous struggle with the current. Even on the keelboat of a missionary the men received "the usual compliment." With their whiskey the boatmen drank river water, first taking a cup of whiskey and then a cup of water. Mark Twain characterized river water as good for steamboating and good to drink, but worthless for all other purposes except baptizing. Even in the day of the bargemen a few fastidious individuals precipitated the mud by sprinkling the water with corn meal, but for most westerners that method removed the "pith." Evidently they agreed with the steamboat captain who informed the note-taking traveler that "the sand in the water scours out the bowels, and the more one drinks of it the healthier he gets."[3]

Wages differed with the circumstances of the voyage and the experience of the hands. In 1765 the oarsmen of a fourteen-oared bateau bound from New Orleans for the Illinois country received sixty Spanish dollars each; the patroon was paid double that amount. Two years later Baynton, Wharton, and Morgan claimed to be paying their bateau men a sum that amounted to about $11 a month. In 1794 Major Isaac Craig was paying $12 a month to boatmen working for the quartermaster service, with no distinction between flatboatmen and keelboatmen. The masters usually received $15 to $20, with the exception of one or two who received $30. A writer in the *Palladium* of September 29, 1804, estimated the annual wages of a barge captain at $300 and of a member of the crew at $240; a supercargo received $250 a year. Christian Schultz found in 1810 that boatmen on the Mississippi were receiving $25 to $40 a month and the patroon $60—sums that he did not consider unreasonable when he took into account the labor of the ascent. Food was always furnished in addition to wages, save for some exceptions in the Missouri fur trade, in which wages were about $120 to $150 a year, and *engagés* were supposed to undertake a great many labors in addition to boating. In 1789 James Wilkinson advertised that he would pay flatboatmen $35 for the trip from Kentucky to New Orleans, and in 1802 another advertiser offered $50 for the same trip. F. A. Michaux quoted the usual wage as $50 for the men and $100 for the captain for the voyage from Kentucky, which generally lasted about a month. Statistics thereafter are vague, but it is likely that the price remained constant until the War between the States. After steamboats had become common, the flatboatmen took passage up river in them and reduced the cost of the trip by helping to carry wood on board. A group of them would sometimes place all their money in a barrel and take turns in standing guard over it.[4]

American commerce on the rivers had scarcely begun before the necessity of finding some means of caring for sick and indigent boatmen became evident; for the transit from the bracing northern spring to the enervating heat of the southern summer produced considerable sickness. Hazardous to health, also, were the intemperance and debauchery that so often accompanied the boatman's voyage and stay in the South. If one may believe the testimony of a contemporary, the boatman's medicine chest contained only whiskey, salt, and pepper—not very efficient remedies for malaria. An eyewitness writing of conditions in 1802 said, "It is really pitiable to see such numbers of distressed objects, as sometimes present themselves to view, in the sickly months, who have been left to shift for themselves, after their employers have made their markets." In New Orleans the Spanish were willing to admit boatmen to the hospital for the poor, but facilities were limited, and, besides, Americans had a prejudice against Spanish doctors. Consequently, the sick lay in their ships or boats or in wretched cabins, in which they died miserably.

In 1802 Congress provided that rivermen should be regarded as seamen and should pay at Fort Adams a tax of twenty cents apiece for the use of marine hospitals. Thereafter arrangements were made for boatmen to be received in a private charity hospital at New Orleans; the government paid seventy-five cents a day for their maintenance and provided medical care. The receipts from taxation of rivermen during the early period were far less than the expenditures: the latter during the four years from 1817 through 1820 amounted to twenty-two thousand dollars, and the former amounted to only seventy-five hundred dollars.

In 1805 Natchez established a hospital for the relief of boatmen and paupers, but it apparently never received support from the marine-hospital fund. Attempts were made to secure the approval of Congress for a special levy on boats touching at Natchez, but they were unsuccessful. The hospital led a hand-to-mouth existence for seventeen years, maintaining its patients on thirty to forty cents a day. It was closed for lack of funds after the epidemic of 1819. When it was reopened the next year, it received, within eighteen months, 318 patients, of whom 51 died. Of the total number, 86 were of European nationalities. The citizens of Louisville in 1816, roused by the sad condition of boatmen and strangers taken ill in the city, and interested in removing the stigma of insalubrity that was often attached to the place, organized a boatmen's hospital and obtained its incorporation by the legislature the next year. The mortality among boatmen from disease continued to be very high. According to reports, it was common for two out of five of a flatboat crew to die, and sometimes the whole crew perished and left boat and cargo deserted. It was not until 1837 that Congress gave much attention to marine hospitals; then at one stroke it provided for establishments that were eventually built at New Orleans, Natchez, Napoleon, St. Louis, Paducah, Louisville, and Pittsburgh.[5]

A happier side of river life is reflected in an institution without which no boat's crew, American or French, seems to have been complete. That was the fiddler, whose ability to scrape a violin gave him certain privileges. James Hall describes one of these men, known to the keelboatmen as Pappy, though he was probably no more than fifty years of age. He was sallow and his hair was tinged with gray, yet his eyes had the fire, and his step the elasticity, of youth. His manner was kind and amicable, he spoke with a drawling accent, and there was always a smile and a jest on his lips. When he came on board he brought "Katy and his plunder"—the first his violin, and the last a few clothes tied up in a bandanna.

While others worked he would sit for hours scraping upon his violin, singing catches, or relating merry and marvelous tales. When he chose to labor he went to the oar . . . but whether at play or work he applied himself with all his heart. If the boat grounded on a sandbar, he was the first to plunge into the water; if a point was to be weathered, or a rapid to be passed, his was always the best oar; if a watch to be kept at night, who so wakeful as he? And on such occasions, he would fiddle and sing the live long night . . . . He kept our own crew in good humor, and hailed every boat we passed with some stroke of pleasantry. More than once he enacted chief musician at dances got up at the hovels along shore, near which we lay by for the night.

When a boat was tied to the shore, there was often dancing on deck, with a fiddle or two scraping an accompaniment. In the morning when the boatmen "set off" from the night's berth at the edge of an eddy, and a part of the crew was sufficient to get the boat under way, the remainder would work off their spirits to the tunes of the ever-present violin. During the day the fiddler amused the crew with his tales and music, and the men joined in singing while they kept time with their rowing. Snatches of boatmen's songs have been preserved, and they must have had a merry swing. It is easy to imagine the oars cutting the water of the reach while the men sang:

> Some rows up, but we rows down,
> All the way to Shawnee town,
> Pull away—pull away!

or to see them dragging a great barge against the swift current of the Mississippi while they panted the lugubrious lament:

> Oh! it's love was the 'casion of my downfall,
> I wish I hadn't never loved none at all!
> Oh! it's love was the 'casion of my miseree;
> Now I am bound, but once I was free.

When the boat had "headed to" and "fastened its bowlines" at night and the men had eaten their rations, they might take their dogs and go on a coon hunt. Otherwise they spent their time in gambling, drinking, or wrestling, or they gathered under the trees and spun yarns of amorous experiences in the cities and on the rivers, or tales of the plains and mountains of the West, where many of them had adventured among the cannibal Indians and the white bears. If they were feeling tuneful they might sing that keelboatman's classic with its swinging chorus:

> The boatman is a lucky man,
> No one can do as the boatman can,
> The boatmen dance and the boatmen sing,
> The boatman is up to everything.

> Hi-O, away we go,
> Floating down the river on the O-hi-o.

> When the boatman goes on shore,
> Look, old man, your sheep is gone,
> He steals your sheep and steals your shote,
> He puts 'em in a bag and totes 'em to the boat.

> When the boatman goes on shore
> He spends his money and works for more,
> I never saw a girl in all my life,
> But what she would be a boatman's wife.

THE BOATMEN

At night, when opportunity offered, a dance was often arranged at a settler's house, and the boatmen swung their disheveled partners and stamped a boisterous accompaniment to their fiddler's scraping.

> Dance, boatman, dance,
> Dance, dance, away;
> Dance all night till broad daylight,
> And go home with the gals in the morning.

Finally, when they had danced and sung themselves out or gambled away what was left from the last frolic, they spread out their blankets on the deck or the bank and, with a smudge to keep off the mosquitoes, slept until dawn. If it was raining they sandwiched themselves together on top of the lumpy cargo in the cabin.[6]

The French boatmen were great singers, far superior to the Americans. John Bradbury and H. M. Brackenridge, who were in the two boats that ran a famous race up the Missouri under Wilson P. Hunt and Manuel Lisa respectively, have described the way in which the arduous toil of those days was made lighter by song. The songs were usually responsive, the patroon leading with the first couplet and the crew joining in with the chorus. The words were frivolous but the tunes were agreeable, and the men were "kept from thinking too deeply" of their situation in a hostile country beyond the frontier "by their songs and the splashing of the oars which kept time with them." One of their songs ran:

> Dans mon chemin j'ai rencontré
> Trois cavalières bien montées,
> L'on, ton, laridon, danée
> L'on, ton, laridon, dai.

Trois cavalières bien montées,
L'une à cheval, l'autre à pied,
L'on, ton, laridon, danée
L'on, ton, laridon, dai.

"Lisa," says Brackenridge, "himself seized the helm and gave the song, and at the close of every stanza, made the woods ring with his shouts of encouragement. The whole was intermixed with short and pithy addresses to their fears, their hopes, or their ambition." Once, when Lisa's party received news of hostile Indians, "gloom overspread every countenance except that of Lisa, who seized the helm, made an encouraging speech, sent round the grog, and then raised the song."[7]

Every boat had its horn for use on foggy days or, for that matter, whenever any of the crew felt like blowing it "to scare off the devil and secure good luck." Time and again one comes across references to the mellow, enchanting notes of the boatman's horn. "The notes were all in a minor key, soft and weird, and when its source was unseen it seemed like the wail of a spirit." General William O. Butler wrote a poem, famous in its day, which deserves a wider audience in the twentieth century:

O, boatman! wind that horn again,
For never did the listening air,
Upon its lambent bosom bear
So wild, so soft, so sweet a strain!
What though thy notes are sad and few,
By every simple boatman blown,
Yet is each pulse to nature true,
And melody in every tone.[8]

Just as ocean sailors have their initiations at the equator, so did the rivermen hold initiations at the Grand Tower on the Mississippi and at the mouth of the Platte on the Missouri. Boatmen who were passing those places for the first time had to submit to being shaved or ducked if they were unwilling to "compromise the matter with a treat."[9]

The expeditions up the Missouri carried hunters, and the crews depended a great deal on the game they killed. Brackenridge in 1811 found the banks of the Missouri as replete with game as those of the Ohio had been thirty years before, and the river often bore on its surface the bodies of hundreds of buffalo drowned in crossing. General Collot describes an incident illustrative of western superstition. The boat's hunter had been bitten by a rattlesnake and had given himself up for lost when he suddenly bethought himself of the general's almanac. Upon consulting it he thought that he perceived favorable signs, and immediately his despair fell away. The wound was treated in the usual manner, and the hunter recovered perfectly.[10]

Next to the westerner's fighting, drinking, and spitting, his curiosity seems most to have engaged the interest of the traveler. No commander of a seventy-four, Timothy Flint asserted, was more "punctiliously greeted" with all kinds of questions than the crew of a flatboat or keelboat descending the Ohio. A classic illustration is found in an occurrence that took place above Limestone (Maysville) when one boat's crew hailed another:

"Where you from?"
"Redstone."
"What's your lading?"
"Millstones."
"Who's your captain?"
"Whetstone."
"Where're you bound?"
"Limestone."

THE KEELBOAT AGE

Mark Twain relates that in later years the flatboatmen in their skiffs would fight their way over a waste of water to his steamer. One of them, to test the good nature of the clerk, would draw near and shout, "Gimme a paper!" and the clerk would throw over a file of New Orleans newspapers. As the others drew near, he would heave over bundles of religious tracts tied to shingles. The result can be better imagined than described. Mark Twain mildly observes that the "amount of hard swearing which twelve packages of religious literature will command when impartially divided up among twelve raftsmen's crews, who have pulled a heavy skiff two miles on a hot day to get them, is simply incredible." People whose ears burned easily were wise to keep out of reach of the boatmen's shafts of wit. Timothy Flint, who traveled with his family and whose crew was called "Flint's civil boat's crew" because the men had agreed not to swear or to get drunk while in his service, confesses that he had often to smile at their whimsicality but oftener was disgusted by their obscenity.

Blackguarding was the boatman's lighter relaxation, and every passing boat or person within hearing on the shore became his target. The westerner of that day, however much one may deplore his lack of culture and cosmopolitan interests, yet was possessed of a vocabulary and a celerity of wit eminently suited to these tilts. The person who finally succeeded in silencing the other became the hero of the occasion, and the silenced party became the butt of his comrades' jokes. Flint tells of a vanquished boatman who became so exasperated that he leveled his rifle at his rival on shore. The latter sprang hastily for the shelter of a tree, and his terror was so plain and so ludicrous that the boatman burst into laughter and dropped his rifle with the exclamation that he had treed the game.[11]

THE KEEL-BOAT.

The Keelboat. From *The History of Travel in America* by Seymour Dunbar. Reprinted by permission of Bobbs-Merrill.

Travellers

The Helmsman

Sketches by Joshua Shaw. From *The History of Travel in America*
by Seymour Dunbar. Reprinted by permission of Bobbs-Merrill.

THE BOATMEN

Like all Americans of their time, the boatmen were given to using metaphors and picturesque expressions. The physical features of the rivers were called by appropriately descriptive names. A peculiarly shaped sand bar was dubbed General Hull's Left Leg; Paddy's Hen and Chickens were a group of islands composed of a large island and several small ones; a particularly bad turn in the Mississippi was called the Devil's Elbow; Muscle Shoals was said to have been so named because of the labor required to pass it.

When a bargee or keeler felt dry he tied his bowlines at "Nu Y'orlins" to realize his ideal of a hell-roaring time by going on a spree. Before a cat could wink its eye he had had galore of drinks, but instead of turnin' nigger he was a good old hoss and split everything with his friends and even skyed a copper to see who'd get his last chaw o' 'baccy; it'd shore be harder'n rowin' up Salt River to find a cleverer parcel o' fellers 'n them keelers. He never seed so many niggers in all his born days as they was there. "They was thicker'n black bugs in spiled bacon ham, and gamblers, thieves and pickpockets was skitin' about the street like weazels in a barnyard."[12] Mannee, it did beat all how that woman put on the fixin's. Made her look right smart, but she had no business acting so fofarrow for she was jist a yaller gal. She was makin' meat all right and doing it slicker'n greased lightnin'. The eyes she was makin' 'd bamboozle a dead Injun into thinkin' she was awful fond o' him but she was only waitin' her chance to lift that keeler's plunder. Might fetch a greenhorn or a flatter but it'd shore be harder nor climbin' a peeled saplin' heels uppard to count any coups on an old dyed-in-the-wool keeler. He'd throw his pole wide and brace off afore he run into a snag. Yes siree! All that and a long chalk more. When a boatman wandered off on his own hook in Injun country, though he was heap brave with plenty of grit and wasn't a bit skeered, he kept his eyes skinned. After all, them red devils mought come down on a feller quicker nor a alligator could chaw a puppy and rub him out deader'n a kilt nigger in a mud hole— to say nothin' o' raisin' his ha'r.

Boatmen's courtesy to their passengers was not always of the highest order. A traveler who missed a knife and accused the crew of taking it received a sarcastic offer to buy the fork. H. R. Schoolcraft tells of laying a valuable mineralogical specimen on the deck for a moment and returning to find it knocked to pieces. He expressed his disapproval of this action, whereupon a boatman remarked that there were more where this came from, and, stretching himself to the full extent of his six feet and displaying muscles tense and hard from the use of the setting pole, he added insolently, "Help yourself!" On the other hand, Timothy Flint found no reason to complain of the courtesy of his "civil boat's crew." E. P. Fordham, who worked with a crew of keelboatmen on a down-river voyage, did not paint them quite as black as did some others and even said that they were careful of their conversation in front of respectable women. "Give them your hand," he wrote, "accost them with a bold air,—taste their whiskey,—and you win their hearts. But a little too much reserve or haughtiness offends them instantly, and draws upon you torrents of abuse, if not a personal assault." Nevertheless, he advised travelers to go well armed and to be accompanied by a stanch, dependable friend. W. T. Harris, however, who descended the Ohio in the barge "Commodore McDonough," found that his captain, a New Englander, was so pious that on the Sabbath he shipped the oars and allowed the boat to drift with the stream.[18]

The reliability of the bargemen and keelboatmen was a moot subject. The desire for further business was an incentive toward honesty in conducting their cargoes, and it is thus probable that whatever their crimes, they retained a certain degree of trustworthiness. It is no doubt fair to assume, however, that there was a difference between the attitude of the harum-scarum crews and that of the more responsible captains. The captains were sometimes the owners of their boats or at least had an interest in them and thus would see to it that there was no pilfering of the cargo. There is, nevertheless, a well-authenticated account that the famous keeler, Mike Fink, and his crew were once detected broaching whiskey barrels that had been entrusted to their care. Brackenridge also relates that the captain of a keelboat on which he traveled refused to pay a boatman his wages and locked up the stock of provisions that the passengers had bought for themselves. His intention was to use the provisions in starting a store. When the owners protested, the captain "showed us his teeth and his pistols." The case was taken before a magistrate at New Madrid before the captain would give up the provisions and the wages. As for flatboats, there may have been many cargoes stolen, or destroyed through carelessness, but here again there is no way of checking the proportion. Schultz gave the Kentucky boatmen a high character for mutual helpfulness and told of the crews of eleven flatboats spending the best part of a day in helping two stranded boats to get afloat.[14]

Schoolcraft relates that some complaining boatmen were paid off during the struggle up the rapid current of the Mississippi above the mouth of the Ohio, and there is Cuming's statement that the French engagés never deserted their boats until their engagements were up; but the Americans frequently did. In the Missouri trade, where conditions were more arduous than on the Mississippi, H. M. Chittenden says that Creoles frequently deserted, though not as often as Americans, and would risk their lives through a thousand miles of hostile country to regain St. Louis. Brackenridge tells of a Creole crew complaining against their *bourgeois* or pa-troon, Lisa, as the result of their strenuous labors during the race with Hunt up the Missouri. Boatmen's contracts were enforceable in Kentucky, and sheriffs and constables were instructed to bring back absconding boatmen.[15]

Among the boatmen's amusements, shooting at a mark was a favorite, and the men could spend a week profitably between that sport and drinking and gambling, with perhaps a fight or two thrown in for variety. Their diversion par excel-lence was fighting, and on a frontier where there were thou-sands of men bubbling over with animal energy, they were bound to find plenty of opportunity. The boatman who wore in his cap the red feather of victory and boasted that he had never been whipped was bound to fight everyone who chal-lenged him. These challenges are, in retrospect, one of the ludicrous features of frontier life, though they were probably not so funny to the law-abiding citizen who had to listen to a "half-horse, half-alligator" boatman telling the world how good he was. A writer in Cist's *Miscellany* has preserved the challenge of one of these frontier berserks. It was on election day, and a crowd was milling about the courthouse when a "screamer from the Mob," about six feet, four inches, in height, sprang out and began his tirade:

This is *me,* and no mistake! Billy Earthquake, Esquire, commonly called Little Billy, all the way from Noth Fork of Muddy Run! I'm a small specimen, as you see—a ramote circumstance, a mere year-ling; but cuss me, if I ain't of the true 'imported breed,' and can whip any man in this section of country! Whoop! Won't *nobody* come out and fight me? Come out some of you and die decently, for I am *spileing* for a fight! I han't had one for more than a week, and if you don't come out, I'm fly blowed before sun-down, to a *certingty!* so come up to taw!

May be you don't know who Little Billy is? I'll tell you: I'm a poor man—its a fact—and smell like a wet dog; but I can't be run

over! I'm the identical individual that grinned a whole menagerie
out of countenance, and made the ribbed nose baboon hang down his
head and blush! W-h-o-o-p! I'm the chap too, that towed the
'Broadhorn' up Salt River, where the snags were so thick that a
fish couldn't swim without rubbing his scales off!—fact, and if any
body denies it, just let 'em make their will! Cock-a-doodle-doo!
Maybe you never heard of the time the horse kicked me and put
both his hips out of jint—if it ain't true, cut me up for cat fish bait!
W-h-o-o-p! I'm the very infant that refused its milk before its eyes
were open, and called for a bottle of old Rye! W-h-o-o-p! I'm that
little Cupid! Talk to me about grinning the bark off a tree!—'taint
nothing; one squint of mine at a Bull's heel would blister it! Cock-
a-doodle de-doo! O I'm one of your toughest sort—live for ever,
and then turn to a whiteoak post. Look at me, [said he, slapping his
hands on his thighs with the report of a pocket pistol,] I'm the
ginewine article—a *real double acting engine,* and I can out-run,
out-jump, out-swim, chaw more tobacco and spit less, and drink
more whiskey and keep soberer than any other man in these localities! Cock-a-doodle-doo!

After all this palaver, no one offered to fight, and "Little Billy"
walked off muttering that there wasn't a man there with
courage enough to collar a hen.[16]

Westerners were not averse to fighting with rifles or knives
or even with the terrible "devil's claws"—metal fingers that
were attached to the hand and that, when drawn across a
man's face, would maim him for life. The two commonest
choices, however, were to "fight fair" or to "fight rough and
tumble." The first was a fist fight, the second a bloody affray
in which the endeavor of each man was to maim and disfigure
the other by gouging out his eyes or by biting off his lips, nose,
or ears. John Melish records that in 1811 the laws of Kentucky
against the bloodier features of the rough-and-tumble fight
were being strictly executed and that stabbing was becoming
the practice. Boatmen's battles were closely supervised to
ensure adherence to the rules, and a cry of "enough" from one

of the combatants was the signal for the company to drag off the winning opponent. It is said that keelers and flatters felt for each other an antipathy that often resulted in fights, but that on these occasions a certain number of champions were chosen by each side and no one else interfered, even though the battle might be turning against his friends.

It was the custom to break each voyage at Natchez, at New Madrid or Shawneetown, and at Louisville or Shipping-port, and at each stop the crews had a holiday. When several keelboats' crews met at a town, a riot was usually the result. There were pitched battles between boatmen and townsmen, in which the former usually won, in the process breaking up the furniture in the taverns and amusing themselves by tearing down fences, outbuildings, and signs. Camp meetings and muster days were especially enjoyed by the boatmen, and many such meetings were turned into stampedes with the rivermen in close pursuit. Frequently, when their boat was tied up at a town, the boatmen amused themselves at night by sweeping the streets with a rope, tripping up whoever happened to be in the way. Archer B. Hulbert cites an instance of some flatboatmen who, wandering around Louisville one night, discovered two parties of Negroes engaged in a corn-husking race. The boatmen went to the river and filled their pockets with stones, then returned, divided themselves into two groups, and took stations in the dark whence they could harass the husking parties with stones. The victims, of course, blamed one another, and it was not long before the wily boatmen were viewing a satisfactorily rousing battle.[17]

By 1815 there were probably between two and three thousand men employed on the river barges and keelboats. It is no wonder that the soberer citizens began to fear that as transportation became more important, the increase in the number of the boatmen would seriously endanger the peace of the country. Fortunately the advent of the steamboat put an end to these rowdy days, but it was said that in the meantime only families of the roughest character dared to live within reach of the boatmen; the more respectable ones chose out-of-the-way locations or settled in the cities.[18] The reputation of the boatmen for rapine and bad manners was so widespread in Louisiana that, according to Cramer, it was next to impossible for a traveler to obtain a night's lodging at the formerly hospitable homes of the French planters. Referring to the boatman's retirement from his profession, Cramer wrote: "He sets himself down in some town or village as a wholesale merchant, druggist, or apothecary, practising physician, or lawyer, or something else that renders himself respectable in the eyes of his neighbors . . . nor is it by anyone known" that he laid the foundations of his fortune in the boating business. In the course of a printer's-ink battle in Natchez, the worst thing one contestant could say of the other was that he had been "detected in the purlieus of this city, drinking, dancing, and supping with *Boatmen,* blackguards, and Prostitutes."[19]

Natchez was one of the chief resorts of the rivermen. Here the descending flatter, since he considered the worst of his voyage over, felt that he could indulge in some dissipation, and on the journey home he had his last fling here before plunging into the wilderness. The town was divided into two parts: the upper town on the bluff was the orderly, respectable section where life and property were safe, and the lower part along the river bank, or "Natchez under the hill" as it was termed, was the resort of every known vice. Boatmen stopped under the hill because of inclination, propinquity of their boats, and lack of money to maintain themselves on the hill. In fact, during the Spanish days no boatmen were allowed above without special permits from the commandant.

As did the ocean sailors, the rivermen spent their money like water for the various pleasures of the flesh. Gambling was a passion with them, and perhaps this was one reason why some of them wore only trousers in the summer. In a community where nearly every building not a warehouse was given over to drinking, gambling, or prostitution, and where robbery or murder was an almost daily occurrence, there was not much room for law and religion. Schultz, however, mentions a case of a boatman being arrested and fined as a gambler for making a wager. A Methodist minister, Thomas Griffin, had the temerity to preach in Natchez one night between two ballrooms and was guarded during the sermon by several strapping Kentuckians.[20]

New Orleans was likewise wide open; the gambling houses operated so publicly that the passer-by could hear the calls of the croupiers. The more provident flatboatmen might be interested in strolling by the churches and courts that formed a striking contrast to their rough background, but most of them seem to have made their way to the "Swamp" on Girod Street, where they could do as they pleased and where the police left them severely alone. Even when rowdies, local or foreign, indulged in riots on the levee and laid out innocent passers-by, the police did not always interfere. There is an account of a battle on Christmas Day, 1817, between some seamen and some Kentuckians in which dirks and clubs were wielded freely. Several of the seamen were killed before troops succeeded in dispersing the rioters.

During the War of 1812, when the upstream trade was increased by the closing of the river by the British navy, it was inevitable that New Orleans at any given moment should hold a large number of reckless bargemen spoiling for a fight, and when Andrew Jackson appeared to defend the city it was only natural that he should make use of this restless crowd.

THE BOATMEN

As a matter of fact, James Girty, one of the most famous of the boatmen, who had just arrived in the city with a load of supplies, claimed that Jackson commissioned him a captain and empowered him to raise a company among the rivermen, which company he commanded during the Battle of Chalmette. No record of their actions has survived, but one may be sure that it was the most enjoyable holiday that that crowd of boatmen ever had.[21]

The actor, N. M. Ludlow, has left a vivid account of a scene enacted one evening in the old French Theater in New Orleans a few years after the Kentuckians had played so decisive a part in defeating the British at Chalmette. Samuel Woodworth's poem on that battle, "The Hunters of Kentucky," fell into Ludlow's hands, and he set it to music. On the night he chose to sing the song, the theater was full of keelboatmen and flatboatmen. Said he:

As soon as the comedy of the night was over I dressed myself in a buckskin hunting-shirt and leggins, which I had borrowed of a riverman, and with *moccasins* on my feet, and an old slouch hat on my head, and a rifle on my shoulder, I presented myself before the audience. I was saluted with loud applause of hands and feet, and a prolonged whoop, or howl, such as Indians give when they are especially pleased. I sang the first verse, and these manifestations of delight were louder and longer than before; but when I came to the following lines:—

> But Jackson he was wide awake, and
>   wasn't scared with trifles,
> For well he knew what aim we take
>   with our Kentucky rifles;
> So he marched us down to 'Cypress
>   Swamp'; the ground was low
>   and mucky;
> There stood John 'Bull,' in martial
>   pomp, *but here was old Kentucky.*

As I delivered the last five words I took my old hat off my head, threw it upon the ground, and brought my rifle to the position of taking aim. At that instant came a shout and an Indian yell from the inmates of the pit, and a tremendous applause from the other portions of the house, the whole lasting for nearly a minute and . . . 'the house rose to me!' The whole pit was standing up and shouting. I had to sing the song three times that night before they would let me off.[22]

During the War of 1812 there were some brushes on the upper Mississippi between American boats on one side, and British and Indians on the other. In the summer of 1813 the Americans built four gunboats and armed them with six-pounders and howitzers. In May, 1814, Governor William Clark make an expedition to Prairie du Chien with five barges and 200 men and left several barges and 135 men to erect Fort Shelby. In July a large force of British and Indians attacked and captured the fort and burned one of the gunboats. Another gunboat, the "Governor Clark," under the command of Captain Yeiser, was attacked at close range from both banks but after running the gantlet for eight miles succeeded in escaping. Meanwhile a Lieutenant Campbell had been sent from St. Louis with three keelboats and a sutler's and contractor's barge; there were about 133 people, including women and children, in the company. At Rock River they were visited by the famous Blawk Hawk and several hundred Sauk and Foxes who appeared to be friendly. Shortly afterward, the sutler's and contractor's barge, which carried the ammunition, reached the head of the rapids and proceeded onward. Four miles behind it were two barges, and two miles farther in the rear was Campbell's boat with about thirty men. Campbell had taken refuge from a high wind on the eastern shore in the lee of some willows, and his men were cooking when a sudden discharge of musketry warned of an attack. Several of the crew were killed before they could reach the boat. Lieutenants Rector and Riggs, in command of the two boats ahead, saw the smoke of the battle and dropped downstream. Riggs's boat stranded about two hundred yards below Campbell's, and Rector, fearing a similar mishap, anchored above. For an hour a heavy fire was kept up by both sides, but the Indians, being under cover, probably received little damage. Finally, when fire arrows, shot into Campbell's sails, had set his boat on fire, Rector cut his cable and took off the survivors. As he had a number of wounded on board and was in danger of running on a lee shore, he could not assist Riggs and decided to retreat to St. Louis. Campbell's burning boat was drawn to shore by the Indians, and Black Hawk puritanically emptied all the whiskey he found into the river. (This did not, however, prevent him and his men from getting gloriously drunk a few days later on a British present of rum.) Soon after Rector's departure, a boat reconnoitering from the "Governor Clark" discovered Riggs's party engaged with the Indians and returned in time to warn the sutler's and contractor's barge. The two together reached St. Louis nine days later. Riggs finally succeeded in getting his boat afloat and followed down river. Campbell's boats lost about a dozen men, and about twenty, including himself, were wounded. Of Yeiser's crew there were seven wounded, one of whom died a few days afterward.[23]

A few weeks later Major Zachary Taylor undertook a retaliatory expedition to Rock River with 334 men and a fleet of eight large barges. He flew a white flag from the masthead of his boat, purposing, as he afterward acknowledged, to tempt Black Hawk and his chiefs to a council where he could follow their example by taking treacherous advantage of them. The fleet arrived at Rock River late in the afternoon of September 5 and anchored for the night near a willow island. That night a sentinel on Captain Whiteside's boat was shot, so that the next morning Taylor hoisted the red flag, signifying that no quarter would be allowed. The Indians had stationed themselves on the island. The Americans landed and drove them below to the next island, and Captain Rector was ordered to drop down and harass them with his cannon. Soon afterward several pieces of artillery manned by British gunners opened fire upon the boats and bade fair to sink them unless they retreated out of range. Simultaneously the Indians attacked, but were repulsed with grapeshot from the guns of Rector, and of Whiteside, who had gone to his aid. It was apparently at this juncture that both boats ran aground and lay helpless under the Indian bullets and the pounding of the British cannon. Finally Captain Whiteside leaped over the rail to the sand bar and called out, "All you who are not cowards, follow me." The men responded with enthusiasm, and the Indians were quickly driven from cover and many of them shot in the water as they tried to reach the mainland. The stranded boats were pushed off, and the fleet made its way downstream about three miles, where it halted to repair the damage to the boats and to care for the wounded. At a council of the officers it was decided to continue the retreat. Two or three men were killed in the Rock River action, and about a dozen were wounded. This proved to be the last battle of the war in this section, though Black Hawk's raids continued for a long time.[24]

In 1827 the Winnebago, who had become angered by the execution of two of their number for crime, attacked a barge or keel called the "Oliver H. Perry" at Bad Axe above Prairie du Chien. Two men of the crew of sixteen were killed before the rest recovered from their fright. An attempt to take the boat by storm failed, but two Indians managed to get aboard and steer it upon a sand bar. A member of the crew finally shot one of the boarders through a crack in the deck; the other Indian succeeded in mortally wounding the patroon, but was finally shot by a sailor named Jack Mandeville. Mandeville then took charge and whipped the malingerers into line. For three hours the boatmen lay prone in the blood and bilge water in the bottom of the boat, with Indian bullets crashing through the sides of the boat and over their heads. Finally, when night had fallen, Mandeville and four others braved a storm of shots and pushed the boat off the bar so that it could float out of range. Another boat that came down the river a few hours later passed without casualties.[25]

The events in the lives of the boatmen have for the most part survived only as traditions and are ascribed in turn to each of the famous members of the brotherhood. Mike Fink, Mike Wolf, James Girty, and Bill Sedley have become legendary figures concerning whom the only certainty is that they once lived. Bill Sedley is one of the few flatboatmen whose fame has survived. This hero, with a "heart as big as an apple bar'l," was an amazing worker and a terrible fighter who made his headquarters at Mother Colby's boardinghouse in the "Swamp" when he was in New Orleans. On the ground floor was a drinking and gambling place run by two Mexican brothers named Contreras. One day in 1822, Bill thought he saw one of the brothers cheat at cards, so he started in to "clean up" the place. The crowd cleared out and left him in the saloon to fight it out with the brothers. For a while there was a great clatter of pistol shots and crashing of furniture, above which could be heard Sedley's bull voice shouting, "I'm the child of the snapping turtle, I am." Presently the commotion died down, the door opened, and Sedley appeared, covered with blood and with one arm hanging limp, but with a smile on his face. "Gentlemen," he said, "walk in. The drinks are free. The proprietors has gone on a journey and left me in charge." Sure enough, amid the wreck and ruin lay the brothers, one of them dead, the other dying. Sedley was hurried out of the city on the road to Kentucky, and though he never returned, it was said that he lived to a good old age.

James Girty, who was a nephew of the famous renegade, was a man of courage and prowess who boasted that he had never been whipped. According to his mistress, said some, he was "not constructed like ordinary men, for instead of ribs, bountiful nature had provided him with a solid, bony casing on both sides, without any interstices through which a knife, dirk, or bullet could penetrate." His headquarters were said to have been on the Monongahela just above Pittsburgh, and there he held high carnival with Indians and with devils. Notwithstanding all this, he had a reputation for honesty in business and was never out of employment. His narrowest escape came when he was in command of the barge "Black Snake" of Maysville. Several of his crew had been fleeced by gamblers in a dance hall at Natchez, and Girty joined his men in a raid on the gambling den in which several of the gamblers were killed and wounded. Girty and one of his crew were arrested and held for manslaughter. The proprietress of the dance hall in which the fight had occurred, however, was a friend and admirer of Girty and succeeded in persuading the witnesses to absent themselves from the trial. Only one refused, and she managed to give him a dose of arsenic in time; thus no one appeared against Girty at the trial, and he was honorably acquitted.[26]

Mike Fink, or, as he preferred to spell it, Miche Phinck, was the Paul Bunyan of the boatmen, and to him were ascribed sooner or later most of the exploits that the young West loved to retell and exaggerate.[27] He was born near Pittsburgh around 1780 and was said to have become a scout in the Indian wars while still in his teens. With the end of the wars he took up keelboating and continued at that until he became a trapper for the Missouri Fur Company, shortly before his death about 1823. Mike was said to weigh about one hundred and eighty pounds and to be three inches under six feet in height. His face was round and pleasant, his eyes blue-gray and expressive, his teeth broad and white, and his skin brown and tanned. He was well built and very muscular and active. He used to epitomize himself after the western fashion by boasting, "I can out-run, out-hop, out-jump, throw down, drag out and lick any man in the country. I'm a Salt-River roarer; I love the wimming an' I'm chock full of fight." On the Ohio he was called "The Snapping Turtle" and on the Mississippi "The Snag." Mike was as mighty a drinker as ever "pushed a keel"; it was claimed that he could absorb a gallon of whiskey in twenty-four hours without showing any effect in his language or actions. He also had his humorous side and was wont to say that "he told his jokes on purpose to be laughed at, and no man should make light of them"—and everyone laughed or paid the penalty. Mike's relative, Captain John Fink, near whose home at Wheeling Mike laid up his boats in the winter of 1815, described him as a strict disciplinarian who visited summary punishment on the man who shirked. Usually he had two boats that traveled together, and he always had his woman with him and would allow no other man to converse with her.

It is recorded that one time when his boats had landed near Marietta, Mike went ashore and scraped up a large pile of leaves; then, taking his rifle, he summoned his current woman to lie down on the pile.

"Now, Mr. Fink"—she always mistered him when his blood was up, says the account—"Now, Mr. Fink, what have I done? I don't know I'm sure—"

"Get in there and lie down or I'll shoot you," reiterated Mike with an oath, drawing up his rifle.

There was nothing for poor Peg to do but obey. Mike piled the leaves over her and then calmly set fire to them. The blaze sprang up and presently found its way to the trembling Peg, who stood it as long as she could, then ran, streaming fire and smoke, for the river, and plunged in.

"There," said Mike, as Peg sizzled, "that'll larn ye ter be winkin' at them fellers on t'other boat."

Mike was a champion marksman, bearing the title of "Bang-all." When he appeared at a shooting match he was always asked to take the "fifth quarter"—the hide and tallow—as the price of not entering. He usually found it his pleasure to accept and immediately to trade his share for whiskey to treat the crowd. One of his favorite amusements was to make his woman place a tin cup on her head or between her knees, and then to shoot at it from a distance of thirty yards or so. He was said to have shot the tails neatly from five pigs that were feeding on shore while his boat was passing. Another exploit of which he liked to boast occurred while he was hunting. He was about to take aim at a deer when he saw an Indian doing the same. Mike shifted his gun, and the instant the Indian shot the deer, Mike bagged the Indian. It was solemnly claimed that there was in the court papers of St. Louis a record of Mike's arraignment for shooting the racial projection from a Negro boy's heel. Mike offered as his defense that "the fellow couldn't wear a genteel boot and he wanted to fix it so that he could." Mike's "practical jokes," as he called them, were the terror of the dwellers along the Ohio. The story is told that he once coveted some fine sheep grazing on a bank; after rubbing snuff into their nostrils, he confided to the owner that they had the dreaded "black murrain." The farmer begged him to shoot them, and Mike finally consented, after being offered a bribe of a couple of gallons of peach brandy. The dead sheep were thrown into an eddy, and after dark Mike fished them out and had mutton chops for supper.

The classic episode of Mike Fink's career was supposed to have occurred at Louisville, where, because of his depredations, a reward had been offered for his capture. It happened that the constable was an old friend, and by playing on Mike's kind-heartedness and representing to him how much his family needed the money and how light were the chances of conviction, he finally persuaded the boatman to appear in court. Mike, however, would not go unless he could go with his crew and in his yawl, and so a long-coupled wagon was pushed under the boat and dragged by oxen up the muddy hill toward the courthouse. On the way Mike began to doubt the wisdom of his surrender and made up his mind to retreat. "Set poles," he ordered, and the crew thrust their poles in the mud, and at Mike's call of "back her," the wagon, yawl, and oxen started backward down the hill. The constable expostulated, and finally Mike consented to go up again, but near the top his heart failed him and he retreated once more. This time the constable succeeded in overcoming the boatman's reluctance sufficiently to get him into the courthouse. There, as his friend had prophesied, Mike was acquitted of the first accusation for lack of evidence. Others were about to be brought against him when Mike decided he had had enough, and, calling his crew about him, he boarded his boat. Fixing his red bandanna on a pole, he waved it to the crowd, promised to call again, and gave the order for retreat to the river.

With the advent of the steamboat and the filling up of the Ohio Valley with settlers, Mike expressed the disgusted opinion that the country was getting too civilized, and he retreated to the West. There, in 1822, with Carpenter and Talbot, his two firmest friends, he joined the Henry and Ashley expedition to the Yellowstone. During the winter, Mike and Carpenter quarreled, presumably over a squaw. The next spring, while they were amusing themselves by shooting at tin cups on each other's heads, Mike "elevated a little too low" and killed his rival. Afterward, Mike, who does not seem to have held his liquor as well as of yore, boasted while in his cups that he had shot Carpenter purposely. Talbot, thus having his suspicions confirmed, drew one of his dead comrade's pistols and shot Mike through the heart.

The boatman's was a life with much hard work but with long spells of ease. There were music and whiskey all along the way, and complaisant women and green-topped gaming tables in the sunny ports to the southward. There were hazards, too, which could be overcome if the boatmen could resurrect the reckless daring of their pioneer fathers—a daring that had been quiescent since the recent passing of the Indian from the region.

The plowboy stops his plow in the furrow and gazes down toward the sparkling river around whose upstream bend a saucy keelboat has just come in view. "The boatmen are dancing to the violin on the deck of their boat. They scatter their wit among the girls on the shore who come down to the water's edge to see the pageant pass. The boat glides on until it disappears behind a point of wood. At this moment, perhaps, the bugle . . . strikes up its notes in the distance over the water."[28] The plowboy turns back to his furrow. His blood has been stirred, and perhaps some morning he is missed from the accustomed duties. The lure of the boatman's horn has drawn him. What he has not seen, perhaps chosen not to see, is that barely thirty years after these waters began to be navigated by keel and barge, there is scarcely a bend, scarcely a high point of the river, where there is not a depression in the ground and a rude memorial carved on an adjacent tree —a memorial which proclaims that there at last one of that

THE BOATMEN

hardy race of men, "half horse, half alligator," was forced by hard work and dissipation to embark on that dark stream whose swift, inexorable current even his indomitable spirit could not stem.

5

River Pirates
and the Natchez Trace

THE colorful history of early navigation on the western waters includes a long series of piracies in many respects as thrilling, if not as heroic, as those of the Spanish Main. The first distinct mention of pirates is found around 1760, when they had begun to center on Cottonwood Creek and at the Grand Tower. At the latter place, according to F. A. Rozier, a keelboat bound from New Orleans for the Illinois country was captured by Indians and renegades, and only one person, a young woman, was allowed to proceed to Fort Chartres. During the Revolution, as has been seen, there was some fighting and plundering, which the Spanish termed piracy, carried on by irregular forces led by the Colberts. When the war was over the Colberts apparently remained in the same occupations, for the depredations of the "Colbert Gang" became notorious. Apparently it was because of the activities of this gang that the Spanish governor in 1788 ordered that all boats bound for St. Louis must sail in company. The flotilla thus formed attacked and captured the pirate stronghold at Cottonwood Creek and recovered part of the plunder taken in former years. This incident gave to 1788 in the annals of Louisiana the name of "l'année des dix bateaux."[1]

This action apparently did no more than force the pirates to change their base of operations, for in the issue of March 29, 1794, the *Pittsburgh Gazette* stated that "the report respecting the armed force at the mouth of the Ohio, stopping boats going to New Orleans, and the Spanish settlements on the Mississippi is now generally believed." Whether this statement referred to the so-called boat wreckers who made their headquarters around Cash River near Fort Massac on the Ohio River, or to the outlaws farther upstream near Cave-in-Rock, it is impossible now to ascertain. The boat wreckers sometimes endeavored to entice the crews of passing boats on shore for games of cards and would cheat them unmercifully. Their special designation, however, came from their habit of offering to pilot boats through dangerous channels and then wrecking them or driving them upon shoals where they could be robbed. If the crews refused pilots, the wreckers gave them directions that would have the effect of bringing the boats into their power. Sometimes, when every artifice had failed, they watched their chance and slipped aboard at night to bore holes in the bottoms or dig out some of the calking. When a boat was sinking, the wreckers flocked about in their skiffs to "save" the cargo. Needless to say, this activity took the form of rowing the goods up the creeks that abounded in that region, and the hapless owners never saw their property again.

The most famous practitioner of the boat-wrecking profession was said to be Colonel Fluger (or Pfluger) of New Hampshire, known familiarly throughout the West as Colonel Plug. His wife was called Pluggy, and boatmen loved to tell of an *opéra bouffe* duel fought between Plug and his lieutenant, Nine-Eyes, with fair Pluggy as the cause. Colonel Plug accused Nine-Eyes of carrying on a "candlestick ammer" (clandestine amour) with his wife, and the two men met straightway upon the field of honor. After each had received a bullet in his anatomy, they confessed themselves satisfied.

"You are all grit!" said Colonel Plug.

"And you waded in like a rale Kaintuck," complimented Nine-Eyes.

Pluggy's virtue thus was vindicated, and a bottle of whiskey was produced, over which the two men swore everlasting friendship.

It was told that on one occasion Colonel Plug met his match. He was playing cards with some boatmen whom, unfortunately for himself, he did not remember having robbed a year before, and when he whistled as a signal for his huskies to appear, some waiting confederates of the boatmen rushed in. Three of Plug's men were tossed in the river, and the rest fled. Plug himself was stripped and tied to a tree and after being beaten within an inch of his life was left to feast the mosquitoes. Not long after this, while the colonel was "engaged in the exercise of his profession, that is, digging the caulking out of the bottom of a boat," a squall parted the mooring and drove the boat out into the river, where it sank with Plug still on board.[2]

RIVER PIRATES

The most widely known center of river piracy was at Cave-in-Rock on the Illinois shore of the Ohio about twenty miles below Shawneetown and just above the modern village of Cave-in-Rock, Illinois. The cave is in a long limestone bluff, and its floor is about forty feet above low water, so that flood waters often reach it. Seen from the river, the opening is an almost perfect arch, and the roof keeps this form in general for the entire one-hundred-and-sixty-foot length of the cave. The floor at the mouth is a shelf of rock about fifty-five feet wide with a cleft in the center affording a gradual approach. The width back of the entrance is about forty feet, but during the last century a sink hole in the ceiling has admitted a considerable quantity of earth that has formed a ramp that covers about half of what was the floor in the days of the pirates. Before 1800 the bank in front of the cave, and the top of the bluff above, must have been more heavily wooded than they are now, yet the situation was a splendid one for spying up and down the river. Cave-in-Rock Island, just above the cave, divided the river and, by turning the main channel to the right, forced boatmen to drift close to the mouth of the cave. Ten miles above the cave was Battery Rock, a bluff on the Illinois side about a quarter of a mile long. Below the cave were Walker's Bar, Tower Rock, and Hurricane Island. Together these hazards formed for about eight miles a dangerous channel for which it was almost always necessary to hire a pilot.[3]

The most elementary ruse employed by the pirates to decoy their victims ashore was to have some member of the gang, man or woman, hail passing boats and either ask for passage or offer to make some purchases of provisions from the cargo. If the boat touched shore it was easy for the gang to rush out and seize it, and the crew was silenced forever by being sent to feed the catfish. Sometimes the pirates adopted the tactics of the boat wreckers and waited until a boat had tied up and the crew had landed for the night, then stole aboard and dug out some of the calking or bored a hole in a bottom plank. It was probably soon after 1806 that they adopted a more subtle scheme. Cramer's *Navigator* for 1806, after describing the channel below Cave-in-Rock, added: "Just below the cave, on the right bank, there is a person who is sometimes employed to pilot boats through this serpentine channel, and it is better for a stranger to pay a dollar or two for this purpose then run the risk of grounding on either one or the other of these bars in low water; when the water is high there is no occasion for a director." At Battery Rock the pirate band would keep one of their men stationed, and when a boat appeared he would hail it and offer to act as pilot, at the same time explaining that the pilot referred to in the *Navigator* was away on a visit. Sometimes he got the job, but if he did not, another confederate at Ford's Ferry, about three miles above the cave, made the same offer. Whichever pilot succeeded in obtaining the direction of the boat used his judgment as to the value of the cargo and decided whether to ground the boat at the cave or on Hurricane Island, or to take it safely through. If both of the upper pilots were rejected and the one mentioned by the *Navigator* was taken on, he invariably discharged his duty faithfully, and the safe trips helped to avert the suspicion of the owners of lost boats from Cave-in-Rock.[4]

Apparently there were several successive bands of outlaws who operated in the vicinity of Cave-in-Rock, but at this late date it is impossible to follow the fortunes of any one of them with much certainty, as their identities are lost in a flood of aliases and traditions. A story of doubtful authenticity, yet which may have had some basis in fact, represents the leader of one of these bands as a certain Jim Wilson. On the river bank he erected a sign that bore the legend, "Wilson's

Liquor Vault and House of Entertainment," and within the cave he set up a hostelry that became infamous for its licentiousness.[5] It soon became apparent to the up-river shippers that their boats were not reaching market and that the reason probably lay in the unfaithfulness of their supercargoes; inquiry developed the fact that many of the cargoes were marketed by crews other than the ones originally entrusted with them. Next it was noticed that no crew was heard from after passing Cave-in-Rock, and the blame was soon pinned on Wilson's gang. The Pittsburgh shippers held a meeting and offered a large reward to anyone who would root the outlaws from their lair. John Waller of Maysville and five companions undertook the task of serving as "inside men" in advance of a large punitive expedition. They set out with a boat and cargo furnished by their backers and upon nearing the cave were attracted to the bank by Jim Wilson's novel sign and by the gestures of several women connected with his establishment. Their boat was seized, but Waller and his men were taken into the band, and after a series of thrilling adventures they managed to lead their waiting confederates in an attack that destroyed the outlaws both at the cave and at Hurricane Island.[6]

The best-known name connected with the outlaw history of Cave-in-Rock was that of Samuel Mason. Though a highwayman and pirate of terrible repute, he had none of the "raw-head-and-bloody-bones appearance which his character would indicate." On the contrary, he was a large man of fine appearance, modest and unassuming. He was born in Virginia about 1750 and as a captain in the Revolution won distinction as an Indian fighter. He was one of the five survivors of the Indian ambush at Wheeling on September 1, 1777. Toward the close of the war he appeared in East Tennessee but was run out by John Sevier for thievery. He migrated to western Kentucky, where at Red Banks (Henderson) he appeared by 1791 as the leader of the rogues and outlaws of that region. About 1796 Captain John Dunn, the law's representative at Red Banks, succeeded in driving Mason away but paid the forfeit with his life. From Red Banks, Mason and his family and followers, amounting to twenty or thirty in number, moved down river about fourteen miles, apparently to make their headquarters on the Kentucky shore opposite Diamond Island. A band of regulators, however, forced the group to leave this point, and it moved on to Cave-in-Rock, seventy miles below, where headquarters were established for the greater part of 1797. It is entirely possible that Mason set up an inn at the cave and, to counteract his evil reputation, changed his name to James Wilson. It is not likely, however, that he was ever driven out by a direct attack on the cave, as was the Wilson in the story. It was during Mason's stay in the vicinity of the cave that he came in contact with a man who was to play a vital part in his later career. This was James May, who had appeared at Red Banks with a lame sister about the time that Mason left there. May stole some horses and with his sister fled to Vincennes, but was overtaken and brought back. On the night of his enforced return he escaped and joined Mason's gang.[7]

It is barely possible that Mason knew the Harpe brothers, who were infamous in the early history of Kentucky and Tennessee; one of them was to share in the drama of Mason's death. Micajah and Wiley Harpe, believed to be brothers, were born around 1770, in a Tory family in North Carolina. Their treatment as Tories and probably some other unknown factors appear to have warped their minds and driven them to take a fearful vengeance on the world. After some time spent with outlaw Indians they appeared at Knoxville, Tennessee, in 1797. Micajah, usually known as Big Harpe, had two women with him named Susan and Betty Roberts, supposedly sisters. He was said to be married to Susan, but each woman bore him a child. At Knoxville, Wiley, usually called Little, or Redheaded, Harpe, married Sally Rice, a girl of good family. Soon afterward the clan was driven out for hog stealing and started for Kentucky along the Wilderness Trail; meanwhile its members began the series of horrible and meaningless murders that marked their path wherever they went. All were apprehended in December, 1798, and imprisoned at Stanford, Kentucky. Less than three months later, however, the two men escaped, and sometime afterward the three women, each having borne a child in jail, were released, and set out by a circuitous route to join their men near Cave-in-Rock.

Whether or not Mason was still there at the time is not clear. At least, according to tradition, there were outlaws there who received the Harpes into their ranks. It seems that this outlaw band, still inherently more decent than the recruits, did not appreciate the Harpes' brand of humor. A boat had stopped on the shore for some repairs, and two lovers had taken the occasion to wander to the top of a bluff to admire the beauties of the river. The brothers, who happened to be passing, saw them and pushed them off the cliff. They fell forty feet, but landed on a sandy beach and fortunately escaped injury. Another time the Harpes bound a prisoner to a blindfolded horse and drove horse and man over a cliff upon the rocks. The outcome of this prank was not so fortunate either for the victim or for the Harpes, for the latter were immediately, so says the tradition, driven away with their women and children. At about the same time, a Kentucky expedition under Captain Young, which had been scouring the country for the Harpes, made the vicinity of Cave-in-Rock so hot that most of the other outlaws left. The next July the Harpes appeared again near Knoxville, and once more a trail of hideous murders led into Kentucky. The country was now thoroughly aroused, and the clan was followed until overtaken about fifty miles south of Henderson. Big Harpe was killed and his head stuck up in a tree, but Little Harpe escaped to play his part in a later drama. Altogether it is probable that about thirty-five people fell before these monsters of the frontier.[8]

According to the elder Audubon, Mason, after his departure from Cave-in-Rock for the Mississippi, lived for some time at Wolf Island, about twenty-five miles below the mouth of the Ohio. Here he engaged in stealing Negroes and horses and in robbing boats; he passed his booty for disposal to a line of confederates that extended from Virginia to New Orleans. In March, 1800, he obtained a pass from the Spanish commandant at New Madrid that would serve as a protection if he were forced to flee from the scene of his robberies on the American side of the river. The exploits of Mason on the Natchez Trace and on the Mississippi are not always easy to follow, because of the natural tendency to lay all crimes to the charge of the best-known criminal. The prevalence of his name in the papers of the time in connection with so many of the robberies in that region is sufficient warrant of his fame.[9]

Until the day of the steamboats, the flatboatman who came down to New Orleans had the choice of three methods for his return homeward. One was to take ship for Baltimore or Philadelphia and cross the mountains to his western home, another was to join a keelboat crew and return the way he had come, and the other and commoner way was to travel by the Natchez Trace.[10] This trace led through a maze of woods trails and over frequent fords from New Orleans to Natchez and then by the old Indian and buffalo trail to Nashville, a total distance of approximately seven hundred miles. It was about five hundred miles between the two last-named points, and before

1800 there were no white settlements for the greater part of the distance. The trace had been used by the white men as early as 1763 and became important thereafter in proportion to the increase in flatboat traffic.

Returning boatmen, with few exceptions, traveled in parties of three to twenty for mutual protection; usually they walked, but sometimes they bought horses or Texas ponies in New Orleans or Natchez. When two or three men could club together and buy a horse, they rode "whipsaw fashion"; that is, one rode the horse for an hour, or any specified time, and then tied it and walked on; the next man, when he came up, rode for the same length of time, then left the horse for the next man; and he in turn tied up the horse to await the man who had ridden first. The nature of the country was such that riding was not always a pleasure, and it was often an easy matter for pedestrians to keep up with the horsemen. The boatmen sometimes walked races with the hard-riding mail carriers, and one called "Walking Johnson" was said to have beaten the mail three times. In the earlier days before the trace was improved, the journey from Natchez to Nashville required from fifteen to twenty days.

Travelers had to provide themselves with food and clothing, for there was no opportunity to buy them on the way at reasonable prices. They carried corn for the horses and the usual frontier rations of hardtack, bacon, rice, and corn, for the men. An emergency ration of a pint of parched and ground corn was carried; a spoonful of this was supposed to keep a man going for a day. Clothing usually consisted of brown overalls, shirt, and brogans, and of course every man had his knife, blanket, canteen of whiskey, and a rifle or pistol. If the improvident flatboatman had not spent all his wages in New Orleans and Natchez, the remainder was converted into specie and sewed into his belt or the seams of his clothes. The captains or owners of cargoes usually bought mules to transport their baggage and the heavy silver dollars for which they had exchanged their cargoes, and in addition they could afford horses for their own use. When they stopped for the night, they first hobbled the horses so that they could not wander far away, then took the saddlebags and money belts outside the camp and concealed them in the leaves or brush, or in hollow logs and trees. When highwaymen raided a camp, their first object, of course, was to look for this concealed money. A watch was always kept at night against robbers and Indian thieves. It is a curious fact, however, that the Kentucky boatmen usually fell an easy prey to the outlaws of the Natchez Trace.

Sixty-two miles beyond Natchez was Grindstone Ford on the Bayou Pierre. Here, in the early days, was the last civilized dwelling before Nashville, almost five hundred miles away. The trail led along the ridge between the Yazoo and Tombigbee rivers and was choked with fallen trees and so obstructed by briers and underbrush that it was necessary to travel in single file. Thirty miles was a good day's journey. Also, water was scarce and the endeavor was always made to stop on the site of an abandoned Indian camp, where there would be a cleared space with water close at hand. At the head of the Tombigbee was the Big Town of the Chickasaw, and near it were many abandoned peach and apple orchards. When a party was on the march in the Choctaw and Chickasaw country, a scout was usually sent ahead, as the Indians sometimes proved troublesome when they were drunk—and they always were when they could get the liquor. At other times they were usually generous and hospitable, though their poverty did not allow them to be of much help to the traveler.

Forty miles beyond the Big Town the trace reached the Tennessee, and there, because the river was too deep and swift to be forded, the traveler had to pay the half-breed, James Colbert, a dollar for ferriage. Colbert's helpers were Indians and were cantankerous, so that if the boatman arrived after bedtime, he had to wait for daylight before they would set him over. Colbert was said to have received an income of two thousand dollars a year from his ferry alone, and this amount suggests that about two thousand persons, mostly flatboatmen, made their way northward on the trace each year. A white man, Jim Allen, had married Colbert's daughter, and their daughter, Peggy Allen, was a famous beauty in the Southwest. Swaney, the mail carrier on the Natchez Trace, said that the number of travelers and boatmen who stopped to gaze upon her was almost incredible. She later married a planter from the vicinity of Natchez.

Between the Tennessee and Duck rivers lay seventy-five miles of the roughest country on the trace. Bumpy hills, dense canebrakes, and swamps of soupy mud, aptly termed "hell holes," united with the mosquitoes to make the transit of this region anything but a pleasure. Between Duck River and the Cumberland the hills were suggestive of camels' humps, and the disgruntled boatman was constrained to alight from his pony and plow through the sand on foot. At Nashville the parties generally broke up, and the boatmen traveled singly or in smaller groups eastward to Knoxville or across the Barrens to Danville, whence there were well-traveled roads to the various parts of the Ohio Valley. The man who knew the Natchez Trace best was probably John L. Swaney, who traversed it as mail carrier from about 1796 to about 1804. He allowed three weeks of hard riding for the round trip of eleven hundred miles from Nashville to Natchez. In addition to the mail, he carried his provisions, an overcoat or blanket, and a tin trumpet. He knew Mason well and saw and conversed with him often, and Mason told him repeatedly that he wanted nothing but money and that if he could get it without violence, he would be glad to avoid shedding blood.[11]

J. C. Guild has preserved for us Swaney's story of one of Mason's first robberies in the territory. A large party of boatmen had camped at Gun Springs in the Choctaw territory. According to custom they were setting out pickets, when one of them stepped on one of Mason's men who was concealed in the grass. The robber jumped up with a yell and fired his gun, and the boatmen were struck with such terror that they fled for the tall timber, leaving their equipment to Mason. Early the next morning Swaney came along and, recognizing the signs of flight, wound his horn to call in the fugitives. They came, still badly frightened and some of them half clothed. One big Kentuckian had only a shirt; his pants with four gold doubloons sewed in the waistband were among the spoils of war. After consultation the boatmen decided to pursue the robbers; arming themselves with clubs, they started on the trail with the big Kentuckian in the lead. About a mile on the way they began to find articles of clothing that the outlaws had tossed aside, among them the Kentuckian's pants with the four doubloons still intact. After that it was noticed that the Kentuckian's enthusiasm oozed away, and he was soon bringing up the rear. Presently the company was halted by a hail from Mason, whose gang was standing behind trees with guns presented. He ordered the boatmen to leave at once or be shot. The ensuing stampede rivaled that of the night before, and the big Kentuckian once more led the van. When the others taunted him for his change of front he only laughed and said that he had more to lose than they. He spent all his rescued money, however, in buying supplies for his comrades.[12]

The most famous robbery was that of Colonel Joshua Baker, a Kentucky merchant who was returning home with four men, five riding horses, and five pack mules carrying provisions

Raftsmen Playing Cards by George Caleb Bingham. Courtesy of the St. Louis Art Museum.

The Jolly Flatboatmen in Port by George Caleb Bingham. Courtesy of the St. Louis Art Museum.

and the money made in his venture to New Orleans. On August 14, 1801, about twenty miles from the site of Jackson, Mississippi, the party was surprised and robbed by four men with blackened faces.[18] A short time later Mason's son, John, was captured with another member of the band and publicly whipped and exposed in the pillory at Natchez. Their crime was participation in the Baker robbery, an accusation that both stoutly denied, crying "innocent" with every blow of the whip. A few days afterward they escaped from jail with the aid of some of their comrades.[14] Meanwhile Mason's depredations had become bolder and more frequent. A Spanish officer later announced his conviction that Mason had confederates throughout the Ohio and Mississippi valleys, and it is known that he had an accomplice in Natchez who received and disposed of his booty. No one can say positively that Mason's methods included murder, for he was usually careful to leave with those victims whom he allowed to escape an impression of good humor rather than ferocity. Nevertheless, it is likely that there were some who did not live to tell the tale. Scores of men might have disappeared in the Southwest and never have been missed, save, perhaps, in their far-away homes.

By the end of the year 1802, Mason had gone on north to Little Prairie, near New Madrid, where he assumed the role of a settler. There were six men in the party: Mason himself, his four sons, and another man, who passed either as John Setton or John Taylor. The only woman was the wife of John Mason, and she was accompanied by three children. In January, 1803, the suspicions of the inhabitants of Little Prairie that their high-handed neighbors were the Masons led to the arrest of the group by Captain McCoy, an Irish-Spanish officer. The prisoners were taken before the commandant at New Madrid. The examination proved beyond a doubt the identity of the Masons, who, however, tried to throw the blame for the river robberies upon others, including John Setton. The latter offered to turn state's evidence against the Masons and claimed that they had been holding him in durance. The puzzled commandant cut the Gordian knot by sending the whole party to New Orleans, where in turn it was decided to turn them over to the United States. During the upward journey, begun under Captain McCoy, the prisoners were held in irons. Near Point Coupée, on March 26, the mast of the barge broke, and while part of the crew was on shore fabricating a new one, the outlaws managed to rid themselves of their irons and seize some guns, and they began firing on the guard. Upon hearing the shots, McCoy rushed from his cabin but was met by Mason, who shot him in the breast and shoulder. McCoy returned the fire and shot Mason in the head. The latter, however, though dazed by the wound, rallied his party, drove the Spanish from the boat, and kept them at bay till nightfall. By that time reinforcements had arrived for McCoy, and the outlaws hastily abandoned the ship and fled, followed by Mason's daughter-in-law and her children.[15]

This thrilling battle and escape caused a great repercussion throughout the West. A reward of a thousand dollars was offered for the leader, dead or alive, and there was a great riding to and fro of regulators investigating reports that he had been seen here or there. About the first of June it was claimed that he had been seen fifteen miles from Natchez. Two months later, James May, who unknown to his neighbors had been a former associate of Mason at Cave-in-Rock, made oath at Old Greenville to a rather incredible story. He had been descending the river when Mason had intercepted and robbed him. Mason, however, had allowed him to join the band. A few days later, during an alarm caused by the firing of guns, the party scattered to hide their horses. May's duty of hiding the boat was effected first; upon returning, he found Mason counting the money to divide among the band, whereupon May shot him above the eye, took the money and property, and fled in the skiff. Evidently his word that he had killed Mason was not believed, for he was allowed to leave. In October he reappeared with John Setton at Natchez, and both men were thrown in jail as Mason's associates, though Setton claimed he had come to act as state's evidence. Though it was proved rather conclusively that both had been concerned in a certain robbery, they were released to join the hunt for Mason. They appeared again, probably in December, after a series of obscure adventures, bearing the head of Mason as evidence of the passing of the great robber. In an interview at Natchez, Governor W. C. C. Claiborne instructed them to call at a certain time for their reward. As soon as they had left the room, a Captain Stump, an old friend of Claiborne's who had just arrived in Natchez and was present at the interview, expressed his opinion that Setton was Little Harpe. In consequence, May and Setton were arrested, and announcement was made at the landing that any boatmen who had known Wiley Harpe should examine the prisoner. Five boatmen recognized him and gave their testimony concerning his identity, and a little later a John Bowman further identified him by the scar of a wound that he had inflicted on Harpe in Knoxville. Harpe's case now was desperate, and May also began to fear that his activities at Cave-in-Rock might become known. Accordingly both seized an opportunity to escape, but they were soon recaptured. The trials were held at Old Greenville in January and February, 1804, and on the eighth of the latter month, both Harpe and May were hanged and their heads placed on poles along the Natchez Trace.[16]

The death or disappearance of Mason by no means made the Natchez Trace a safe highway. Mason had demonstrated the profits to be gained thereon, and there were plenty of men to take his place. In 1807, near Bayou Pierre, fifteen robbers surprised a large party and took four or five thousand dollars, and though the pillaged men overtook the outlaws they did not have the courage to attack. Stack Island, or Crow's Nest, in the middle of Nine-Mile Reach, at what is now the south-eastern corner of Arkansas, which had been frequented more or less by Mason, remained a piratical center for several years. According to the southwestern tradition, however, the pirati-cal activities of the freebooters were brought to an end in a summary fashion by lynch law. The winter of 1808–9 had been characterized by an unusual number of raids, and several boats and their crews had disappeared. During the following April it chanced that seven keelboats were detained by heavy winds at the head of the reach, and the crews took advantage of the opportunity to attack Crow's Nest. Shortly before daylight, eighty or ninety well-armed men descended in their skiffs to the island and after a short skirmish killed several of the outlaws and captured nineteen men. A boy and two women were allowed to leave, but the men were executed—how, the tradition does not say.[17]

Two or three years later, according to Cramer, the island was sunk in the earthquake or swept away by flood. It was Number 94 in his scheme of Mississippi islands. There is fairly good evidence that it was a piratical nest till the last. Captain Sarpy of St. Louis, with his family, tied up at the island on the evening of December 15, 1811, but, finding that a band of men was waiting to rob him, he dropped downstream. That night came the earthquake, and in the morning, island and robbers had been swallowed up. Thomas Nuttall speaks of the robbers in this vicinity before 1811 as numbering about eighty men and as being divided into two gangs, one at Stack Island and the other at the mouth of the Arkansas. They were accustomed to buying goods and paying for them with counterfeit money. In the fall of 1811, so one account runs, the Arkansas gang under a leader named Clary worked this trick on the crew of a flatboat, and the owner, upon demanding restitution, was driven away by gunfire. Soon afterward eleven other flatboats arrived, and their crews agreed to help in wiping out Clary's gang. They attacked that evening and in spite of resistance broke open Clary's house and seized him and two others. Clary was sentenced to receive a number of lashes, and the two other prisoners were forced to help work the boats in place of two men who had been wounded. When the party reached Natchez the prisoners were committed to prison, but were acquitted for lack of evidence. Clary, who was apparently released after his lashing, was said to have confessed that in the week previous to the attack he had bought eighteen hundred dollars' worth of goods with counterfeit money and had sent his spoils up the Arkansas.

Nuttall, whose visit to this region was made in 1819 and 1820, stated that the Stack Island gang had never been routed but were still in the neighborhood, passing counterfeit money. Seemingly he had not heard of Stack Island's disappearance. The country was still infested by worse men than counterfeiters, however. In 1817, when the members of Ludlow's theatrical troupe passed Plum Point below New Madrid, they were so firmly convinced of their peril that they ransacked one of their properties trunks and armed each man and woman with a saber. Two years later, while passing Little Round Island, Nuttall's boat was hailed by some men on shore "mimicking distress to draw us to land, but in vain. We had been well assured of the existence of gangs of pirates occasionally occupying these solitudes."[18]

The Immigrant

It has been seen that during the Revolution the population of the West was swelled by a horde of immigrants, a great many of whom were Tories and neutrals seeking a haven from economic and political persecution. This does not mean that they were opposed to the patriot's concept of liberty. They had left the East because they saw no advantage in unseating a ruler three thousand miles away only to enthrone their next-door neighbor in his place. The desire, even the demand, for freedom and an opportunity for themselves and for their children persisted. Zadok Cramer, one of the most zealous advocates of western progress, waxed lyrical in the stilted, long-winded fashion of his day when he saw the immigrants launching their boats in ever increasing numbers at the thriving little village of Pittsburgh. They seek, he said, "places of settlement in these new countries where their prosperity may rest in safety, having plenty of all the necessaries, and many of the luxuries of life, where their children's children may enjoy the rich and prolifick productions of the land, without an over degree of toil or labour, where the climate is mild and the air salubrious, where each man is a prince in his own kingdom, and may without molestation enjoy the frugal fare of his humble cot; where the clashing and terrifick sounds of war are not heard; where tyrants that desolate the earth dwell not; where man, simple man, is left to the guidance of his own will, subject only to laws of his own making, fraught with mildness, operating equally just on all, and by all protected and willingly obeyed."[1]

During the Revolutionary years, the Wilderness Road through Cumberland Gap was probably the principal route from Virginia and North Carolina. Yet the Ohio River was by no means neglected, and the family boat was already a common sight in spite of the peril from Indians. It is recorded that no less than three hundred large boats arrived at Louisville during the spring of 1780, and in the six stations of the Bear Grass region centering around Louisville alone, there were six hundred fighting men. There may have been ten thousand people in Kentucky, but whatever the number, the fighting force was a striking contrast, as one writer suggests, to the one hundred and two hard-pressed men and boys who had composed the total force two years before. At the same time, in spite of Virginia's prohibition against settlement, Americans were occupying the Illinois country. By the end of the war, Bellefontaine had become a sizable American village, and in 1787 there were recorded the names of about one hundred and thirty-five English-speaking men living in and about that place. Even as early as 1768 the Americans in Illinois had been numerous enough to muster a militia company of sixty.[2]

Immigrants usually endeavored to reach the headwaters in early spring or fall. In the first season they took advantage of the high water that continued for several months after the breaking up of the ice. Those who crossed the mountains in September usually had the advantage both of dry roads and of the rise in water that came with the October rains. Circumstances, of course, varied from year to year. Now and then, travel on the upper rivers during the summer was possible immediately after a heavy rainfall, and on these occasions waiting immigrants sometimes embarked in such haste that they left part of their goods. There were other reasons for the choice of spring and fall as the seasons of migration. The guidebooks of the time warned against the malaria that had given the rivers a bad reputation for unhealthfulness in the summer time. Moreover, the odors wafted from decaying vegetation in the shore waters were not very pleasant to sensitive nostrils.[3]

There were three principal points of embarkation: Brownsville (Redstone), Pittsburgh, and Wheeling. The first, being closest to the East, was likely to be favored in seasons when the water was running high. At low stages it was impracticable. Wheeling was safest at such times, but it had the disadvantage of being nearly sixty miles farther by land from the East, and moreover it was difficult to purchase an outfit there. Pittsburgh, by and large, was the best point of departure; a boat might have a little difficulty in getting over the shoals in low water, but there were adequate storage and out-fitting facilities. There were boat yards at these three places and others at near-by towns. Sometimes a fortunate immigrant could pick up at a reduced price a flatboat that had come down the Allegheny or the Monongahela laden with salt, lumber, or produce. During the early years of the nineteenth century, Olean in New York was a point of departure for immigrants from New York and New England. In March, 1815, there were about twelve hundred people waiting there for the breaking up of the ice.[4]

The flatboat and its furnishing depended, of course, upon the purse and character of the owner. The better boats had brick fireplaces and were very comfortably furnished. Christian Schultz described one as being neater than half the houses on shore. In one end was the family room, where the cooking and eating took place, and in the opposite end was a room in which furniture was stored. Between the two, down the middle of the boat, was a passage five feet wide, and along each side were little bedchambers about twelve feet by six, each separated from each other by clean white curtains.[5] When the horses, cattle, and poultry shared one end of the family boat, there was no doubt a very unsavory odor and a great amount of noise. One can visualize the lighter farming tools piled in the cabin, and the grain and hay in the middle of the boat, next to the partition screening off the cattle. Chests of clothing and dishes, barrels of provisions brought to use or to sell, and miscellaneous articles of everyday use cluttered up the living room. On the roof there might be a wagon and a plow. A boat as neat as the one described by Schultz was hardly the rule, for Americans of that day were far from germ conscious. In fact, the typical family, either afloat or ashore, was likely to be living in squalor and to be afflicted with parasites and "Scotch fiddle," as the itch was commonly called.

Immigrants did not always travel on stout, seaworthy flatboats. Often their craft were only wretched imitations with leaky bulwarks two or three feet high. Perhaps as many immigrants went down river on pine rafts as on flatboats. If they were ambitious enough or if the season demanded it, they might have on the raft a shed for the horses and cattle and one for the family. Otherwise they traveled with a tent or

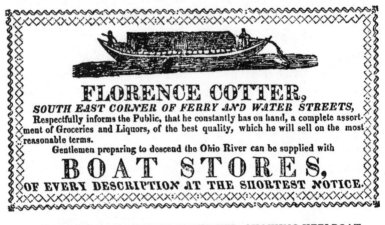

ADVERTISEMENT OF BOAT OUTFITTER, SHOWING KEELBOAT

From Riddle and Murray, "Pittsburgh Directory of 1819"

an awning, or, if they were especially shiftless or indigent, perhaps made no pretense at shelter.

By no means all the craft that went down river with immigrants on board were rafts or flatboats. The pioneers of the Marietta settlement left the Youghiogheny in 1788 on a fine new forty-five-foot galley that they named the "Mayflower" in memory of the other "Mayflower" that had brought their ancestors to New England. In earlier years, some immigrants traveled in the new mail packets that plied the Ohio between Pittsburgh and Louisville, the proprietors of which guaranteed that "no danger need be apprehended from the enemy as every person on board will be under cover, made proof against rifle or musket balls."[6]

Charles Sealsfield described a passenger keelboat on which he traveled as a "machine fifty feet long and ten feet broad, shut up on every side; with two doors, two and a half feet high. It forms a species of wooden prison, containing commonly four rooms; the first for the steward, the second a dining room, the third a cabin for gentlemen, and the fourth a ladies' cabin. Each of these cabins was provided with an iron stove. . . . On the sides were our births [*sic*], in double rows, six feet in length and two broad. . . . Our passage to Trinity, 515 miles by water, including provisions, &c., was twenty five dollars." Two of the berths had to be lengthened in order to accommodate two Kentuckians of more than normal stature. On board were ten women and eleven men passengers, a captain, a mate, a steward, twelve oarsmen, and forty slaves.

The slaves were huddled on the roof of the cabin in a space seven and a half feet by forty-two feet, and their lot was pitiable, exposed as they were to the weather. The kitchen was also on deck. The passengers' food was good, because they had taken the precaution to stipulate that they could order such provisions as they thought proper. Breakfast was at eight, luncheon at eleven, dinner at three, and supper at six. The ladies and gentlemen alternately gave tea parties at nine in the evening. The voyage was enlivened by various incidents; among them was a boat race to overtake a deer that was swimming the Ohio. A slave girl belonging to a sick Kentuckian escaped at Shawneetown and could not be located until a reward was offered, when a residenter, who had shortly before sworn ignorance of her whereabouts, promptly brought her aboard. Soon afterward, during an altercation, the cabin caught fire from an overheated stove, and the invalid Kentuckian would have been badly burned had not his Negro man dashed a bucket of water over him. Instead of being grateful, the Kentuckian heaped abuse on the luckless slave for his rough treatment.[7]

Frequently two or three individuals traveled together in a skiff equipped with oars, setting pole, and sail. This was as cheap a method as any, and it is said that on one occasion two young men floated seven hundred miles, and their total expenses, including the skiff, amounted to only fourteen dollars. It was not necessary to pay even that much, for there is a record of an independent young hunter who, being denied passage on a boat unless he would work his way, embarked on a makeshift raft and actually reached Kentucky.[8]

One can envisage the scene that must have been enacted time after time at a score of places along the Ohio and its upper tributaries as the immigrants gathered to await the spring thaw. Taverns are teeming with tipplers and gamesters, and even the private residences are pressed into service by the mob of transients. Along the bank is a line of rafts and flatboats, each occupied by immigrants or merchandise, or both. Here on one end of a giant raft is a little house, before which a woman bends wearily over a washtub. At the other end is a haystack, around which several horses and cows munch contentedly. The open space between is occupied by a wagon, a plow, and some other articles of husbandry, and pigs and chickens and children running about make it look for all the world like a real barnyard.[9] A rooster, with one eye upon his harem and the other upon a rival on the roof of a neighboring flatboat, mounts the plow handle and crows defiance to all comers. It is a warmish day and the break-up of the ice is very near, so that the old lady in the next flatboat can sit on the roof in her rocking-chair and knit and watch the panorama of life on the shore. A score of makeshift huts, each

THE IMMIGRANT

with a curl of smoke drifting from crude stick-and-mud chimneys, rise above a conglomeration of wagons, poultry pens, pigsties, picketed horses and cattle, and youngsters shouting rowdily at their play. From the crowded village farther up the bank, a merchant and his flatboat captain pick their way through the fetid mud and teeming smells to look at the ice. As they stand at the river's edge there is a sound of a crack farther upstream, and the captain, who is an old riverman, says, "We should soon be on our way."

That night the ice breaks and rushes by the camp, grinding and crashing as though in rage that its day of domination is past. At daybreak the river is clear and rising fast, and the denizens of boats and rafts and huts, who in the excitement have scarcely closed an eye all night, are working feverishly to get their belongings on board. Half-clad children, bright-eyed with anticipation, tug at the halter of the family cow to urge her up the frail gangplank of their clumsy Kentucky boat. Another family, amid the laughter of neighbors, frantically chases the hens from an overturned coop. Here a harassed mother boxes the ears of a youngster who has dropped a pile of linen in the mud. The boy puckers his face and has half a mind to cry, but thinks better of it. There is too much a-doing to waste time in weeping. Today we start West! By noon every craft has cleared, and the river for a mile downstream appears to be a solid mass of boats and rafts. On the shore, where a few hours before there seemed to be a populous village, now appear only some broken-down huts with a handful of poverty-stricken inhabitants. Another convoy has gone West.

Naturally, most of the immigrants were young or at least not beyond middle age, but there were occasional older persons who struck out for themselves. James Hall, the most prolific chronicler of the West, tells of meeting near the Guyandot an old couple chatting together while they tugged at the oars of their flatboat. Questioned about venturing out at that age to new settlements, the old man answered: "Why, Sir, our boys are all married and gone off . . . and our neighbors, a good many of 'em's gone out back, and so the old woman and me felt sort o' lonesome, and thought we'd go too, and try our luck. . . . better late than never . . . and maybe the old woman and me'll have as good luck as any of them."[10]

Indian raids did not come to an end with the close of the Revolution, but the expectation of a cessation of hostilities caused the stream of immigration to shift in a large degree to the Ohio River. About half the settlers followed that route. The usual terminus of the river voyage was at Limestone, Kentucky, where a blockhouse was erected in 1784. From there a road led into the Blue Grass country. Another road, important to the Bear Grass region, touched the river at Louisville. Legal settlement was begun north of the Ohio with the planting of a New England colony at Marietta in 1788 and the foundation of Cincinnati shortly afterward. These encroachments confirmed the Indians' view of the white man's intention not to stop at the southern bank of the Ohio, and in 1789 the raids on settlements and boats, which had never stopped for very long at a time, began to increase in number. From then until the American armies carried the scene of hostilities northward in 1794, the raids on river traffic were almost constant.[11]

Travelers on the river were thus forced to go in armed bands. Companies were gathered at certain points, sometimes by advertisement. Every advantage was taken of the boat's cargo to form a barrier, and two instances are recorded in which salt pans being transported to salt licks were ranged along the sides as bullet-proof defenses. When several boats traveled together they often adopted a certain formation for mutual protection. In a convoy of sixteen Kentucky boats and two keels that passed down the river in 1790, the flatboats were lashed together three abreast and kept in one line. The women, children, and stock were placed in the center boats, and only the outside ones were worked. Each block of boats had its own commanding officer, and the keels, which were more mobile, were kept to the flanks. A storm broke upon the flotilla near the Scioto, and the lashings had to be cut while the boats made helter-skelter for the shores. Fortunately the travelers escaped attack and in the evening were able to go on. The principal danger point on the southward journey was the mouth of the Scioto River, opposite which on the Kentucky side rose the famous Watch Tower, a high rock from the summit of which the Indians could scan the river for boats. John Heckewelder, usually dependable, says that within the two years previous to July, 1792, 150 people had been killed or captured near that place. The wary immigrant never stopped there but floated on even during the nighttime.[12]

Indians preferred to lure their victims to the shore, but when the means were at hand they did not hesitate to make their attack on the water. The usual method of enticing the immigrant ashore was for a white renegade to pretend that he was escaping from the Indians and to run along the shore pleading to be taken on board. Boatmen of course soon became aware of this trick and were suspicious of anyone hailing them. Yet, as timeworn as the trick became, people continued to be taken in by it. When in 1790 Colonel John May, for whom Maysville was named, was descending the river with four men and two women, he was hailed near the Watch Tower by two white men who begged piteously to be taken aboard. May refused but at the demand of the women and one of the men finally touched shore. Indians instantly appeared, and in the ensuing hail of bullets May and one of the women were killed and the rest of the party captured. As a result of such experiences, those who really were escaping from the Indian country had difficulty in convincing boatmen of their sincerity. Colonel Downing of Kentucky once followed a boat for two miles before a man would come after him in a canoe, and then the rescuer held his rifle ready and warned Downing that if he saw an Indian he would shoot him (Downing) dead in his tracks.[13]

Immigrants were not always of the bold, daring nature often attributed to the pioneers. They might meet an attack with a single volley and then give up in craven fear, or the men might leap overboard and abandon the women and children to their fate. It is recorded that not far from the Scioto River, the companies from five boats endangered by the Indians spent the evening in fiddling and dancing instead of preparing for battle. Fortunately for the merrymakers, the Indians had attacked another boat nearby, and had received such a drubbing that they did not choose to interfere with the five. Three Frenchmen and an American who were attacked by Indians decided "to present a handkerchief, with other demonstrations of friendship, and surrender without resistance." The Indians, however, butchered two of them. The other two escaped by swimming ashore. Another party that surrendered without resistance was treated with civility, and blankets were spread for them to sit upon.

An attack sometimes had its humorous aspects. On one occasion a grown man lay down in the bottom of the boat and howled prayers at the top of his voice; he allowed a boy to take his place at the oars, only to find that the Indians, who proved to be friendly, were bursting with laughter at his expense. In a bloody encounter between some Indians and a boatload of travelers under James Ward of Kentucky, a Revolutionary captain lay terror stricken on the floor of the flatboat groaning, "Oh, Lord! Oh, Lord!" An enormously fat Dutchman cravenly cleaving to the bottom boards was painfully aware that his generous posterior extended above the gunwales. "In vain he shifted his position. The hump still appeared, and the balls still flew around it, until the Dutchman, losing all patience, raised his head above the gunnel, and in the tone of querulous remonstrance called out, 'Oh, now! Quit tat tamned nonsense, tere, will you?'" Fortunately for him, it was a shore attack, and the Indians gave up after following the boat a few miles.[14]

Resolution and coolheadedness sometimes routed attackers without a shot. In April, 1784, near Green River, two lashed boats under the command of a settler named Rowan passed an Indian encampment at night. The seven men of the boats stood ready behind the concealment of the bulwarks, but without a sound, for Mr. Rowan had given orders to that effect. As the boats came opposite the central fire, they were discovered, and the yelling savages took to their canoes.

The boats floated on in silence—not an oar was pulled. The Indians approached within less than a hundred yards, with a seeming determination to board. Just at this moment, Mrs. Rowan rose from her seat, collected the axes, and placed one by the side of each man, where he stood with his gun, touching him on the knee with the handle of the axe, as she leaned it by him against the side of the boat, to let him know it was there, and retired to her seat, retaining a hatchet for herself. The Indians continued hovering on the rear, and yelling, for nearly three miles, when, awed by the inference which they drew from the silence observed on board, they relinquished farther pursuit.[15]

One of the most famous boat battles was fought in May, 1778, on Salt River, when 120 Indians attacked a flatboat loaded with kettles intended for the saltworks at Bullitt's Lick. There were twelve men and a woman on board. The boat belonged to Henry Crist and Solomon Spears, who were with the company. Early one morning while the boat was still chained to the shore, though it had drifted a little distance from it, two of the men who had gone out to hunt came running back pursued by Indians. The attackers, foiled in an attempt to force their way on board, retired to the bank and opened fire from behind trees. The salt kettles had been lined up along the gunwales, but unfortunately both ends of the boat were open so that the enemy fire swept its length with terrible effect. Five men were killed and four wounded. For an hour the battle continued; then one of the wounded men succeeded in working the hook of the mooring chain loose from the link into which it was slipped, and the survivors managed to get the boat out into the stream and to the opposite shore, where they hastily took to the woods. The Indians followed them, and a hand-to-hand conflict ensued from which only three men, including Crist, escaped; these made their way with great difficulty to the salt licks. One of them died of his wounds soon afterward. The woman was captured and taken to Canada. Some years later she was ransomed and returned to Kentucky. According to her story, thirty Indians had been killed in that desperate encounter.[16]

Another epic of the river was Captain William Hubbell's battle in March, 1791, near the mouth of the Scioto. There were nine men, three women, and eight children in his party. Just before daylight one morning, an attempt was made to lure the travelers ashore, and when that failed, the sound of paddles forewarned them of an attack. Chairs and tables were thrown into the stream, blankets were hung up fore and aft, and the women and children lay down on the floor of the cabin with the baggage placed around them. Hubbell cautioned his men to wait until the savages were so near that "the flash from the guns might singe their eyebrows" and to fire at intervals so that they would not be left helpless after one volley.

THE IMMIGRANT

There proved to be three canoes with twenty-five or thirty Indians, and these canoes arranged themselves one at each end and the other at the right side, so that the boat was under a cross fire. The firing on both sides now became general. Hubbell, having fired his gun, took up that of a wounded man, but a shot carried away the lock. Instantly he reached for a coal from the fire kettle and discharged the weapon. A moment later he was shot through the arm, but, spying some Indians clambering in at one end of the boat, he rushed upon them and, after discharging his pistols, heaved chunks of firewood at them until they gave up the attempt.

The savages next attacked a boat under a Captain Greathouse, which was behind Hubbell's; they captured it easily, for its occupants fled to the cabin without any attempt at resistance. The men were killed, and the women were placed in the centers of the Indian canoes, which then returned to the attack of the Hubbell boat. Ignoring the danger of shooting the captive women, the four able men remaining resisted with such resolution that the Indians gave up a second time. The boat was now drifting near shore, and several hundred Indians came running down to fire upon it. Two white men only were left unwounded, and they, hidden by blankets and high gunwales, managed to work the craft back into the stream, though the Indians tried to hinder them by firing at the oars. One of the wounded men, incautiously exposing himself, was shot in the mouth and fell dead among the carcasses of the horses that had been killed. When they were out of reach of the shore, the little band—men, women, and children —gathered together and gave three hearty cheers and called to the Indians to come on again if they were fond of the sport. Three men died as a result of the battle, and of the rest, four were severely wounded. One of the boys received two wounds but heroically refrained from saying anything about them until after the battle. When the boat arrived at Limestone the holes in the blankets were counted. A space five feet square was found to bear 122 bullet holes. The bodies of the women captives of the Greathouse boat were found a few days later tied to trees and marked with lashes. These unfortunates appeared to have been literally whipped to death.[17]

If these tales were epics, then certainly the voyage of Colonel John Donelson's party down the Tennessee River in 1779–80 was the Odyssey of the West. Donelson, more than sixty years of age at the time, was a prominent resident of East Tennessee who, with Richard Henderson and James Robertson, had taken up land on the Cumberland near Nashville. A party had gone ahead the previous spring to plant corn for the prospective immigrants, who were to follow in two groups. One group, under Robertson, was to be composed of men and was to escort the horses and cattle by land; after reaching its destination it was to send scouts to Muscle Shoals and leave signs so that Donelson, who was coming by water with the rest of the men and was in charge of the women and children and household goods, would know whether or not it was safe to abandon his boats and cross to Nashville by land. Unfortunately, because of the severity of the winter and the wildness of the country, the connection was not made, and Donelson's party had to go on by water. Donelson's boat, the "Adventure," was probably a keelboat of some kind and was equipped at the boat yard in what is now Kingsport, Tennessee. There were about thirty boats in the convoy when it started, most of them flatboats or pirogues, and a number of others were picked up on the way. The voyage was not, as is sometimes intimated, made through an unknown wilderness, for the Tennessee River was familiar to traders and had been traversed by immigrants a number of times since 1764. On the voyage down the Tennessee and up the Cumberland,

THE IMMIGRANT

Donelson kept a journal that presents a starkly realistic picture of river immigration that no modern pen could hope to equal:

JOURNAL OF A VOYAGE, intended by God's permission, the good boat *Adventure,* from Fort Patrick Henry, on Holston river, to the French Salt Springs on Cumberland river, kept by John Donelson . . . .

March 2d.—Rain about half the day; passed the mouth of French Broad river, and about twelve o'clock Mr. Henry's boat, being driven on the point of an island by the force of the current, was sunk, the whole cargo much damaged, and the crew's lives much endangered, which occasioned the whole fleet to put on shore, and go to their assistance, but with much difficulty baled her out and raised her, in order to take in her cargo again. The same afternoon Reuben Harrison went out a hunting, and did not return that night, though many guns were fired to fetch him in.

Friday, 3d.—Early in the morning fired a four-pounder for the lost man, sent out sundry persons to search the woods for him, firing many guns that day and the succeeding night, but all without success, to the great grief of his parents and fellow-travelers.

Saturday, 4th.—Proceeded on our voyage, leaving old Mr. Harrison, with some other vessels, to make further search for his lost son: about ten o'clock the same day found him a considerable distance down the river. . . .

Wednesday, 8th.—Cast off at ten o'clock, and proceeded down to an Indian village, which was inhabited, on the south side of the river: they invited us to "come ashore," called us brothers, and showed other signs of friendship, insomuch that Mr. John Caffrey and my son, then on board, took a canoe which I had in tow, and were crossing over to them, the rest of the fleet having landed on the opposite shore. After they had gone some distance, a half-breed, who called himself Archy Coody, with several other Indians, jumped into a canoe, met them, and advised them to return to the boat, which they did, together with Coody, and several canoes, which left the shore and followed directly after him. They appeared to be friendly. After distributing some presents among them, with which they seemed much pleased, we observed a number of Indians on the other side embarking in their canoes, armed and painted with red and black. Coody immediately made signs to his companions, ordering them to quit the boat, which they did, himself and another Indian remaining with us, and telling us to move off instantly. We had not gone far before we discovered a number of Indians armed and painted, proceeding down the river, as it were to intercept us. Coody, the half-breed, and his companion sailed with us for some time, and telling us that we had passed all the towns, and were out of danger, left us. But we had not gone far until we came in sight of another town, situated likewise on the south side of the river, nearly opposite a small island. Here they again invited us to come on shore, called us brothers, and observing the boats standing off for the opposite channel, told us that "their side of the river was better for boats to pass." And here we must regret the unfortunate death of young Mr. Payne, on board Captain Blackemore's boat, who was mortally wounded by reason of the boat running too near the northern shore, opposite the town where some of the enemy lay concealed; and the most tragical misfortune of poor Stuart, his family and friends, to the number of twenty-eight persons. This man had embarked with us for the Western country, but his family being diseased with the small-pox, it was agreed upon between him and the company that he should keep at some distance in the rear, for fear of the infection spreading; and he was warned each night when the encampment should take place by the sound of a horn. After we had passed the town, the Indians having now collected to a considerable number, observing his helpless situation, singled off from the rest of the fleet, intercepted him, killed and took prisoners the whole crew, to the great grief of the whole company, uncertain how soon they might share the same fate: their cries were distinctly heard by those boats in the rear.[18] We still perceived them marching down the river in considerable bodies, keeping pace with us until the Cumberland Mountain withdrew them from our sight, when we were in hopes we had escaped them. We are now arrived at the place called Whirl, or Suck, where the river is compressed within less than half its common width above, by the Cumberland Mountains, which juts in on both sides. In passing through the upper part of these narrows, at a place described by Coody, which he termed the "boiling pot," a trivial accident had nearly ruined the expedition.

THE IMMIGRANT

One of the company, John Cotton, who was moving down in a large canoe, had attached it to Robert Cartwright's boat, into which he and his family had gone for safety. The canoe was here overturned, and the little cargo lost. The company, pitying his distress, concluded to halt and assist him in recovering his property. They had landed on the northern shore, at a level spot, and were going up the place, when the Indians, to our astonishment, appeared immediately over us on the opposite cliffs, and commenced firing down upon us, which occasioned a precipitate retreat to the boats. We immediately moved off. The Indians, lining the bluffs along, continued their fire from the heights on our boats, below, without doing any other injury than wounding four slightly. Jenning's boat is missing.

We have now passed through the Whirl. The river widens with a placid and gentle current, and all the company appear to be in safety, except the family of Jonathan Jennings, whose boat ran on a large rock projecting out from the northern shore, and partly immersed in water immediately at the Whirl, where we were compelled to leave them, perhaps to be slaughtered by their merciless enemies. Continued to sail on that day, and floated throughout the following night. . . .

Friday, 10th.—This morning about four o'clock we were surprised by the cries of "Help poor Jennings," at some distance in the rear. He had discovered us by our fires, and came up in the most wretched condition. He states, that as soon as the Indians had discovered his situation, they turned their whole attention to him, and kept up a most galling fire on his boat. He ordered his wife, a son nearly grown, a young man who accompanied them, and his two negroes, to throw all his goods into the river, to lighten their boat for the purpose of getting her off; himself returning their fire as well as he could, being a good soldier and an excellent marksman. But before they had accomplished their object, his son, the young man, and the negro man jumped out of the boat and left them: he thinks the young man and the negro were wounded. Before they left the boat, Mrs. Jennings, however, and the negro woman succeeded in unloading the boat, but chiefly by the exertions of Mrs. Jennings, who got out of the boat, and shoved her off; but was near falling a victim to her own intrepidity, on account of the boat starting suddenly as soon as loosened from the rocks. Upon examination he appears to have made a wonderful escape, for his boat is pierced in numberless places with bullets. It is to be remarked that Mrs. Peyton, who was the night before delivered of an infant, which was unfortunately killed in the hurry and confusion consequent upon such a disaster, assisted them, being frequently exposed to wet and cold then and afterwards, and that her health appears to be good at this time, and I think and hope she will do well. Their clothes were very much cut with bullets, especially Mrs. Jennings'.

Saturday, 11th.—Got under way after having distributed the family of Mrs. Jennings in the other boats. Rowed on quietly that day, and encamped for the night on the northern shore.

Sunday, 12th.—Set out, and after a few hours' sailing we heard the crowing of cocks, and soon came within view of the town: here they fired on us again without doing any injury. After running until about ten o'clock, came in sight of the Muscle Shoals. Halted on the northern shore at the upper end of the shoals, in order to search for the signs Captain James Robertson was to make for us at that place. . . . But to our great mortification we can find none, from which we conclude that it would not be prudent to make the attempt; and we are determined, knowing ourselves to be in such imminent danger, to pursue our journey down the river. After trimming our boats in the best manner possible we ran through the shoals before night. When we approached them they had a dreadful appearance to those who had never seen them before. The water being high made a terrible roaring, which could be heard at some distance among the drift-wood heaped frightfully upon the points of the islands, the current running in every possible direction. . . . Our boats frequently dragged on the bottom, and appeared constantly in danger of striking: they warped as much as in a rough sea. But, by the hand of Providence, we are now preserved from this danger also. . . .

Tuesday, 14th.—Set out early. On this day two boats, approaching too near the shore, were fired on by the Indians; five of the crew were wounded, but not dangerously. Came to camp at night near the mouth of a creek. After kindling fires and preparing for rest, the company were alarmed on account of the incessant barking our dogs kept up; taking it for granted the Indians were attempting to surprise us, we retreated precipitately to the boats, fell down the river about a mile, and encamped on the other shore. In the morning I prevailed on Mr. Caffrey and my son to cross below in a canoe, and return to the place, which they did, and found an African negro we had left in the hurry, asleep by one of the fires. The voyagers then returned and collected their utensils which had been left.

Wednesday, 15th.—Got under way, and moved on peaceably on the five following days, when we arrived at the mouth of the Tennessee on Monday the 20th, and landed on the lower point, immediately on the bank of the Ohio. Our situation here is truly disagreeable. The river is very high and the current rapid, our boats not constructed for the purpose of stemming a rapid stream, our provision exhausted, the crews almost worn down with hunger and fatigue, and know not what distance we have to go, or what time it will take us to our place of destination. The scene is rendered still more melancholy, as several boats will not attempt to ascend the rapid current. Some intend to descend the Mississippi to Natchez; others are bound for the Illinois—among the rest my son-in-law and daughter. We now part, perhaps to meet no more, for I am determined to pursue my course, happen what will.[19]

Donelson reached the French Licks on April 24 after incredible dangers and privations during this voyage of more than four months.

Immigrants did not necessarily settle first along the river shore. The Blue Grass region of Kentucky was fairly well populated before more than two or three settlements were founded on the river. What is now the West Virginia shore was free of settlement until the 1790's. The Indian shore in what is now Ohio received its immigrants after 1785, though there were some squatters before that time. Illinois, as has been seen, was being penetrated even before the Revolution, and at the same time, the shore of the lower Mississippi was receiving individuals, families, and various companies and groups. It was not until after the Louisiana Purchase that the great rush into the latter region began.[20]

THE KEELBOAT AGE

During the later years of immigrant travel, in good weather and when the water was at a reasonable stage, navigation on the Ohio was not very difficult for the strong and alert. After the immigrants had performed their few simple household tasks and had fed and watered the stock, they could talk or sleep, or jig to the tunes of some backwoods musician. In the reaches, if they were so disposed, the flatboat people could seek a refuge from the sun under a canopy of green boughs. Then there was fishing to occupy their time—a recreation that in the early days was a practical source of food—and there was the banter from boat to boat, for at certain times of the year a boat was scarcely ever out of sight of at least one other. An American in those days did not hesitate to ask for information when his curiosity was aroused, nor did he hesitate to answer when questioned. A witty retort was best received, and an Englishman paid the westerners the compliment of saying that since he had left England they were the first Americans he had found who could appreciate a joke. There was also the adventure of buying food, unless a traveler had come supplied with every necessity for the voyage.

On the Kentucky shore there was a wariness of "Yankee tricks," and on the northern shore, a watchfulness for "Kentuck" thievery. The honest immigrant passing between these files might be insulted by the overcautious settler, for the flatboaters came to bear the sobriquet of "chicken thieves," and no doubt many of them earned it. At night, when the immigrant tied up, he, too, had to be on the lookout. If he spent the night in a riverside dwelling or tavern, he had to take everything movable with him, and even then he couldn't be sure that the boat would not disappear during the night. In addition to human thieves, there were the wolves to be taken into consideration. John Melish tells of missing a ham from the larder one morning and, upon examination, finding wolf tracks and hair upon the skiff. This was as late as the summer of 1811.

If the immigrant was a skillful hunter he might be fortunate enough to bag a wild turkey or at least a few pigeons. After 1790, however, game rapidly became scarcer. The days when the voyager took along salt and barrels for his surplus buffalo meat were long past. Yet, though some of the pioneer conditions no longer existed, the immigrant still had many of the earlier hazards to contend with. Natural forces remained to dispute his progress. The roofs of the flatboats were too often makeshifts and so far from waterproof that during a driving rain the immigrant family could do nothing but spend the night huddled together under heavy blankets and hope to counteract the effect next day by onion syrup and foot baths. On the other hand, a heated roof in warm weather might prove fully as dangerous. Malaria was a constant menace in the summer, and pneumonia in the winter.

Francis Baily has left an account of a passage down the Ohio in December, 1796, which can scarcely find its equal in the annals of Indian perils of a few years before.[21] A short distance below Wheeling, three boats had been frozen in, and the companies, aggregating a total of about fifteen persons, were forced to make the best of the situation. Baily's boat was protected upstream by a felled tree; nevertheless, on the night of the twenty-first, a sudden rise in the river burst the ice and ripped a great hole in the boat. Threatened with the total loss of their cargo, the men worked for three hours, waist deep in ice and water, until the rise of the water drove them ashore. Here the water, threatening to engulf what they had saved, forced them to move their goods up the steep bank, but, exhausted and chilled as they were, they could only manage to move them a few feet at a time and lodge them behind trees, and they continued this operation till the river ceased rising.

Their first shelter was a lean-to, but within a few days they removed to a rude log shelter intended for cattle. Meanwhile the other two boats that had survived the ice crush moved on, and Baily's party of seven English men and women was left to fight the winter. After two months of labor, during which their house narrowly escaped being burned down and their only food was gained by hunting, they succeeded in constructing another boat and continued their interrupted voyage.

When Nicholas Roosevelt and his wife went down the rivers on the exploratory voyage that preceded the building, in 1811, of the "Orleans," the first steamboat on the Ohio, they were awakened one night by two Indians who had entered their sleeping room and were calling for whiskey. Mr. Roosevelt had to get up and satisfy their demand before he could prevail on them to leave. At Baton Rouge they slept in a filthy room opening off a barroom, "which was filled with tipsy men looking like cutthroats." The Roosevelts threw their cloaks on the bed and lay down, but the noise of the drunken, fighting crowd prevented their sleeping. When the travelers slept in their boat, the alligators would scratch against it, taking it for a log, and when a cane alarmed the beasts, they would splash noisily into the water. It is no wonder that when the travelers wrapped up in buffalo robes and lay down on the beach, they fancied every moment that something terrible was going to happen.[22]

The Reverend Timothy Flint, that indefatigable missionary of the West, has left an account of a poignant day and night in his own life in the year 1819 while he and his family were voyaging down the Mississippi in a keelboat.[23] With a storm approaching and his wife beginning to feel the pangs of travail, he moored the boat securely to the shore opposite a cypress swamp. The children were wrapped in blankets and laid themselves down on a sand bar. At eleven in the morning the storm broke in a fury of rain and wind and hail and threatened at every moment to tear the boat loose and drive it into the river. Mrs. Flint, though confident that the hour of death was near, remained tranquil even when the wind burst in the roof of the cabin and flooded her bed with rain. The storm finally passed, and that evening she was delivered of a child. Two days later it died, and the father and children laid it in a small trunk and made a grave amid the rushes on the river bank. The prayer made by the father, with the children for concourse and mourners, if not eloquent, was, to them at least, "deeply affecting." This unmarked grave of a pioneer's sacrifice in serving the young West is on a high bank opposite the second Chickasaw bluff.

What was the condition of the immigrants upon their arrival in the land of milk and honey? The thrifty ones with a little cash to tide them over the first months prospered. The shiftless, improvident, and unfortunate suffered. Timothy Flint has left us a picture of them as he saw them in Cincinnati in 1815. Whole families were crowded into a single room, penniless, friendless, many of them sick, perhaps dying. When they did die they were buried by charity. Widows and orphans were left to battle a world grown used to the sufferings of immigrants. Even if a man were fortunate enough to escape the perils of the voyage and to buy a stretch of rich bottom to farm, there might be other handicaps. Thieving squatter neighbors might take the fruits of his labor, and there might be no law worth appealing to. Wolves and wildcats might do their share to deplete the stock. The ornithologist, Alexander Wilson, contrasted the squatter and the settler as he observed them in 1810:

Nothing can add more to the savage grandeur . . . of the scenery along the Ohio, than these miserable huts of . . . the squatter lurking at the bottom of a gigantic growth of timber. . . . And it is truly amusing to observe how dear and how familiar habit has rendered these privations, which must have been first the offspring of necessity; yet none pride themselves more on their possessions. The inhabitants of these forlorn sheds will talk to you with pride of the richness of their soil—of the excellence and abundance of their country—of the healthiness of their climate and the purity of their waters, when the only bread you find among them is of Indian corn coarsely ground in a horse mill, with half of the grains unbroken; even their cattle are destitute of hay, and look like moving skeletons; their own houses worse than pig styes; their clothes an assemblage of rags; their faces yellow and lank with disease, and their persons covered with filth and frequently garnished with . . . the 'seven-years itch.' . . . All this is the effect of laziness. The corn is thrown into the ground in the spring, and the pigs turned into the woods, where they multiply like rabbits. The labour of the *squatter* is now over till autumn, and he spends the winter in eating pork, cabbages, and hoe-cakes. What a contrast to the neat farm, and snug, cleanly habitation of the industrious settler, that opens his green fields, his stately barns, gardens, and orchards, to the gladdened eye of the delighted stranger.[24]

7

Shipbuilding
on the Western Waters

HENRY CLAY, that tireless promoter of industrial progress, once described, in the course of an address before the House of Representatives, an incident illustrative of the spirit of commercial enterprise on the western waters:

A vessel, built at Pittsburg, having crossed the Atlantic . . . entered a European port (he believed that of Leghorn). The master of the vessel laid his papers before the proper custom-house officer, which, of course, stated the place of her departure. The officer boldly

159

denied the existence of any such American port as Pittsburg, and threatened a seizure of the vessel, as being furnished with forged papers. The affrighted master procured a map of the United States, and, pointing out the Gulf of Mexico, took the officer to the mouth of the Mississippi, traced the course of the Mississippi more than a thousand miles, to the mouth of the Ohio, and conducting him still a thousand miles higher, to the junction of the Allegany and Monongahela,—there, he exclaimed, stands Pittsburg, the port from which I sailed! The custom-house officer, prior to the production of this evidence, would have as soon believed that the vessel had performed a voyage from the moon.[1]

In 1761, even before the Philadelphia traders had begun their penetration of the Illinois, a writer in the Quaker City was boosting Pittsburgh as a shipbuilding center. In 1770, in their address to Lord Hillsborough, secretary of state for the American department, Benjamin Franklin and his associates foretold that "whenever the farmers or merchants of the Ohio shall properly understand the business of transportation, they will build schooners, sloops, &c., on the Ohio, suitable for the West-India or European markets."[2]

As the Northwest began to fill with settlers, the prophecies became more florid. J. C. Symmes advertised that vessels of one hundred tons burden could be built on the Ohio and navigated, fully freighted, to any seaport. Manasseh Cutler, a forerunner of the plague of lobbyists that afflicts Congress, claimed to look forward to seeing the Ohio and the Mississippi more frequented than any other rivers on earth. Hugh Henry Brackenridge wrote that before he went West, he and his friends calculated "that a farm in the neighborhood of these rivers was nearer the market of any part of the world than a farm within twenty miles of Philadelphia." These hopes of making the Ohio a great shipbuilding center seem at a casual glance to have been justified. Black oak, white oak, black walnut, cherry, locust, and yellow pine grew plentifully and to sizes that made it possible to obtain cheap planks and masts of any desired dimensions. Iron ore was common; hemp and flax could be raised in the country; and tar was being made on the Allegheny.[3] The materials were at hand and experienced workmen were on the way. What these pioneer enthusiasts failed to take into consideration were the perils of river navigation. Far from being always the gentle streams of which certain purblind optimists wrote, these rivers contained sand bars that clutched relentlessly at the unwary boatman; snags and sawyers lay hidden at every turn, threatening to crush the frail bottom of his craft; and in escaping the falling bank waiting to overwhelm him, the boatman might rush into the jaws of a crevasse. Moreover, at certain seasons the calm river could become a lashing, storm-driven expanse of choppy waves or a white inferno of grinding, crashing ice.

By 1792, however, the optimistic prophecies concerning western shipbuilding had begun to take form in reality. The first seagoing vessel from the upper waters was probably the one named in the *Kentucky Gazette* of May 5, 1792: "The sloop Western Experiment, Captain, Charles Nicholson. Built on the Monongahela and bound for Philadelphia—passed limestone on Saturday the 20 April, navigated by Isaac Brown, Samuel Moor, Walter M'Morris, Joseph Woods and Andrew Mitchel." Albert Gallatin stated in 1808 that a schooner built on the Monongahela had reached New Orleans in 1793, and Francis Baily recorded that a Dr. Waters of New Madrid had built a schooner at the head of the Ohio and that in 1797 it was engaged in ocean commerce out of Philadelphia. Gallatin and Baily may have referred to the same vessel. Nevertheless, there seem to have been at least two ships, for the *Kentucky Gazette* of October 12, 1793, quoting the *General Advertiser*, stated that on its passage from New

Orleans to Philadelphia, "the vessel built on the Ohio, within the state of Pennsylvania" had been captured at sea. This circumstance was cited as proof of the need of a treaty with Spain concerning the navigation of the Mississippi.[4]

Unless the row galleys "President Adams" and "Senator Ross" found their way into service on blue water, no further mention of ocean-going vessels from the upper waters is to be found for eight years. Early in 1800 a group of farmers and others living near Elizabeth on the Monongahela organized themselves into the Monongahela Company and began the construction of a vessel, with a John Scott as designer and master builder. It was built of white oak and black walnut and decked with yellow pine. Meanwhile another boat, the schooner "Redstone," forty-five feet in keel, owned by Samuel Jackson and Company, was being built at Joseph Chester's shipyard below Brownsville. "With spars, rigging, etc., of the growth and manufacture of this western country," she was riding at anchor at Pittsburgh on March 28, six weeks before the appearance there of her Elizabeth rival.[5] It is possible that the "Redstone" was intended only for river commerce, but if it was an ocean craft it may well have reached the Gulf before the "St. Clair" of Marietta, to be mentioned later, which reached Cincinnati on the twenty-second of April.

The Elizabeth boat was launched on April 23, 1801, and christened the "Monongahela Farmer." It was of perhaps 100 tons burden, and a schooner rig was planned for use after it reached New Orleans. Under the command of John Walker, the vessel loaded about 750 barrels of flour and began its voyage down the rivers, touching at Pittsburgh on May 13. Adding whiskey, hides, hemp, and flax to her cargo on the way, the "Monongahela Farmer" drifted downstream; but at Louisville she had to wait three months before the river rose enough to carry her over the falls. Just below Cave-in-Rock she went aground on a shoal, which the famous pilot book, the *Navigator,* thereafter called Walker's Bar. When New Orleans was reached, it was found that the flour had soured, so that it had to be sold to cracker-makers. The vessel itself was sold and used in the trade between the eastern coast and the West Indies and New Orleans. In 1808 a "Monongahela Farmer," burden 120 tons, was at New Orleans waiting to take on cargo for New York. According to one account, this boat broke the record for speed between the Balize and New York by making the voyage in twelve days.[6]

John Walker later took the brig "Ann Jane" or "Ann Jean," said to have a burden of 450 tons, to New York in 1804. It was owned by Robert and James McFarland. A brig owned by the same men was aground below Pittsburgh in the spring of that year. It also was built at Elizabeth and, though of only 200 tons burden, may well have been the "Ann Jane," since tonnage statistics were notoriously inaccurate.[7] Though no other names of vessels built at Elizabeth have been ascertained, it is possible that some of those accredited to Pittsburgh actually came from the former place.

During the period of trouble with France at the close of the eighteenth century, fear of a conflict with Spain, a French ally, caused the building of two row galleys at Pittsburgh under the supervision of Major Isaac Craig. As nearly as can be judged from the mutilated account book, these galleys were forty-five feet in length and thirteen in beam. They had two masts and were equipped with sails and rigging brought from the East. There were thirty oars of differing lengths, and the row benches were constructed so that they could be folded away. The first galley, the "President Adams," was launched on May 19, 1798, with General Wilkinson presiding at a celebration, the expenses of which were paid by the government. The boat departed on June 8 bearing the commander in chief and escorted by a fleet of Kentucky boats and smaller craft. The other galley, the "Senator Ross," was not launched until March of the next year, because of ice and low water. Her armament consisted of a twenty-four-pounder and several swivel guns.[8]

Shipbuilding at Pittsburgh was carried on principally by Eliphalet Beebe and by the firm of John A. Tarascon Brothers, James Berthoud & Company. The Tarasçons, originally from Bordeaux, were established as merchants in Philadelphia when they realized that large profits might be gained by building ships at the headwaters of the Ohio in the midst of as fine and cheap timber as the country produced. Accordingly they sent two of their clerks, Charles Brugiere and James Berthoud, to investigate conditions around Pittsburgh and to report upon the navigability of the Ohio and the Mississippi. The result was that they established at Pittsburgh a shipyard with dependent smith shops and rigging and sail loft, as well as a store and warehouse where they carried on a merchandising business.[9]

The Tarasçons, however, were not to have the honor of launching Pittsburgh's first merchant ship. In January, 1803, the brig "Dean," 170 tons, built at an unidentified yard on the Allegheny, sailed from Pittsburgh for the Cumberland to take on a cargo of cotton bound for Liverpool. She passed the falls on February 27 at the same time as the brig "Muskingum" of Marietta. A Louisville paper recorded that "a number of citizens went over in those vessels to assist in keeping them in the current and were entertained with various refreshments by the captains." According to the *Western Spy,* a Liverpool paper spoke of the "Dean" as "the first vessel which ever came to Europe from the western waters of the U.S."[10] The same year there followed the ship "Pittsburgh," 270 tons, and the schooner "Amity," about 100 tons, built under the direction of Captain Beebe in the Tarascon yard. Both were laden with flour and sailed about May 1, the first bound for Lisbon and the other for St. Thomas. In 1804 the Tarascons launched the brig "Nanina," about 150 tons, and the ship "Louisiana," of perhaps 200 tons. Beebe's yard also built the schooner "Conquest," owned by James O'Hara, and a brig that may have been the "Allegheny." The next year the brig "General Butler," owned by O'Hara, sailed for Liverpool with a cargo of flour. After unloading she departed for Philadelphia but was supposed to have foundered at sea, as she was never heard from again. Other ships were built in the succeeding years; according to J. T. Lloyd, one belonging to the Tarasçons was lost at the Falls of the Ohio in 1805.[11]

What gala occasions the launchings of Pittsburgh's ships must have been, and how local toastmasters must have pointed with pride and boasted of civic progress! An old resident tells of seeing one of these new ships sailing up and down the river "with a crowd of gaily dressed ladies and their escorts on board" while the sailors ran nimbly up the masts and scampered about amid the billowy clouds of snowy-white canvas.[12]

Some of the records of one Pittsburgh ship, the "Louisiana," have been preserved. Built in the Tarasçon yard under the direction of Abraham Marpole, she was launched in April, 1804, and left soon after for the mouth of the Cumberland River, there to take on a load of cotton bound for Liverpool. Registered at Marietta and probably owned there, she was known as the "Louisiana of Marietta" during her ensuing triumphs and misfortunes. Of the two, the latter seem to have been her more usual lot, judging by the surviving papers. On May 11 the vessel ran ashore a few miles below Fort Massac and lay aground until a rise on the twenty-fifth enabled her to float free. To escape being held responsible for the accident, Captain Minor and others of the crew swore to a "protest" before Commandant Bissell at the fort and gave the circumstances of the mishap: "The said brig was at the time nearly in the middle of the River and the Water was far more than sufficiently deep just before she struck."

On July 23, 1804, the "Louisiana" sailed from New Orleans with cotton, skins, and staves, but was detained in the Mississippi by contrary winds until August 5. After she had entered the gulf there came several weeks of alternate calms, light winds, and squalls, which greatly hampered her progress. In addition, the crew became so sick that they could hardly make sail and were forced to put into Norfolk, where on September 7 another protest was indited recounting the experiences of the voyage and blaming "the Calms and Weather, the sickness of the Crew and all other Events and occurrences aforesaid for all the Losses, Costs, Charges, Damages and Expenses." The "Louisiana" finally reached Liverpool and probably took on another cargo for Messina. At any rate, on February 28, 1805, another protest was made at that port to the effect that the hatches had opened on the passage from Liverpool and the cargo had been damaged—all of which had been caused not by the neglect of the master but "by the Labour of the said Brig in the repeated Gales and bad weather." On April 24 a clearance was granted to the "Brigantine *Louisiana* built in Marietta" to return to Liverpool with a cargo of oil, fruit, and the like. At the latter place a cargo of white salt was shipped, and the vessel departed for Philadelphia.[18]

The principal center of shipbuilding in the West was Marietta. The town had been partly settled by seamen and shipwrights from Connecticut and Rhode Island, who cannily planned on triple coups—building ships cheaply from the abundant timber of the Ohio Valley, transporting low-priced farm produce in them to the markets of the world, and selling both ships and cargoes at good rates. Scarcely had the town been well established before these activities were begun and several river craft were built. These were followed in 1801 by the brig "St. Clair," 104 tons burden, built by Stephen Devol and said to be the first square-rigged vessel built on the Ohio.[14] Laden with pork and flour and under the command of the intrepid old Commodore Abraham Whipple of "Gaspée" fame, the little ship was given a grand send-off by the citizens of Marietta. Doubtless they felt that they saw before them the germ of what was destined to become a shipbuilding center as great as Philadelphia or Boston. Captain Jonathan Devol rose nobly to the occasion with a poetic effusion which, with top-heavy capitals and tangled feet, tripped through a realm of classic fancy. Scene and cast were "mouth ye Mississippi Neptune God of the Sea Trittons, Sirens, etc. a Ship Descending."

The Tritton crieth who is that from Shore
Neptune Replieth its the old Commodore
its Long Since Ere I Saw him
in 75 from Columbia Shore he came
to attack Britain Power was his Aim
his Gun Awaked me from my Coazy Bed
he Often Crossed my Domain
on the Gallick Coast I have seen him
his Thundering Cannon Lulled my Waves
he was One of them his Country Saved
in War of Revolution
But now he is from the western woods
Dcending with their Gentle Floods
he hath Oped the way to Commerce
Attend my Sons to Let him pass
Present your Arms unto him
his Gray Hair Shows, Life is near a Close
Lets pay the Honours Due Him
Sirens attend with Flute & Lyre
& Bring your Conks my Trittons

THE KEELBOAT AGE

in Chorus Blow to the Aged Sire
in Welcome to my Dominions.[15]

It is said that on April 27 at Cincinnati, "the banks were
crowded with people" to greet what was mistakenly announced as the first vessel to descend the Ohio equipped for
sea. The "St. Clair" reached New Orleans during the first
part of June after a passage that must have been a great trial
to the old seaman. "Commodore Whipple thinks it the greatest thing he ever did," wrote a correspondent, "and deserves
more credit than his going out of Newport in a frigate with
dispatches from Congress, after passing seven British frigates.
. . . He is seventy years of age, and was six weeks coming
down." At New Orleans the "St. Clair" anchored in the stream
to avoid the payment of duty and after a short stay went on
to Havana, where the flour was sold at forty dollars a barrel
and a duty of half that amount was paid. She then sailed for
Philadelphia with a cargo of sugar and netted her owners a
handsome profit.[16]

Shipbuilding in Marietta now entered a halcyon period that
lasted for six or eight years. The price for ships completely
equipped and ready for sea was fifty dollars a ton—a price
that made the venture well worth while, at least until the
Falls of the Ohio began to take their toll. The principal
builders of Marietta were Jonathan Devol and James Whitney, and the chief owners were Charles Green, B. I. Gilman,
Abner Lord, and E. W. Tupper. It was probably in the spring
of 1802 that the ship "Muskingum," of about 220 tons burden,
and the brig "Eliza Green," about 130 tons, were launched.
While the "Muskingum" was lying to at Blennerhasset Island,
a sudden storm struck her; the main mast was shivered by
lightning, and some men were knocked into the water or to
the deck, one remaining insensible for more than an hour.
In floating down the Ohio, each ship went stern first, keeping

William Mason's map of Pittsburgh, 1805. From the original in the possession of the Historical Society of Western Pennsylvania.

Vessels shown include the following: schooners *Allegany*, *Amity*, and *Conquest*; brigs *Ann*

...ne, Bison, Fayette, and *Nanina;* ships *Western Trader, General Butler,* and *Pittsburgh.*

in the current by dragging an anchor. So many cables were broken and anchors lost that stones were finally substituted for the latter. After the ships reached the Mississippi, platforms were built three feet above the decks, and from these the vessels were kept in the channel by sweeps. This occurred considerably later, however, for the "Muskingum" and the "Eliza Green" were detained at Louisville by low water for months. The former went over the falls with the "Dean" of Pittsburgh on February 27, 1803. Even then the cargoes had to be sent over the falls in flatboats. Once on the Mississippi, both Marietta ships took on cargoes of cotton at Governor Winthrop Sargent's plantation and departed for Liverpool.[17]

From 1802 to 1807 inclusive, there were a score of vessels built at Marietta,[18] and half again as many at other points. In April, 1803, the secretary of the navy advertised for proposals to build some galleys at Pittsburgh, Marietta and Louisville. They were to be built of white oak and black walnut, to be fifty-eight feet in length and fourteen and a half in beam, and to be rowed with twenty-eight oars. Their armament was to consist of a twenty-four-pounder and four six-pound brass howitzers each. In later years other gunboats were constructed on the western waters, including two at Marietta in 1806, two at Columbia (near Cincinnati) in 1807, and several in the yard of Matthew Lyon of Eddyville, Kentucky.[19] Doubtless after 1803 the gunboats were built for service on the coast. Among the places where shipbuilding was attempted were Wheeling, Charleston (near Maysville, Kentucky), Belville, Limestone, Frankfort, and Louisville. Port Gibson in the Mississippi Territory had two or more ships.[20]

The ships built on the western waters were not inferior in size to those built in other parts of the world. The exact meaning of the term "tonnage" is open to question in most instances, as obviously the burden a vessel could carry varied with the nature of the cargo. Probably, however, the standard practice was to calculate a ton for each ninety-five cubic feet of capacity. But again there is the problem of whether the builders and editors figured gross or net capacity. If the lowest tonnages claimed are to be accepted, western vessels averaged close to 170 tons; the American vessels trading from New Orleans in 1802 and in the first half of 1803 averaged about 135 tons; the French, 115 tons; and the Spanish ships, 105 tons.[21]

By 1808, however, a combination of adverse factors had begun to discourage Ohio shipbuilding. The vessels built for ocean commerce were necessarily of deep draft and consequently found it difficult to pass the bars in which the river abounded. The most serious obstacle of all and the one probably most to blame for the decline of Ohio shipbuilding was the falls at Louisville. The greatest catastrophe at this place was in April, 1807, when the ships "John Atkinson," 320 tons; "Tuscarora," 320 tons; and "Rufus King," 300 tons, all of Marietta, attempted passage. The *Western Spy, and Miami Gazette* of May 18, 1807, gives a graphic account of the episode:

Louisville, April 20—Shipwrecks at the Rapids of Ohio. A spectacle so distressing to the generous heart, was never presented in the western country as that of this day, in front of Louisville—On Saturday four large ships, all new and bound to New-Orleans, lay in a line in the bason [sic] above the rapids waiting the rise of water, which was then on the swell; and promised a safe passage over the obstructions, so that all calculated on passing on Sunday—Sunday was a boisterous day which prevented a possibility of managing a ship in so straight a passage—The water at a stand during the day began to fall in the evening.—Monday the water had fallen two or three inches, and very little hope obtained of its swelling to that height again during the year.—The owners of the ships who were present, felt the consequence too sensibly to remain idle a moment if a possibility existed of passing—soundings were made and hope revived. Col. Lord owner of the ship John Atkinson, bore down for the head grand shoot, and passed handsomely by, rubbing the rocks two or three times, and anchored below. By this time the wind had increased a little in a direction somewhat unfavorable, but not sufficiently to prevent the attempt by the Tuscarora, who got under way and the Rufus King followed her wake. At this moment the shores, terraces, and windows were filled with anxious spectators enjoying a doubtful pleasure, but in a few minutes their suspence was decided with the fate of the ships, which lay wrecks upon the rocks! until they filled with water, which was in a short time after they struck. The apparent perilous situation of the crews and gentlemen on board was dreadful; in ships without rudders or keels tumbling from rock to rock and rolling from side to side, in a current which rates twelve or fourteen miles an hour, without a possibility of being relieved from the shore. Fortunately for the lives on board, the ships filled on the rocks without going to pieces.

The Rufus King endeavored by casting her anchors after the Tuscarora struck to avoid the like blow, but the strength of the current was too powerful, she struck near the same place and drawing a few inches less water bounded past the bow, and carried away the head of the Tuscarora and part of her railing, lodged about her length below.

Col. Lord had returned from his ship with the pilot and was on board the Rufus King, during this time, his ship the John Atkinson which had passed without damage, dragged her anchor or parted with it, and in spite of the exertions of the hands on board stranded on Sandy Island shoal, which will be perfectly dry in a few days if the water continues to fall at the present rate—'tis presumed she may be got off the next rise of the water without sustaining any material damage—these three ships drew nearly the same depth of water. The Penrose which draws more made no attempt to pass, and now lies safely in the bason; where she has already weathered out one year.

Tuesday, April 21. To close the misfortune of those gentlemen, whose enterprize entitles them to the extreme reverse of what has befallen them and the best wishes of their countrymen; a large covered boat (a lighter) belonging to the owner of the Rufus King, and lying in the bason laden with tobacco and cordage, took fire and was destroyed. The flame spread so rapidly that the only alternative was to extinguish it by sinking her—what part of the cargo, was not entirely lost is very much damaged. The place was crowded with small crafts, some of which received injury.

One solitary consolation is that no lives have been lost—a man of the Rufus King was severely bruised with the tiller, perhaps mortally.[22]

Apparently neither the "Tuscarora" nor the "Rufus King" was a total loss. Schultz speaks of one of them, worth $10,000, being sold for $1,500. Cramer mentions that in the spring of 1808 the "Tuscarora" grounded on Flint Island about one hundred miles below the falls and was there stripped by thieves of two thousand dollars' worth of bolts, bands, rings, and other equipment.[23] The *Louisiana Gazette* of January 27, 1809, noted the arrival at New Orleans of the ship "Rufus King" of Marietta.

The embargo was the second reason for the decline of Ohio shipbuilding, or at least so it appeared to the budding capitalists of Marietta. A poet a little more polished than the bluff old shipbuilder who celebrated Marietta's first venture now struck his lyre to add a discordant note to the western hymn to democracy:

> Our ships all in motion
> Once whiten'd the Ocean
> They sailed and returned with a cargo;
> Now doomed to decay
> They have fallen a prey
> To Jefferson, worms, and embargo.[24]

Samuel P. Hildreth stated that the embargo put a stop to all mercantile operations and ruined a number of the merchants of Marietta. One of them who at the time had a ship and cargo in New Orleans lost more than ten thousand dollars on the venture. With a few belated exceptions, the building of seagoing vessels on the Ohio may be looked upon as dead after 1808, although schooners were built in Marietta in 1809, 1812, and 1816. Pittsburgh sent out a brig in 1810, and Columbia in 1817 launched the brig "Cincinnatus" of 170 tons. The shipyards turned to the building of river barges that in size compared favorably with the schooners and brigs of the early days; after 1812 they devoted themselves to steamboats. It was not until the 1840's that there came a revival of the building of ocean craft on the Ohio. Marietta, as before, was the center of activities.[25]

It is well for the present-day observer to avoid overestimating the importance of western shipbuilding. Even as a psychological factor it should not be overrated. The westerners themselves, after the first blush of enthusiasm, regarded it as a subject for oratory rather than financial investment. The pioneers' hopes of making the Ohio a great shipbuilding center were formed in blissful ignorance of the numerous obstacles that the courses of the Ohio and the Mississippi offered to the navigators of unwieldy ocean craft. The experiences encountered between 1801 and 1808 did much to dampen the ardor, and one can scarcely avoid a suspicion that the shipbuilders were glad to cast the blame for the wrecks of their ships and their hopes upon the broad shoulders of Jefferson.

The shipbuilding ventures of the early days in the West were not of very great economic importance. Making due allowance for western optimism by placing the average tonnage at 150, and counting the 67 known ships, exclusive of gunboats, it can be estimated that there were at least 10,050 tons of ocean shipping launched on the western waters. This, at $50 dollars a ton, would make a total valuation of more than half a million dollars. The cargoes, when spread over twenty years and compared with the 500,000 or more tons carried by barge, keel, and flatboat, could not have been very important.

The $500,000 presumably received for the ships was likewise a small sum when placed beside the $150,000,000 probably received for western goods shipped to New Orleans in the first two decades of the century.[26] Thus, shipbuilding on the western waters, whatever its romantic interest, can scarcely be regarded as more than a minor phase of the westward movement.

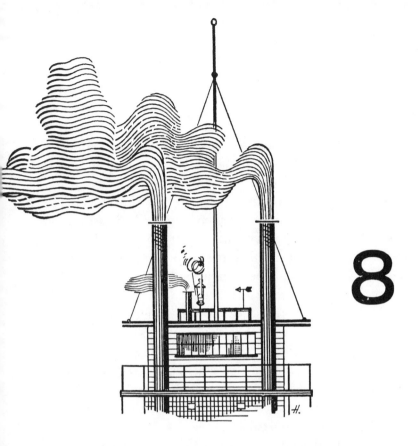

8

The Boatman Has His Day

THE first reference to a packet on the western waters is found in an advertisement in the *Pittsburgh Gazette* of September 2, 1786. In it John Blair announced that he expected to pass up and down the Monongahela every week with a boat and would deliver newspapers at a reasonable rate. This service extended for thirty-five miles above Pittsburgh. In the same issue John McDonald, with an eye to the business of the flour mills up river and to the carrying trade between Pittsburgh and the Monongahela landing nearest Washington, announced that he had started weekly trips and would deliver the *Pittsburgh Gazette* to subscribers. He also proposed to erect a storehouse at his landing for goods. McDonald remained in the packet business for a number of years.

In October, 1793, Jacob Myers inaugurated a fortnightly passenger service between Pittsburgh and Cincinnati. The first boat left Pittsburgh on October 14, and the second on November 5. His plan was to add two more boats so that there would be weekly service. Myers stated in his advertisement that "the Proprietor . . . being influenced by a love of philanthropy and desire of being serviceable to the public, has taken great pains to render the accommodations on board the Boats as agreeable and convenient as they could possibly be made." Protection against the Indians was provided by high bulwarks thick enough to withstand rifle shots and pierced with portholes. Each boat carried six one-pounders, probably swivels, and a number of muskets. The number in the crews is not stated but was supposed to be sufficient for defense. To obviate the necessity of landing in dangerous vicinities, the boats were provided with sanitary conveniences. Passengers were boarded and "liquored" by the management "at the most reasonable rates possible," and a separate cabin was provided for the women passengers. There was a set of "Rules and Regulations for maintaining order on board, and for the good management of the Boats." Unfortunately no copy of these rules seems to have survived, nor any statement of the schedule on which the boats ran. Freight and letters were carried, and insurance was sold, at a "moderate" rate, but none of the schedules of rates survives. Myers' boats were propelled by oars and sails and were intended to serve not only as conveyors of freight and passengers but also as convoys for other boats. Two additional boats were put in service by January, 1794.[1]

THE BOATMAN HAS HIS DAY

In July, 1794, a line of mail packets was established between Wheeling and Limestone. Major Isaac Craig, who was experienced in river navigation, and Colonel James O'Hara, the army contractor, were in charge of the arrangements. The boats were bateaux, twenty-two to twenty-five feet long, steered with oars, and provided with tarpaulins for protection in rainy weather. Each crew consisted of four rowers and a captain, who were well armed; their muskets were stowed in weatherproof boxes alongside their seats. At night the crews landed at the head of an island to cook and sleep. Upstream a boat was able to make thirty miles a day, and downstream it might make twice that. It is probable that passengers were sometimes carried. As originally established, the line consisted of three boats. The mail was carried from Pittsburgh to Wheeling by postriders; from there the first boat carried it to Marietta and handed it over to the second boat, which took it to Gallipolis, and the third boat took it on to Limestone. Each boat was to make a round trip weekly between its two termini. Mail service by river never proved satisfactory, as it was slower than overland mail, not as punctual, and incurred great expense; moreover, it was held up by ice for some weeks during the winter. It was continued, however, until 1797, when the passing of the danger of Indian attacks made possible the substitution of postriders.[2]

Pittsburgh early began to profit by its strategic situation and built up a variety of manufactories for utilizing western materials. A great number of keelboats were employed in transporting goods to and from that city. In 1810, between May 1 and November 14, Pittsburgh imported from downriver 689 tons of spun yarn and hemp, worth about two hundred thousand dollars. Ten tons of tobacco were imported and 120 tons of cotton. The passing domestic trade of Pittsburgh was estimated by Zadok Cramer at one million dollars.

During the boating season of 1812 there were said to have been 1,000 tons of Kentucky goods shipped from Maysville to Pittsburgh. About 1805 there were 50 keels of 30 tons each plying from the latter city to Cincinnati, and ten years later, according to Morgan Neville, there were 150 keels engaged in the upper Ohio trade. The round trip from Pittsburgh to Louisville occupied two months, and each boat was supposed to make it at least three times a year. Trips from New Orleans to Pittsburgh were made frequently, and in June, 1814, a firm advertised the cargoes of six keelboats expected from New Orleans that month. In 1817 a two-masted barge of 150 tons burden was in the trade, and in 1814 Cramer recorded that "a great number of barges constantly ply between this and the country below." Probably most of them were small, since it was difficult for large barges to ascend above Wheeling in low water.[3]

It is impossible to estimate the value of this trade, but the advertisements in the Pittsburgh newspapers show the importance to the city of southern and western goods. The manufacture of cotton, tobacco, rope, and bagging was directly dependent upon the West and the South for raw materials. Missouri lead, Mexican copper, Spanish hides, Kentucky glazed powder, whiskey, country linen, saltpeter, bacon, sugar, Spanish wool, and West Indian products came up the river. A traffic in Onondaga salt by way of Lake Erie and French Creek was begun. Most important of all, Pittsburgh became an iron manufacturing center and headquarters for cast and wrought iron, wire, nails, and tools. In addition, the city began the manufacture of glass, leather goods, white lead and paints, chemicals, flour, and other products too numerous to mention. In spite of difficulties, trade across the mountains flourished, and the Conemaugh and Youghiogheny rivers became important waterways leading respectively into the

THE BOATMAN HAS HIS DAY

Allegheny and the Monongahela. The War of 1812, by cutting off the sea route, caused the main route of commerce from South to North to flow through Pittsburgh, and this movement retained some of its impetus until the day of the railroad. The trade of 1813 was estimated at four million dollars, and over four thousand wagonloads of goods crossed the mountains between Pittsburgh and Philadelphia. Bosler and Company alone imported 275 tons of goods from New Orleans between April 1 and September 1 of that year.[4]

It is found upon examining the trade of Cincinnati that by 1806 a merchant named Reed was importing goods from New Orleans by a regular line, and that in later years several other lines were formed. These boats ordinarily made one trip a year, but in wet seasons sometimes made two. The "Triton" accomplished that feat in 1816 and was said to have been the first to do it. There were probably three boats named "Cincinnati" trading from the city of that name. The *Louisiana Gazette* of May 27, 1806, mentions one and gives the master's name as Moore. Five years later, on May 26, the "elegant" sloop "Cincinnati," the first rigged vessel to reach Cincinnati from below, with Beale as commander, dropped anchor before the town. She had taken seventy-eight running days in the ascent from New Orleans and had been warped over the falls in half a day by eighteen men. This was not an unusually large boat; it was only 100 feet in length and 16 in beam and had a burden of 65 tons. In 1815 a "Cincinnati" under the command of Jonathan Horton arrived from New Orleans in eighty-seven days, another good record. This boat had a burden variously reported as 100, 115, and 120 tons. In 1815 she was owned by Jacob Baymiller and Jonathan Horton, and in 1816 by J. and W. Teatman. "The finest barge that ever floated on the Ohio" was the "Missouri," which was built at Cincinnati, carried 170 tons burden, and was propelled by 44 oars. She accomplished the 180 miles between Cincinnati and Louisville in twenty-two hours and twenty-four minutes, with a cargo of sixteen hundred barrels of flour besides other lading.[5]

Barges from New Orleans made their way past the falls to the home ports of Frankfort and Maysville. John Palmer tells of the merchants at the latter place greeting a newly arrived boat with salutes of cannon fire from both sides of the river. Lexington, the emporium of the West before the War of 1812, was served by land from Frankfort, but declined in importance after the invention of the steamboat and the movement of manufacturing establishments to the Ohio. Louisville was the natural entrepôt of Kentucky and the logical place for the transshipment from barge to keelboat of goods destined for the shallower waters away from the river. There is no way of knowing how many barges made regular trips to Louisville, but in 1806 and 1807 the "Ship News" column of the *Louisiana Gazette,* which listed perhaps one quarter of the arrivals and departures at New Orleans, recorded about twenty-five barges as arriving from or clearing for Louisville or unnamed Kentucky ports.[6]

Eddyville, Kentucky, had a prominent citizen who operated at least one barge, the "Union," between his landing and New Orleans. Nashville, farther up the Cumberland, had a line of barges owned by a merchant named Spriggs. Among the boats listed as engaged in the Tennessee trade are the "Minerva," the "Clem Hall," the "Nashville Packet," the "Willing Maid," and the "Perseverance." Regular trade was carried on between St. Louis and Pittsburgh and St. Louis and New Orleans, but how extensive it was it is impossible to say. The *Louisiana Gazette* mentions the "Parassena," the "Vigilina," the "Betsy," and the keelboat "Missouri" as trading with St. Louis.[7]

It would be difficult to estimate the number of barges and

keelboats that plied the western waters during the years before the triumph of the steamboat. The life of a boat was probably limited to a few years, and the same name was borne by a succession of boats or by several at the same time. In 1806, in addition to the thirty boats that periodically departed from New Orleans for Natchez, there were probably twice as many plying between New Orleans and the Ohio and the upper Mississippi. From 1810 to 1817, in spite of the introduction of the steamboat, there seems to have been an increase in the number of upstream boats; at the peak there may have been about three hundred of them, including the small craft that penetrated to the headwaters. There were probably between two thousand and three thousand men regularly employed on these boats.[8]

It is fully as hopeless a task to endeavor to estimate the total number of flatboats that descended the western rivers, and the statistics of arrivals at New Orleans are incomplete. In fact, it is probably within the truth to suggest that only about half the boats built on the rivers were intended to reach New Orleans. From August, 1800, to August, 1801, while Americans were still suffering from Spanish restrictions, there were between 350 and 400 arrivals at New Orleans. The Fort Adams customhouse registered 696 flats between January, 1801, and April 14, 1802. This number probably increased a little each year, for in 1807, by the New Orleans "List of Barges and Flats in Port," 755 arrived, and by 1813 the number had jumped to 1,306. During the war there was a decline that reached 308 in 1814, then a recovery to 1,263 in 1817. The depression that lasted for the next five or six years showed in another decrease in arrivals. The steamboat by no means put a sudden end to the flatboat era, for from the time of its introduction until 1846, the number of flatboat arrivals at New Orleans continued to grow until it reached a total of

2,792. After that a decline set in, and by the opening of the War between the States, probably not more than 500 were arriving.[9]

May was usually the month with the most flatboat arrivals at New Orleans, and April and June were next. There were arrivals nearly every month in the years covered by the New Orleans register, but from August to November there were generally very few. The incomplete list of arrivals kept by the *Louisiana Gazette* during 1805, 1806, and part of 1807 would seem to show that Kentucky led as the place of origin of flatboats with almost 30 per cent of the total; Mississippi was next with 24 per cent; and Pennsylvania was third with 17 per cent. Tennessee, Virginia, and Ohio followed with 9, 8, and 7 per cent respectively. It is interesting to compare this estimate with the figures given for the fiscal year 1850–51 in De Bow. At that time Indiana led with almost 32 per cent, Pennsylvania had 24, Ohio 23, Tennessee 11, and Kentucky 6 per cent. The number of flatboats originating in other states was negligible.[10]

It was a frequent complaint that buyers at New Orleans, in order to beat down prices, took advantage of the boatmen's haste or inability to seek other markets, or they delayed buying until the boatmen's expenses had eaten up profits. It was estimated that in 1802 alone, the sum of sixty thousand dollars was lost to the western country by these means. One owner told of staying in New Orleans three months waiting for flour to rise three dollars on a barrel.[11] The tremendous fluctuations in prices made shipping to New Orleans a speculation at best. These fluctuations were caused, of course, by supply and demand, but in those days the seller had no means of taking advantage of a rise since he could not sell farm produce at a distance, and upon his arrival at New Orleans the market price might be below the cost of production. Middlemen had established themselves at New Orleans as early as the Revolution and were a great help in expediting and simplifying commercial transactions for the small speculator and in acting as permanent agents for merchants. Often they ran retail and wholesale businesses of their own in addition, and were thus able to take advantage of any choice bargains that might offer. They advertised their willingness to serve in their own towns and at likely shipping points. Sometimes their business relationships were farflung. Thus in the *Pittsburgh Gazette* of June 8, 1816, Vernon and Skidmore of Louisville advertised that they would receive consignments, procure freights for New Orleans or Pittsburgh, make purchases, and store or forward goods. Merchants and agents frequently advertised for freight or boat hands, or that they had warehouse space to let or boats to sell, that shipments of goods had arrived, or that they wanted to buy goods.

The perils of river navigation early beckoned to the insurance broker as a fruitful field for speculation. On January 15, 1784, Daniel Brodhead at Louisville agreed to insure against loss, for forty-two pounds, Virginia currency, a cargo worth seven hundred pounds belonging to James Wilkinson, on its way from Pittsburgh. With the advance of commerce, companies were incorporated to sell insurance as well as to handle financial affairs in general. The Kentucky Insurance Company, incorporated in 1802, seems to have been the first and to have had the legal monopoly on marine insurance in Kentucky until 1818. The premium of 6 per cent charged by Daniel Brodhead was reduced to 3½ per cent by the Kentucky Insurance Company. In New Orleans the rate on Kentucky flatboats rose by 1807 to as much as 10 per cent, and then sank to 5 per cent five years later. In that city the rate on barges from Kentucky was usually about 5 per cent. The strict requirements of the Kentucky monopoly led its secretary, William Macbean, to offer his services in obtaining policies with private underwriters. It is not apparent how far this private business was carried on, or to what extent privately granted policies were enforceable by law.[12]

Rates of transportation were very high, especially from the Atlantic coast to Pittsburgh. The roads from Pittsburgh to Baltimore and Philadelphia were traversed by Conestoga wagons drawn by four or more horses, which took about three weeks for the journey, depending on the weather. Each wagon carried 3,000 to 4,000 pounds. The number of wagon-loads reaching Pittsburgh from the East each year ran into the thousands; the *Gazette* placed it at 4,055 in 1813, and 5,800 in 1815. The freight rates from Philadelphia to Pittsburgh depended upon the state of the roads; until 1820 they usually hovered between 6 and 10 dollars a hundredweight. A wagon carrying two tons thus received at least $240 for its trip. The eastward journey, however, might have to be undertaken with an empty box, since the tendency was to ship western goods down the Ohio. The rate from Baltimore to Pittsburgh was a dollar or two less than that from Philadelphia, but Philadelphia succeeded in getting most of the business. Until about 1820 there seems to have been a feeling among Philadelphia merchants and the Pennsylvania freighters that they controlled the only feasible road to the West, but the development of the Mohawk River and Lakes route and the completion of the Erie Canal rudely awakened them.[13]

Arrived at Pittsburgh, goods could be shipped either by flatboat or by keelboat. The former method was less expensive, but the risk was greater, so that most merchants preferred the keelboats, which were speedier, more easily managed, had more experienced crews, and were thus safer. In 1813 Manuel Lisa contracted to carry two keelboat loads of goods from St.

Louis to Brownsville; compact articles such as boxes and barrels were freighted for $4.00 a hundredweight, and the bulkier and lighter bales and packs for $5.50 a hundredweight. From New Orleans, freight to St. Louis, Louisville, Cincinnati, or Nashville commanded about the same rate until 1820: approximately $5.00 a hundredweight, with variation of a dollar or so to suit the cargo or the occasion. To Pittsburgh the rate was about $8.00 a hundredweight, if the estimate is made by adding $3.00 for the freight from Louisville to Pittsburgh. From Cincinnati to Pittsburgh, bulky articles such as hemp and yarn were carried for $1.25 a hundredweight. The downstream rate was roughly a quarter to a third of that upstream.[14]

From all accounts, goods could be transported to any of the upriver cities (except possibly Pittsburgh) more cheaply from New Orleans than from Philadelphia. John Filson, writing in 1784, stated that goods had been brought to Louisville from New Orleans for one-third of what it cost to bring them from Philadelphia. General Collot, who descended the Ohio in 1796, made elaborate calculations to prove that a round trip could be made from New Orleans to St. Louis or Knoxville for about two-thirds of the rate from Philadelphia or Baltimore to those points. In spite of the apparent advantage of the all-water route, the land route seems to have been well traveled. After all, New Orleans was not a manufacturing city and was handicapped by having to pay the freight on goods imported to send upriver. The Louisville merchants found it almost as cheap to import Philadelphia goods by way of Pittsburgh as by way of New Orleans—and incidentally saved two or three months' time. For European and tropical goods that could make a long haul directly to New Orleans, the river route may have been the cheapest, a supposition strongly supported by the prevalence of these wares in the surviving manifests and advertisements of cargoes coming upstream. At any rate, fine goods could be taken to the West and sold at a reasonable profit in stores whose overhead expenses were remarkably low. Fashions, it is said, appeared in Frankfort, Kentucky, three months after they had reached Philadelphia.[15]

Passenger rates probably depended upon the whim of the master, the type and speed of the boat, the accommodations expected, and upon whether the passenger provided his own food. Very few statistics remain. Christian Schultz paid two dollars to a flatboat master for a passage from Wheeling to Marietta and recorded that the fare to New Orleans on a trading boat, by which he probably meant a flatboat, would have been five to ten dollars. Local fares were probably cheap. In 1815 the "Monongahela Packet" was carrying passengers the twenty-two miles between Pittsburgh and Elizabeth for twenty-five cents.[16]

A considerable portion of the flatboats that left the upper towns bore cargoes destined to be disposed of from place to place along the river. These trading boats carried a calico flag to indicate their character and would respond to a hail from some dweller on the banks or would tie up near a plantation or hamlet too small to afford a store. Their arrival was announced by a blast on a tin horn, and the inhabitants with money to spend or goods to barter would flock to the landing. The part of the boat dedicated to trade was outfitted with shelves and counters, often arranged with attractiveness and ingenuity. Since they served as the department stores of the rivers, the boats carried large stocks of groceries, liquors, dry goods, and hardware. The small merchant with a distaste for a settled life could thus find his niche in the world of finance, and there was nothing to prevent his making an annual pilgrimage. The ambitious immigrant could pay his way to his new home and arrive with a little money in his pocket, or he might ply his trade aboard his flatboat, moving from place to place as occasion offered.

Tinsmiths, toolmakers, and blacksmiths could exercise their trades on the river and often did. Millers fitted up flatboats with gristmills operated by the force of the current, and earned their way and a little profit by grinding the corn of the riverside farmers. These contrivances, however, had no great amount of power and so were not useful for heavy gristmills and sawmills. The *Kentucky Gazette* was said to have had its first issue set up on a flatboat floating down the river to Kentucky, and there are records of flatboats traveling with libraries, wax-figure exhibits, raree shows, and theatrical troupes. It is asserted that at one time a flatboat theater was moored near a certain Indiana village with an audience aboard and a play in progress when some mischievous boys cut the ropes. The boat landed some miles downstream, and the audience was forced to walk home. Trading boats were not an unmixed blessing; it was claimed that after a visit from one of them, farmers and planters were likely to notice gaps on the hen roosts. The picturesqueness of tavern, retail store, and dram shop, "together with the inhabitants and no small number of very merry customers," floating on the same bottom was not always appreciated. The Reverend Timothy Flint wrote that the boats were too often the resorts of all kinds of bad company, and suggested severe inquiry "respecting the inmates and practices of these floating mansions of iniquity."[17]

Goods transported over the mountains for shipment down the rivers were brought in time to take advantage of the flood season. This fact, together with the local demand, necessitated the erection of warehouses at a very early date. The New Store at the site of Elizabeth, about twenty-two miles above Pittsburgh on the Monongahela, was a warehouse, and here George Rogers Clark prepared for his western expeditions. Pittsburgh's first nonmilitary warehouse was apparently built by George Morgan in 1764. A storehouse at Buffalo Creek had the advantage of being built out over the water, so that boats could be brought under the door to be unloaded. Another one like it belonged to Jesse Reeder at Cincinnati, and one at Charlestown, Brooke County, Virginia, was four stories high. It let flour down into boats by pulleys and windlasses at the rate of three to five barrels a minute.[18]

Goods were usually landed in the mud of the riverbanks and carried by the boatmen or longshoremen or hauled in wagons to the warehouses. Regulations were few during the early years, and boats were free to tie up and remain as long as they pleased. In time, as the number of boats increased, this custom began to work hardship. On a bank lined with boats, many of them empty, descending craft were unable to find room and were forced to go on downstream and land their goods where they could. The problem was usually solved by giving a local official power to make regulations, or by limiting the time allowed for unloading. It is uncertain to what extent docks were built. The freshet of November, 1810, carried off the public wharf on the Monongahela River at Pittsburgh, but there is no indication as to whether it was floating or built on piles. Another wharf on the Allegheny side of town was built on piles in 1798 and was washed away; it was rebuilt fifteen years later. At Louisville the best anchorages were in Bear Grass Creek and at Shippingport. The property owners there charged whatever rates they pleased. Tarascon's charge was one cent for each hundredweight loaded or unloaded. Thus a barge carrying fifty tons would be liable to a twenty-dollar charge, which, it must be admitted, was exorbitant. These tactics helped to build up business on the Indiana side, where wharfage was free. Conditions, however, were even worse in St. Louis, where a prohibitive tax was laid upon boats and barges coming from outside the territory and bearing goods for sale. An exception was made for market boats from Illinois.[19]

The New Orleans *batture* on which business centered included the river front of New Orleans proper and the fronts of the lower suburb, Marigny, and of the upper suburb, Ste. Marie. During the latter part of the keelboat era, keels unloaded in the space just above the present Canal Street, and flats occupied the rest of the shore line of the suburb Ste. Marie above. The part of the river occupied by the flats is now land. At one time in the heyday of the flatboat it was said that the boats were clustered so thickly along the shore that one could walk almost a mile on their decks. Shipping lay opposite the Place d'Armes, now Jackson Square. The Spanish had had a harbor master to collect fees from the craft entering port, but the practice was abandoned soon after the cession. Four years later the city levied a wharfage duty and after some legal disputes succeeded in collecting it. Flatboats paid six dollars and keels and barges three dollars, but the fee for keeled craft was changed from time to time.[20]

The levees of the river towns must have presented an interesting cross section of western life. Timothy Flint, who for all his New England Puritanism took a keen interest in the picturesque, has left a graphic description of the bayou at New Madrid with its teeming transient population:

One hundred boats have landed here in a day.—The boisterous gaiety of the hands, the congratulations of acquaintances, who have met here from immense distances, the moving picture of life on board the boats, in the numerous animals, large and small, which they carry, their different ladings, the evidence of the increasing agriculture above, and, more than all, the immense distances, which they have already traversed, afford a copious fund of meditation. In one place there are boats loaded with pine plank, from the pine forests of the southwest of New York. In another quarter there are numerous boats with the "Yankee notions" of Ohio. In another quarter are landed together the boats of "old Kentucky", with their whiskey, hemp, tobacco, bagging and bale rope; with all the articles of the produce of their soil. From Tennessee there are the same articles, together with boats loaded with bales of cotton from Illinois and Missouri, cattle, horses, and the general produce of the western country, together with peltry and lead from Missouri. Some boats are loaded with corn in bulk and in the ear. Others with barrels of apples and potatoes, and great quantities of dried apples and peaches. Others have loads of cider, that has been strengthened by boiling, or freezing. Other boats are loaded with furniture, tools, domestic and agricultural implements; in short, the numerous products of the ingenuity, speculation, manufacture and agriculture of the whole upper country of the West. . . . The surface of the boats cover some acres. Dunghill fowls are fluttering over the roofs, as invariable appendages. The piercing note of the chanticleer is heard. —The cattle low. The horses trample, as in their stables. The swine utter the cries of fighting with each other. The turkeys gobble. The dogs of an hundred regions become acquainted. The boatmen travel about from boat to boat, make inquiries and acquaintances, agree to "lash boats", as it is called, and form alliances to yield mutual assistance to each other on the way to New Orleans. After an hour or two passed in this way, they spring on shore, to "raise the wind" in the village. If they tarry all night, as is generally the case, it is well for the people of the town, if they do not become riotous in the course of the evening; in which case strong measures are adopted, and the proceedings on both sides are summary and decisive. With the first dawn all is bustle and motion; and amidst shouts, and trampling of cattle, and barking of dogs, and crowing of the dunghill fowls, the fleet is in a half hour all under way; and when the sun rises, nothing is seen, but the broad stream rolling on as before. The boats unite once more at Natchez and New Orleans; and although they live on the same river, it is improbable that they will ever meet again on the earth.[21]

In 1810 the progressive author of the *Navigator* wrote that there was on foot a new mode of navigating the western waters. Steam had been applied to a boat on the Hudson

River in such a manner as to drive it against wind and tide at the rate of four miles an hour, and now there was a similar boat building at Pittsburgh, and another at Frankfort. "It will be a novel sight," he concluded, "and as pleasing as novel to see a huge boat working her way up the windings of the Ohio, without the appearance of sail, oar, pole, or any manual labour about her—moving within the secrets of her own wonderful mechanism, and propelled by power undiscoverable!" A few months later the editor of the *Pittsburgh Gazette* wrote, "With pleasure we announce, that the Steam Boat lately built at this place . . . fully answers the most sanguine expectations that were formed of her sailing." When the "Orleans" steamed down the river and the keelboatmen dropped their poles to watch her pass at the terrific speed of eight miles an hour, she was acting as the harbinger of a new era in western transportation.[22]

The supremacy of the steamboat, however, was not to be won without difficulty. For almost a decade the keelboats and barges flourished. Business increased so consistently that merchants found it profitable to build their barges larger and larger, until river craft actually rivaled in size the smaller ocean trading vessels. The keelboatmen, moreover, anchored by self-interest to the old ways, were frankly contemptuous of the steamboat. In their eyes it was "a scheme to destroy their business and expose people's lives. . . . They would like to see that new fangled machine try 'Horsetail Ripple' or 'Letart's Falls', to get up them without the aid of good setting poles, or 'cordelles . . . it could not be done nohow.'" As a matter of fact, the keelboatmen were not far wrong. The first steamboats were clumsy, unwieldy affairs, hard to manage on a curve and too deep set in the water to battle successfully the swift western currents, even had their engines been more perfect. To complete the caricature, it was supposed that only sea captains could manage them, so that the West had the ludicrous spectacle of bluff old salts with trumpets clapped to their mouths shouting nautical phrases at deck hands who had never seen the ocean. Then when they were misunderstood the captains went into spasms of blasphemy that must have aroused the admiration of western connoisseurs of billingsgate.[23]

For some time it was not at all certain that steamboats would win. The danger of explosion and the delays caused by low water and rapids made them distrusted. The fifth steamboat in the West, the "Etna," in 1815 entered the business of towing ships between the mouth of the Mississippi and New Orleans because she could not gather a cargo for Louisville at $4.50 a hundredweight for light goods and $6.00 a hundredweight for heavy goods. The stubborn fact was that at that particular moment shippers preferred to pay $8.00 a hundredweight to ship their goods in barges. Toward the close of the year the "Etna" succeeded in gathering a scanty cargo for Louisville, but found difficulty in obtaining fuel and sometimes had to lay by for two or three days. Somewhere on the way she broke a shaft and arrived at Louisville under the power of one wheel. Her record was sixty days, which, considering the dangers involved, was not greatly to be preferred to a barge's three months.[24]

In 1816 Captain Henry Shreve, who had received his river training as a keelboatman, built the "Washington" (the ninth steamboat in the West), which carried its boilers on deck and traversed the surface of the water instead of plowing the depths. To the surprise of the country, the "Washington" made the round trip between Louisville and New Orleans in forty-one days, including delays. The success of this boat, due to improvements both in hull design and in machinery, was what roused the drooping courage of the West and struck the first telling blow at the supremacy of the barge. In addition to speed and dependability, the steamboat brought by 1820 what seemed to be unbelievably low rates. From New Orleans to Louisville the best a barge could do was to transport goods in three months at $5.00 a hundredweight. The steamboat now carried them in two weeks at $2.00. Fares were $150, a sum that, considering the saving in time, was quite reasonable. Within a very few years they would be less than $25. By 1829 Morgan Neville could write that goods that a few years before had been brought over the mountains from Philadelphia to Cincinnati at a cost of $5.00 to $8.00 a hundredweight could now be brought around by way of New Orleans at $1.00.[25]

There was an interval of perhaps twenty years during which the keelboat came more and more to be used as an auxiliary carrier towed by the steamboat. Thus the Creek Indians, when they were taken West, went on keels lashed to a steamer. Other keelboats were loaded with supplies for the forts on the upper Mississippi, and still others were employed in transporting lead. At least once, a keelboat was equipped with a steam engine, and this experiment may have been tried oftener. Towing, however, did not become the rule. The usual explanation given was that the steamboatmen opposed it. No doubt their opposition arose from the danger involved in handling such awkward appendages in the comparatively unimproved rivers of that day. In the present day of dams and dredge boats, a river steamboat has become little else than a barge pusher.

The triumph of the steamboat meant the death of the Mississippi barge. In 1815 Daniel Drake optimistically forecast the end of barges and keels. Eleven years later a relative of his wrote that they had been almost entirely superseded by steamboats.[26] It was true that barges had disappeared, but keels had merely retreated to the upper tributaries, where they continued to act as carriers for the goods brought to the heads of steamboat navigation. Nevertheless, the color and romance were gone, appropriated by the stately white packets that traversed the deeper waters. The hoarse voice of the steamboat had taken the place of the boatman's horn, and the farmer boy now dreamed of reigning in a texas instead of pushing a keel. Thus stripped of their occupations, bargemen and many of the keelboatmen turned to other businesses. Some of them, like Mike Fink, followed the Indian and the buffalo westward. Others, who had the capacity, became steamboat pilots and captains.

But at the river cities that were close to the shallower streams, the keelboats continued to arrive. In 1825, when the supremacy of the steamboat was assured, there were 470 keelboat arrivals at Pittsburgh, and in 1840 there were 415. In 1838, with the steamboat in full sway, there were enough keelboats in town to form a pontoon bridge between the shore and a bar in the Monongahela River, where the adherents of David R. Porter held a barbecue in celebration of his election as governor. There were 108 keelboat arrivals at St. Louis in 1841, 88 in 1842, and 55 in 1843. In 1847 there were still 55 keelboats plying the waters of the upper Mississippi. In seasons when the water was too low for steamboats to run, the keelboats stole out of their retreats, and once more the boatman's horn echoed among the hills along the old channels. In 1862 it was possible for the chronicler to say that "the keelboatmen have it their own way on the Allegheny again as it is entirely too low for steamboats," and as late as 1885 we read that the keelboat "is still used on the Ohio and upper Mississippi in low stages of water and on all the boatable streams where steamboats do not yet run."[27]

Defeated by the steamboat, but not eliminated, the keel-

THE BOATMAN HAS HIS DAY

boat continued to ply the shallow waters of the tributaries until the shriek of the locomotive presaged its final disappearance. Far up in the mountains at the headwaters of the Kentucky, a primitive flat-bottomed craft called the push boat still moved along the streams, as had the keelboat more than a century before. Falling back slowly before the railroad, it retreated deeper and deeper into the mountain valleys until it seemed that the railroad could follow it no farther. But then a third menace appeared. In the not distant past, scarcely twenty years ago, when hard roads made the remotest valley accessible to the raucous blast of the truckman's horn, the push boatmen laid aside their poles—gladly, no doubt—altogether unconscious that they were the last survivors of that picturesque race, the western boatmen.

NOTES

BIBLIOGRAPHY

INDEX

Notes to Chapter I

THE ROLE OF THE WESTERN WATERS

1. Anthony Trollope, *North America*, 2:109 (Philadelphia, 1863).

2. Hulbert, *Ohio River*, 212.

3. *Kentucky Gazette* (Lexington), April 12, 1790.

4. The English traders had reached the Mississippi well before 1700, as is shown in the "Mémoire de Dennonville à Seignelay," November 6, 1688, in Archives Nationales, colonies, C 11, A 10, f. 100–111, a transcript of which is in the Clements Library. This memoir states that the English had three times appeared at the mouth of the Ohio (Ouabache) and were attracting the trade of the Illinois. For information on the English traders on the lower Mississippi, see Verner W. Crane, *The Southern Frontier, 1670–1732* (Philadelphia, 1929); and for the westward ventures of the Albany traders, see Helen Broshar, "The First Push Westward of the Albany Traders," in *Mississippi Valley Historical Review*, 7:228–241 (1920).

5. Volwiler, *George Croghan*, 21–42.

6. Volwiler, *George Croghan*, 78–80.

7. Alvord, *Illinois Country*, 238–240; N. M. Miller Surrey, *The Commerce of Louisiana during the French Régime 1699–1763*, 298 (Columbia University, *Studies in History, Economics and Public Law*, vol. 71, no. 1—New York, 1916).

8. "Bouquet Papers," in *Michigan Pioneer and Historical Collections*, 19:27–295, *passim*.

9. Savelle, *George Morgan*, 20–28.

10. Alvord and Carter, *Trade and Politics*, 140, 435; Alvord and Carter, *New Régime*, 476.

11. Savelle, *George Morgan*, 31–75; Alvord and Carter, *New Régime*, 387.

12. Alcée Fortier, *A History of Louisiana*, 2:37–39 (New York, 1904).

13. Arthur P. Whitaker, *Documents Relating to the Commercial Policy of Spain in the Floridas,* 5, 7, 13, 17 (Deland, Fla., 1931); Clarence E. Carter, ed., *The Correspondence of General Thomas Gage with the Secretaries of State, 1763–1775,* 1:297 (New Haven, 1931); François X. Martin, *History of Louisiana,* 2:26 (New Orleans, 1829); Williams, *Early Travels in the Tennessee Country,* 232; Peter J. Hamilton, *Colonization of the South,* 402 (Philadelphia, 1904); Abiel Holmes, *Annals of America,* 1:183 (Cambridge, 1829). The large amount of traffic on the western waters is indicated in Cresswell, *Journal,* 77–81. While Cresswell was on the Kentucky River from May 22 to June 4, 1775, he met thirteen canoes, all bound for Wheeling, Fort Pitt, or Redstone. There were fourteen men in his own company: two Englishmen, two Irishmen, one Welshman, two Dutchmen, two Virginians, two Marylanders, one Swede, one African Negro, and a mulatto.

14. Morgan to Hancock, January 4, 1777; Morgan to the Board of War, May 12, 1778, Morgan Letter Book, no. 1, p. 3.

15. Oliver Pollock's narrative to Congress, September, 1782, in Draper MSS, 60J283, mentions specific shipments in September, 1778, January, 1779, and February, 1780. See letters and statements in Draper MSS, 37J22, 37J44, 60J277, 60J331; Butler, *Kentucky,* 155; *Michigan Pioneer and Historical Collections,* 19:328–338 (Lansing, 1892); Clarence W. Alvord, ed., *Cahokia Records, 1778–1790,* xxxv (*Illinois Historical Collections,* vol. 2—Springfield, 1907); Thwaites and Kellogg, *Revolution on the Upper Ohio,* 226–228, 252 n.; *Wisconsin Historical Collections,* 7:407 (Madison, 1876).

16. For Willing's exploits, see Caughey, "Willing's Expedition down the Mississippi, 1778," in *Louisiana Historical Quarterly,* 15:5–36 (1932); Draper MSS, 60J283; Claiborne, *Mississippi,* 1:118–121; Andrew Ellicott, *Journal,* 130–132 (Philadelphia, 1803). Claiborne gives Harrison's name as Harriman.

17. Claiborne, *Mississippi,* 1:127–134; Siebert, "The Loyalists in West Florida and the Natchez District," in *Mississippi Valley Historical Review,* 2:475–481 (1916).

18. For data on Pourée and Madame Cruzat, see Houck, *Spanish Régime in Missouri,* 1:211–213, 221–233; Houck, *History of*

Missouri, 2:44–46; Howe, *Historical Collections of the Great West*, 1:171; Claiborne, *Mississippi*, 1:133–135; *Pennsylvania Magazine of History and Biography*, 37:124 (1913).

19. Kellogg, *Frontier Advance*, 122; J. A. James, *Clark Papers, 1771–1781*, 41, 254; J. A. James, *George Rogers Clark*, 124; Draper MSS, 30J, 30J55, 30J73, 30J74, 60J313–324.

20. J. A. James, *Clark Papers, 1771–1781*, 98, 100, 139, 156, 162–164, 170, 268, 334.

21. Kellogg, *Frontier Retreat*, 79–94; Draper MSS, 6NN139, 30J79, 31J; Martindale, "Loughery's Defeat," in Indiana Historical Society, *Publications*, 2:106–108, 111, 112. Martindale includes in his article the diary of Captain Isaac Anderson, who was involved in the defeat.

22. J. A. James, *Clark Papers, 1781–1784*, 16, 45, 51, 64, 66, 67, 70, 77–79, 86, 88, 137, 310, 333, 393.

23. Consul W. Butterfield, ed., *Washington-Irvine Correspondence*, 202, 206 (Madison, 1882); *Michigan Pioneer and Historical Collections*, 10:575 (Lansing, 1888); Houck, *Spanish Régime in Missouri*, 1:224; Whitaker, *Spanish-American Frontier*, 95.

24. Butler, *Kentucky*, 156; L. Collins and R. H. Collins, *Kentucky*, 2:358, 723; Clarence W. Alvord, ed., *Cahokia Records, 1778–1790*, cxxxvii (*Illinois Historical Collections*, vol. 2—Springfield, 1907); *History of the Ohio Falls Cities and Their Counties*, 1:188 (Cleveland, 1882). Yoder's tombstone credited him with having taken to New Orleans the first flatboat ever to descend the Mississippi.

25. J. A. James, *Clark Papers, 1781–1784*, 141, 143, 195–197; Verhoeff, *Kentucky River Navigation*, 65; Butler, *Kentucky*, 142; Perkins, *Annals of the West*, 419; Filson, *Kentucke*, 40, 45.

26. United States Continental Congress, *Secret Journals of the Acts and Proceedings of Congress*, 4:320–328 (Boston, 1820–21); Draper MSS, 1M114, 1M137, 53J53. For an able discussion of the reasons why the westerners never undertook to carry out their threats to seize New Orleans, see Whitaker, *Spanish-American Frontier*, 26–28.

27. Beatty, "Diary," in *Magazine of American History*, 1:177 (1877); Hildreth, "Voyage from Marietta to New Orleans," in

American Pioneer, 1:133 (1842); Winsor, *Westward Movement,* 355. Wilkinson, however, states in his *Memoirs,* 2:112, that he first descended the Mississippi in 1787. Of course he may have gone overland to Natchez in 1786.

28. Whitaker, "Wilkinson's First Descent to New Orleans in 1787," in *Hispanic-American Historical Review,* 8:86 (1928); "Daniel Clark's Memoir," in Wilkinson, *Memoirs,* vol. 2, apx. 6, and in *Annals of Congress,* 18:2731–2733. The account as given above mainly follows that of Daniel Clark.

29. James Wilkinson, "Wilkinson's Memorial and Expatriation Declaration," in Temple Bodley, ed., *Reprints,* cxix–cxxxix (*Filson Club Publications,* no. 31—Louisville, 1926); Shepherd, "Wilkinson and the Beginnings of the Spanish Conspiracy," in *American Historical Review,* 9:503 (1904); Wilkinson, *Memoirs,* 2:115.

30. Whitaker, *Spanish-American Frontier,* 95; Clark, *Proofs of the Corruption of General James Wilkinson,* 55, n. 27; Charles Gayarré, *History of Louisiana: The Spanish Domination,* 211 (New York, 1854); Verhoeff, *Kentucky River Navigation,* 58.

31. Wilkinson, *Memoirs,* 2:115, and apx. 6; *Annals of Congress,* 18:2733; *American Museum,* 5:417 (1789); "Decision of the Council of State on Wilkinson's First Memorial," in *American Historical Review,* 9:750 (1904).

32. Verhoeff, *Kentucky River Navigation,* 62 n., 226–229. The journal of John Halley, 1789 and 1791, in the Durrett Collection, gives an interesting description of a boatman's visit to the Spanish commandant at the mouth of the Arkansas.

33. *Annals of Congress,* 18:2734, 2736; letter dated February 10, 1790, in miscellaneous manuscripts, 1786–92, Durrett Collection; John B. McMaster, *History of the People of the United States,* 1:524 (New York, 1927–29); Verhoeff, *Kentucky River Navigation,* 65; Winsor, *Westward Movement,* 413; J. A. James, *George Rogers Clark,* 400; Charles Gayarré, *History of Louisiana: The Spanish Domination,* 277, 285 (New York, 1854); Shepherd, "Wilkinson and the Beginnings of the Spanish Conspiracy," in *American Historical Review,* 9:505 n. (1904).

34. Shepherd, "Wilkinson and the Beginnings of the Spanish Conspiracy," in *American Historical Review,* 9:504 (1904). On this

point, however, see Whitaker, *Spanish-American Frontier*, 103–107.

35. "Decision of the Council of States on Wilkinson's First Memorial," in *American Historical Review*, 9:749 (1904); *Kentucky Gazette* (Lexington), December 26, 1789; Wilkinson, *Memoirs*, vol. 2, apx. 6, 13; Houck, *Spanish Régime in Missouri*, 1:275–315; J. A. James, *George Rogers Clark*, 395; Savelle, *George Morgan*, 200–228.

36. Pope, *Tour*, 41; Verhoeff, *Kentucky River Navigation*, 224–226; Charles Wilkins' statements at the Innes trial, 1808, Innes Papers, no. 604; deposition of Samuel South, Innes Papers, no. 680; Houck, *History of Missouri*, 1:331; Winsor, *Westward Movement*, 543; Whitaker, *Spanish-American Frontier*, 159.

37. *American Museum*, 5:417 (1789).

38. Pope, *Tour*, 22–36.

39. Byars, *B. and M. Gratz*, 23, 256; Denny-O'Hara Papers, *passim;* A. Michaux, "Journals," in Thwaites, *Early Western Travels*, 3:31. The Reed and Forde papers are preserved in the manuscript division of the Historical Society of Pennsylvania. See "Notes of a Journey from Philadelphia to New Madrid, Tennessee, 1790," in *Pennsylvania Magazine of History and Biography*, 36:209 (1912).

40. "Invoice of Stores Forwarded to Fort Washington"; day book, June 29, 1791; "Quarter Master's Stores Issued at Fort Pitt, June 29, 1791"; memorandum book, November 30, 1792–May, 1794; disbursements, nos. 1010, 1011, 1016, 1034, 1189ff., all in Craig Papers. See also Brackenridge, *Recollections*, 41.

41. James A. Robertson, *Louisiana under the Rule of Spain, France, and the United States, 1785–1807*, 1:298 (Cleveland, 1911); *Annals of Congress*, 18:2736–2738; Baily, *Journal*, 286–292, 331.

42. Houck, *Spanish Régime in Missouri*, 2:123–132.

43. Stoddard, *Sketches*, 296–298; Perrin du Lac, *Voyage*, 229; James McFerron to James O'Hara, April 26, August 2, November 8, 1800, Denny-O'Hara Papers; United States Territorial Papers, 3377BRL.

44. *Tree of Liberty* (Pittsburgh), November 7, 1801; *American State Papers, Commerce and Navigation*, 1:493; *American State Papers, Foreign Affairs*, 2:527; Walker, "Commerce of the Missis-

sippi River," in 50 Congress, 1 session, *House Executive Documents,* no. 6, part 2, p. 184 (serial 2552).

Notes to Chapter II

BOATS AND BOATBUILDING

1. Walter B. Stevens, *St. Louis,* 341 (St. Louis and Chicago, 1909).

2. Elliott Cones, ed., *New Light on the Early History of the Greater Northwest. The Manuscript Journals of Alexander Henry . . . and of David Thompson,* 1:181, 331 (New York, 1897); Brackenridge, "Journal," in Thwaites, *Early Western Travels,* 6:86; Josiah Gregg, "Commerce of the Prairies," in Reuben G. Thwaites, ed., *Early Western Travels,* 19:214 (Cleveland, 1905); Chappell, "Missouri River," in Kansas State Historical Society, *Transactions,* 9:271. The white men often made their "buffalo boats" by stretching hides over the beds of wagons.

3. Spelled variously pirogue, periogue, piragua, periagua, piroque, peroque, perrogue, pirog, pirogua, and pettiauger.

4. Eron Rowland, *Life, Letters, and Papers of William Dunbar,* 86 (Jackson, Miss., 1930); Perrin du Lac, *Voyage,* 148; Chappell, "Missouri River," in Kansas State Historical Society, *Transactions,* 9:270; T. Flint, *Recollections,* 3; Brackenridge, "Journal," in Thwaites, *Early Western Travels,* 6:66; J. Hall, *Notes on the Western States,* 218.

5. Howells, *Recollections,* 84; Baxter, "Rafting on the Alleghany and Ohio, 1844," in *Pennsylvania Magazine of History and Biography,* 51:27 (1927); Hulbert, *Waterways of Westward Expansion,* 127–129.

6. T. M. Harris, "Journal," in Thwaites, *Early Western Travels,* 3:341; Cuming, "Sketches," in Thwaites, *Early Western Travels,* 4:88; Peter Kalm, *Travels into North America,* 2:242 (London, 1771); Crèvecœur, *Lettres,* 3:396, and "History of Louisville," in *Louisville Monthly Magazine,* 1:32 (1879); Samuel P. Hildreth, *Pioneer History,* 114 (Cincinnati, 1848).

7. The material concerning keelboats is gathered from Schultz,

Travels, 1:130; J. Flint, "Letters from America," in Thwaites, *Early Western Travels,* 9:109, 112; "Pedestrious Tour," in Thwaites, *Early Western Travels,* 8:245, 256; Chouteau, "Reminiscences," in Kansas State Historical Society, *Transactions,* 8:428; Strickland, *Pioneers of the West,* 195; J. Hall, *Letters from the West,* 323; Ker, *Travels,* 35; *Western Spy* (Cincinnati), January 8, 1806. The following contain specific references to the external keel: W. Dunbar, "Journal of a Voyage," in Rowland, *Life . . . of William Dunbar,* 232; S. Dunbar, *History of Travel in America,* 1:281; *Catalog of the Watercraft Collection in the United States National Museum,* 102.

8. Imlay, *Topographical Description,* 329; Schultz, *Travels,* 2:131; *Louisiana Gazette* (New Orleans), October 1, 1805; November 4, 1806; Cist, *Cincinnati Miscellany,* 1:125; *Courrier de la Louisiane* (New Orleans), November 1, 1811; *Commonwealth* (Pittsburgh), August 23, 1809; Palmer, *Journal,* 66–72; Buttrick, "Voyages," in Thwaites, *Early Western Travels,* 8:59; Evans, "Pedestrious Tour," in Thwaites, *Early Western Travels,* 8:256; Maximilian, "Travels," in Thwaites, *Early Western Travels,* 23: 24ff. The *Palladium* (Frankfort, Ky.), September 29, 1804, contains an interesting estimate of the cost and running expenses of thirty-ton barges. The barge "Missouri" had a burden of 170 tons as mentioned in the *Pittsburgh Gazette,* April 1, 1815, and stowed 1,600 barrels. Palmer mentions one at Cincinnati in 1817 with two masts and a tonnage of 150. Scharf, in his *Saint Louis,* 2:1088, speaks of 400-ton barges, which were, however, unwieldy and too large to land except in high water. For capacities, see the *Louisiana Gazette* (New Orleans), April 16, June 21, 1805; August 8, November 4, 1806.

9. Scharf, *Saint Louis,* 2:1089; Flagg, "Far West," in Thwaites, *Early Western Travels,* 26:265; Stoddard, *Sketches,* 303; Chappell, "Missouri River," in Kansas State Historical Society, *Transactions,* 9:271; Chouteau, "Reminiscences," in Kansas State Historical Society, *Transactions,* 8:428.

10. Flatboat names deriving from the destination of the boats were "Arkansas," "Mississippi," "Missouri," and "Louisiana." Sometimes they were called "tobacco," "flour," "horse," or "cattle" boats from their cargoes, and often they received the name "family boat" from another kind of cargo. The simplest names were "boxes"

and "sheds." Other local or temporary names were common. One of them was "chicken thieves," from the reputation of the flatboatmen for thievery. The ark, as first used on the Susquehanna, was built in the shape of an elongated box with sharp V-shaped ends and with a steering oar at each end. See Gilpin, "Journal of a Tour from Philadelphia," in *Pennsylvania Magazine of History and Biography*, 50:76 (1926). David B. Warden, in his *Statistical, Political, and Historical Account of the United States*, 3:332 (Edinburgh and Philadelphia, 1819), says that arks were first employed in 1793 by a Juniata River miller named Dryder. T. M. Harris credits their invention to a Mr. Krudger of the same vicinity. See T. M. Harris, "Journal," in Thwaites, *Early Western Travels*, 3:335.

11. Cramer, *Navigator*, 163 (1814); "Contract Book," Craig Papers; Melish, *Travels*, 2:85; Evans, "Pedestrious Tour," in Thwaites, *Early Western Travels*, 3:239; David B. Warden, *Statistical, Political, and Historical Account of the United States*, 3:329 (Edinburgh and Philadelphia, 1819); Fordham, *Personal Narrative*, 79; Gould, *Fifty Years on the Mississippi*, 209. Gould tells of Indiana hay boats 150 by 24 feet, which carried 300 tons. Bradbury, in his "Travels," in Thwaites, *Early Western Travels*, 5:301, makes the statement that flatboats were limited to 14 feet in breadth because the Indian chute in the Falls of the Ohio had in low water a passage where two rocks were only 15 feet apart.

12. "Contract Book," Craig Papers; Verhoeff, *Kentucky River Navigation*, 60 n.; Schultz, *Travels*, 1:130; J. Hall, *Letters from the West*, 324; Basil Hall, *Travels in North America*, 3:321 (Edinburgh, 1829); Baily, *Journal*, 146; J. Flint, "Letters from America," in Thwaites, *Early Western Travels*, 9:96; Evans, "Pedestrious Tour," in Thwaites, *Early Western Travels*, 8:257.

13. Woods, "Two Years Residence . . . on the English Prairie," in Thwaites, *Early Western Travels*, 10:245; Dewees, "Journal from Philadelphia to Kentucky," in *Pennsylvania Magazine of History and Biography*, 28:188 (1904); Thwaites and Kellogg, *Frontier Defense*, 257; "Receipt Book," Craig Papers.

14. D. Augustin, *A General Digest of the Ordinances and Resolutions of the Corporation of New Orleans, Banquettes*, 13, 99 (New Orleans, 1831); *Orleans Gazette* (New Orleans), February 2, 1807; A. Wilson, "Letter from Lexington," in *Port Folio*, third series,

3:510; Fordham, *Personal Narrative,* 79; Cramer, *Navigator, 33* (1814); Lyell, *Second Visit to the United States,* 2:130; Gould, *Fifty Years on the Mississippi,* 209.

15. Chappell, "Missouri River," in Kansas State Historical Society, *Transactions,* 9:273; Chittenden, *American Fur Trade,* 1:34.

16. The material in the last three paragraphs is based on Volwiler, *George Croghan,* 33; Keyser, "Memorials of Col. Jehu Eyre," in *Pennsylvania Magazine of History and Biography,* 3:296–307 (1879); Alvord and Carter, *Critical Period,* 531, 533; Alvord and Carter, *New Régime,* 166, 218, 328, 348, 349–359, 476; Alvord and Carter, *Trade and Politics,* 140, 435; Morgan to Hancock, March 2, 1777, and agreement of Richard M'Machen (McMahon), February 25, 1777, in Morgan Letter Book, no. 1; Thwaites and Kellogg, *Frontier Defense,* 257, 276; Kellogg, *Frontier Advance,* 107, 108; letters in Draper MSS, 30J. It appears that the method of swelling the timbers of a bateau to make it watertight was to sink it in the river for some time.

17. May, *Journals and Letters,* 32; *Pittsburgh Gazette,* September 30, 1786; February 9, April 19, 1788; October 4, 1794; May 21, 1802; *Kentucky Gazette* (Lexington), December 18, 1804; Cramer, *Navigator,* 19 (1808); Verhoeff, *Kentucky River Navigation,* 60 n. The contracts and receipts in the Craig Papers give the names of numerous boatbuilders.

18. Information on boat prices will be found in Disbursements, *passim;* "Memorandum Book," 1800–1801; "Contract Book," *passim;* "Account Book D," *passim,* all in Craig Papers; Collot, *Journey,* 1:33; Baily, *Journal,* 147; Schultz, *Travels,* 1:132, 143; Cramer, *Navigator,* 35 (1814); Bradbury, "Travels," in Thwaites, *Early Western Travels,* 5:302; A. Wilson, "Letter from Lexington," in *Port Folio,* third series, 3:501; Melish, *Travels,* 2:84; Fordham, *Personal Narrative,* 79. A receipt in the Denny-O'Hara Papers prices a Mississippi keelboat of twelve feet beam, four and one-half feet depth, and fifty-seven feet length at $6.50 a foot. The terms barge and keel must have been used very loosely.

19. Cramer, *Navigator,* 34, 39, 276 (1814); Scharf, *Saint Louis,* 2:1091; Gould, *Fifty Years on the Mississippi,* 55. Ker, in his *Travels,* 37, tells of a somewhat similar incident, though the wreck

occurred on the Mississippi and the trial at Nashville. He concludes with the statement that at the time he wrote, boats were being inspected when they were launched.

Notes to Chapter III
THE ART OF NAVIGATION

1. E. Wilson, *Pittsburg*, 188; McMurtrie, "Early Printing in Pittsburgh"; advertisement in an undated fragment of the *Palladium* (Frankfort, Ky.), a reproduction of which is in the possession of Mr. Otto A. Rothert, secretary of the Filson Club.

2. Cramer, *Pittsburgh Magazine Almanack*, 64 (1816); Dahlinger, *Pittsburgh*, 162; *Commonwealth* (Pittsburgh), October 28, 1811; Schultz, *Travels*, 1:133. Edmund Blunt was the author of *The American Coast Pilot*, first published in 1796 and often revised and reissued.

3. McMurtrie, "Early Printing in Pittsburgh"; *Pittsburgh Gazette*, February 26, April 30, 1802; *Tree of Liberty* (Pittsburgh), March 13, 1802. The edition of 1814 of the *Navigator* is the only one that has been reprinted, and is found in Leahy's *Who's Who on the Ohio River*, 83–201. Nearly eighty pages of notes dealing with the Mississippi and the country through which it flows are omitted.

4. The material in the last three paragraphs is gleaned from the various editions of the *Navigator* and from Melish, *Travels*, 2:58; T. Flint, *Recollections*, 19; Cuming, "Sketches," in Thwaites, *Early Western Travels*, 4:88, 304; Nuttall, "Journal," in Thwaites, *Early Western Travels*, 13:81; *Pittsburgh Gazette*, March 13, 1812.

5. The proposal for the publication of the *Notes* appears in the *Pittsburgh Gazette* of July 1, 1803, and is dated June 1, 1803, Frankfort, Kentucky. The book was to have sixty to one hundred pages and nine plates showing the most difficult passages in the river. The price was to be thirty-seven and a half cents. The notice of publication dated March 10, 1804, appears in the *Kentucky Gazette* (Lexington), of April 24, 1804. The price had been raised to fifty cents.

6. T. Flint, *Recollections*, 15; Ker, *Travels*, 35.

7. Cuming, "Sketches" in Thwaites, *Early Western Travels*, 4:126; Melish, *Travels*, 2:145; Cramer, *Navigator*, 252 (1814);

Brackenridge, *Views of Louisiana*, 44; Baily, *Journal*, 329; Audubon, *Delineations of American Scenery*, 26; Ker, *Travels*, 35.

8. George Washington, *Diaries . . . 1748–1799*, 1:440 (edited by John C. Fitzpatrick—Boston and New York, 1925); Crèvecœur, *Lettres*, 3:434; Schultz, *Travels*, 1:6; Lewis Evans, *Analysis of a General Map of the Middle British Colonies in America*, 26 (Philadelphia, 1755).

9. The material concerning the manipulation of poles is based on Neville, "The Last of the Boatmen," in J. Hall, ed., *Western Souvenir*, 111 (1828); Casseday, *Louisville*, 78; Scharf, *Saint Louis*, 2:1090; Audubon, *Delineations of American Scenery*, 24; Peck, *Forty Years of Pioneer Life*, 83; Schoolcraft, *Scenes and Adventures*, 23–28; Travis, "Navigation on the Muskingum," in *Ohio Archæological and Historical Publications*, 14:410; T. Flint, *Recollections*, 15, 24; Monette, "Progress of Navigation and Commerce," in Mississippi Historical Society, *Publications*, 7:481; Wilkeson, "Early Recollections of the West, in *American Pioneer*, 2:271 (1843); Jacob Ferris, *States and Territories of the Great West*, 202 (New York and Auburn, 1856); Strickland, *Pioneers of the West*, 196; Chittenden, *American Fur Trade*, 1:33; Chappell, "Missouri River," in Kansas State Historical Society, *Transactions*, 9:272.

10. Scharf, *Saint Louis*, 2:1090; Peck, *Forty Years of Pioneer Life*, 83; Chittenden, *American Fur Trade*, 1:33; J. Hall, *Notes on the Western States*, 221; T. Flint, *Recollections*, 91, 94, 96; Musick, *Stories of Missouri*, 88.

11. Hildreth, "Voyage from Marietta to New Orleans," in *American Pioneer*, 1:99 (1842); James T. Lloyd, *Steamboat Directory*, 33 (Cincinnati, 1856); Monette, "Progress of Navigation and Commerce," in Mississippi Historical Society, *Publications*, 7:481; T. Flint, *Recollections*, 86, 107.

12. J. Hall, *Notes on the Western States*, 221; F. A. Michaux, "Travels," in Thwaites, *Early Western Travels*, 3:160; T. Flint, *History and Geography*, 1:151; Filson, *Kentucke*, 45; Audubon, *Delineations of American Scenery*, 26; Monette, "Progress of Navigation and Commerce," in Mississippi Historical Society, *Publications*, 7:492; Fearon, *Sketches of America*, 249.

13. *Kentucky Gazette* (Lexington), June 18, 1811; *Liberty Hall*

(Cincinnati), May 29, 1811; *Cincinnati Gazette*, July 15, 1815; *Cincinnati Gazette*, December 2, 1816, quoted in Leahy, *Who's Who on the Ohio River*, 59; Jacob Burnet, *Notes on the Early Settlement of the North-Western Territory*, 400 (Cincinnati, 1847); *Commonwealth* (Pittsburgh), August 23, 1809.

14. Brackenridge, *Views of Louisiana*, 43; Perrin du Lac, *Voyage*, 165; T. Flint, *History and Geography*, 1:97; Scharf, *Saint Louis*, 2:1088, 1090; Houck, *History of Missouri*, 1:306; Cramer, *Navigator*, 252 (1814).

15. Pope, *Tour*, 25; Baily, *Journal*, 231, 267; Cramer, *Navigator*, 166 (1814); Schultz, *Travels*, 2:98–101, 180; Nuttall, "Journal," in Thwaites, *Early Western Travels*, 13:68; T. Flint, *Recollections*, 104; L. Collins, *Kentucky*, 511.

16. J. Hall, *Notes on the Western States*, 34; T. Flint, *History and Geography*, 1:96, 399; Hulbert, *Pioneer Roads*, 2:71; Melish, *Travels*, 2:144; Drake, *Natural and Statistical View*, 14; Nuttall, "Journal," in Thwaites, *Early Western Travels*, 13:67; F. A. Michaux, "Travels," in Thwaites, *Early Western Travels*, 3:239; Hulbert, *Ohio River*, 237; Cramer, *Navigator*, 21, 225 (1814); Collot, *Journey*, 1:213; Brackenridge, *Views of Louisiana*, 44.

17. Foreman, "River Navigation in the Early Southwest," in *Mississippi Valley Historical Review*, 15:35–55 (1928); T. Flint, *Recollections*, 105; Baily, *Journal*, 327; Cuming, "Sketches," in Thwaites, *Early Western Travels*, 4:264; Woods, "Two Years Residence . . . on the English Prairie," in Thwaites, *Early Western Travels*, 10:242; *American State Papers, Commerce and Navigation*, 2:741; Thomas Hutchins, *Topographical Description of Virginia, Pennsylvania, Maryland, and North Carolina*, 79–81 (Cleveland, 1904); Melish, *Travels*, 2:151; William Amphlett, *The Emigrant's Directory to the Western States*, 132 (London, 1819).

18. The material on the Falls of the Ohio is taken from Strickland, *Pioneers of the West*, 192–195; Cramer, *Navigator*, 97, 116, 118 (1814); J. Hall, *Notes on the Western States*, 42; J. Hall, *Letters from the West*, 184–186; Kentucky, *Statute Law*, 1:605; 3:221; William Amphlett, *The Emigrant's Directory to the Western States*, 132 (London, 1819); Casseday, *Louisville*, 104; E. James, "Account of an Expedition," in Thwaites, *Early Western Travels*, 14:71;

Imlay, *Topographical Description,* 329 n.; Karl Bernhard, *Travels through North America,* 2:130 (Philadelphia, 1828). Thomas Ashe has left a vivid account of a passage over the falls during a thunderstorm. See Ashe, *Travels,* 214. The Jefferson County, Kentucky, Court minute book no. 5, 1796–1801, March term, 1797, records the appointment of James Patten as the first pilot. The Kentucky state line extended to the low watermark on the Indiana shore, so that Kentucky could license pilots for the Indian chute. In 1802 James Patten advertised in the *Tree of Liberty* that Aaron Bowman, living in the Indiana Territory, was piloting boats without authority and was damaging many of them. As "I am authorized by the State of Kentucky to prevent impositions on strangers," Patten went on, "I hope every person who wishes to pass the Rapids will land on this side the River, where the greatest attention shall be given for their safe passage. If the government of the Indiana territory shall deem it *lawful* or expedient to appoint a Pilot on that side of the River, they will undoubtedly appoint some person more capable of the business, and a man of some respectability." *Tree of Liberty* (Pittsburgh), May 1, 1802.

19. Flagg, "Far West," in Thwaites, *Early Western Travels,* 26:89; J. Hall, *Notes on the Western States,* 48; Schoolcraft, *Scenes and Adventures,* 30; T. Flint, *Recollections,* 95–97.

20. H. Quick and E. Quick, *Mississippi Steamboatin',* 18.

21. J. Flint, "Letters from America," in Thwaites, *Early Western Travels,* 9:158–160; "Notes of a Journey from Philadelphia to New Madrid, Tennessee, 1790," in *Pennsylvania Magazine of History and Biography,* 36:214–216 (1912). The sum mentioned as the rent of the pirogue probably amounted to about $265.

22. J. Flint, "Letters from America," in Thwaites, *Early Western Travels,* 9:158–160.

23. Cramer, *Navigator,* 144, 210 (1814); T. Flint, *Recollections,* 219; Baily, *Journal,* 277; Cumings, *Western Pilot,* 44 (1825); Cuming, "Sketches," in Thwaites, *Early Western Travels,* 4:309; "Austin Papers," in American Historical Association, *Annual Report,* vol. 2 part 1, p. 74 (1919).

24. Joseph D. Shields, *Natchez; Its Early History,* 29 (Louisville, 1930).

25. Nuttall, "Journal," in Thwaites, *Early Western Travels*, 13:92-94; Cramer, *Navigator*, 165 (1814); Schultz, *Journal*, 2:134; Ker, *Travels*, 38, 46.

26. "Notes of a Voyage from Pittsburgh to New Orleans," in Thwaites, *Early Western Travels*, 4:360; Brackenridge, "Journal," in Thwaites, *Early Western Travels*, 6:38, 53; Scharf, *Saint Louis*, 2:1089; Collot, *Journey*, 1:138; Ker, *Travels*, 39; Gould, *Fifty Years on the Mississippi*, 192. It was claimed that five hundred miles were lost in crossing between New Orleans and St. Louis, and this may well have been true if one adds the width of the river to the distance drifted during the crossings.

27. Norman Walker, "Commerce of the Mississippi River," in 50 Congress, 1 session, *House Executive Documents*, no. 6, part 2, p. 252 (serial 2552); Gould, *Fifty Years on the Mississippi*, 312, 338; Schultz, *Travels*, 2:120; Lyell, *Second Visit to the United States*, 2:131; Cramer, *Navigator*, 21, 164 (1814). Cutoffs might save as much as forty miles of navigation, but they seldom failed to affect adversely the lands and tributaries below. Point Coupée (cut point) traditionally was the work of some Canadian boatmen who desired to shorten their voyages and labor. Baily, in his *Journal*, 259, says that backwaters were sometimes sufficient to propel a boat for fifty to a hundred miles upstream.

28. Cramer, *Navigator*, 164 (1814); Schoolcraft, *Journal of a Voyage*, 223; Evans, "Pedestrious Tour," in Thwaites, *Early Western Travels*, 8:301; Nuttall, "Journal," in Thwaites, *Early Western Travels*, 13:68, 80, 83; J. Hall, *Notes on the Western States*, 37; *American State Papers, Commerce and Navigation*, 2:745.

29. Musick, *Stories of Missouri*, 89-91.

30. Ludlow, *Dramatic Life as I Found It*, 129; J. Augustus Lemcke, *Reminiscences of an Indianian*, 140 (Indianapolis, 1905).

31. David Crockett [?], *Life of David Crockett, the Original Humorist and Irrepressible Backwoodsman*, 152-154 (New York, c1902). For other accounts of wrecks, see Schultz, *Travels*, 2:27-30, and Chouteau, "Reminiscences," in Kansas State Historical Society, *Transactions*, 8:424.

32. Foreman, "River Navigation in the Early Southwest," in *Mississippi Valley Historical Review*, 15:47-55 (1928); Hardin,

"The First Great Western River Captain," in *Louisiana Historical Quarterly*, 10:39–64 (1927).

33. Collot, *Journey*, 1:56–59; T. Flint, *Recollections*, 218; *Western Spy* (Cincinnati), August 13, 1805; *Mississippi Herald & Natchez Gazette*, supplement, September 24, 1806; *Mississippi Messenger* (Natchez), September 30, 1806; *Pittsburgh Gazette*, September 25, 1812; *Kentucky Gazette* (Lexington), September 29, 1812. For other accounts of storms and losses of boats, see T. Flint, *Recollections*, 81; Baily, *Journal*, 248, 253, 328; Bradbury, "Travels," in Thwaites, *Early Western Travels*, 5:187; *Kentucky Gazette* (Lexington), May 7, 1805; June 10, 1806.

34. Drake, *Natural and Statistical View*, 14; Nuttall, "Journal," in Thwaites, *Early Western Travels*, 13:74; E. James, "Account of an Expedition," in Thwaites, *Early Western Travels*, 14:85; Cramer, *Navigator*, 37, 276 (1814); Heckewelder, "Journey to the Wabash in 1792," in *Pennsylvania Magazine of History and Biography*, 12:183 (1888); *Western Spy* (Cincinnati), February 26, 1805.

35. E. James, "Account of an Expedition," in Thwaites, *Early Western Travels*, 17:88; Bradbury, "Travels," in Thwaites, *Early Western Travels*, 5:204–210; *Argus of the Western World* (Frankfort, Ky.), March 11, 1812; *Pittsburgh Gazette*, March 13, June 26, 1812; Sampson, "The New Madrid and Other Earthquakes in Missouri," in Mississippi Valley Historical Association, *Proceedings*, 6:218–238.

36. Hulbert, *Ohio River*, 237.

37. Norman Walker, "Commerce of the Mississippi River," in 50 Congress, 1 session, *House Executive Documents*, no. 6, part 2, p. 252 (serial 2552); Gould, *Fifty Years on the Mississippi*, 204; De Bow, *Industrial Resources*, 2:137; price-current columns, in *Louisiana Gazette* (New Orleans) *passim; Pittsburgh Gazette*, April 30, 1802; Nuttall, "Journal," in Thwaites, *Early Western Travels*, 13:87; T. Flint, *Recollections*, 93.

Notes to Chapter IV

THE BOATMEN

1. Chittenden, *American Fur Trade*, 1:55–58; Brackenridge,

"Journal," in Thwaites, *Early Western Travels*, 6:33; Howe, *Historical Collections of the Great West*, 1:80; Philip S. Cooke, *Scenes and Adventures in the Army*, 312 (Philadelphia, 1859); Stoddard, *Sketches*, 304. For an exception to their dependability, see John H. Fonda, "Reminiscences of Wisconsin," in *Wisconsin Historical Collections*, 5:207. According to George F. Ruxton's *Life in the Far West*, 88 (Edinburgh and London, 1851), the French Canadians were called "bad Medicine" by the Indians, who accounted them "treacherous and vindictive, and at the same time less daring than the American hunters."

2. T. Flint, *Recollections*, 93; Ludlow, *Dramatic Life as I Found It*, 237; Neville, "The Last of the Boatmen," in J. Hall, ed., *Western Souvenir*, 107–122 (1828); Chittenden, *American Fur Trade*, 1:56–67; Cist, *Cincinnati Miscellany*, 1:125; Levi Woodbury, *Writings*, 3:439 (Boston, 1852).

3. J. Hall, *Letters from the West*, 48; Palmer, *Journal*, 63; Wilkeson, "Early Recollections of the West," in *American Pioneer*, 2:272 (1843); W. T. Harris, *Remarks Made during a Tour*, 90; Gould, *Fifty Years on the Mississippi*, 635; T. Flint, *Recollections*, 86; Schoolcraft, *Scenes and Adventures*, 36; Tyrone Power, *Impressions of America*, 2:185 (London, 1826); Richard S. Elliot, *Notes Taken in Sixty Years*, 199 (St. Louis, 1883).

4. Alvord and Carter, *Critical Period*, 407; Alvord and Carter, *New Régime*, 476; disbursements and contracts, Craig Papers; Schultz, *Travels*, 2:108; Chittenden, *American Fur Trade*, 1:62; Philip S. Cooke, *Scenes and Adventures in the Army*, 313 (Philadelphia, 1859); *Kentucky Gazette* (Lexington), April 25, 1789; *Palladium* (Frankfort, Ky.), July 15, 1802; F. A. Michaux, "Travels," in Thwaites, *Early Western Travels*, 3:239.

5. The material on boatmen's hospitals is gathered from Cist, *Cincinnati Miscellany*, 1:126; *American State Papers, Commerce and Navigation*, 1:493; 494, 667; 2:36, 514, 658, 756, 772; United States, *Statutes at Large*, 2:192; 5:189; *Louisville Correspondent*, October 7, 21, 1816; March 3, 1817; Kentucky, *Statute Law*, 5:574; United States Marine Hospital Service, "First Annual Report of the Supervising Surgeon," 1872, in 42 Congress, 3 session, *House Executive Documents*, no. 131, p. 9 (serial 1566).

6. J. Hall, *Letters from the West*, 91–94, 182; H. Quick and E. Quick, *Mississippi Steamboatin'*, 234; Strickland, *Pioneers of the West*, 198. Hall relates that one night while at Parkersburg, Virginia, some boatmen plucked up the whipping post (long disused) and flung it into the river proclaiming that "them that wanted to be whipped mought go after it." Then they sat down on the bank in the moonlight and sang several songs, excerpts of two of which are given. Neville's "The Last of the Boatmen," in J. Hall, ed., *Western Souvenir*, 114 (1828), cites the following typical song:

> Hard upon the beach oar!—
> She moves too slow!—
> All the way to Shawneetown,
> Long while ago.

7. *Pageant of America*, 2:198; Howe, *Historical Collections of the Great West*, 1:81; Brackenridge, "Journal," in Thwaites, *Early Western Travels*, 6:63, 89; Bradbury, "Travels," in Thwaites, *Early Western Travels*, 5:39.

8. Howells, *Recollections*, 84. Butler's poem appeared in the *Western Review*, 4:372–374 (1821). A different version, from which the quotation is taken, is in the *Western Pennsylvania Historical Magazine*, 1:26 (1918).

9. Brackenridge, "Journal," in Thwaites, *Early Western Travels*, 6:77; Lewis and Ordway, *Journals*, 65.

10. Brackenridge, "Journal," in Thwaites, *Early Western Travels*, 6: *passim;* Collot, *Journey*, 2:9.

11. T. Flint, *Recollections*, 30; W. T. Harris, *Remarks Made during a Tour*, 98; Samuel L. Clemens, *Life on the Mississippi*, 80 (New York, 1904); Kirkpatrick, *Timothy Flint*, 85.

12. Quoted in Franklin J. Meine, *Tall Tales of the Southwest*, 255 (New York, 1930).

13. J. Flint, "Letters from America," in Thwaites, *Early Western Travels*, 9:113; Schoolcraft, *Scenes and Adventures*, 24; Kirkpatrick, *Timothy Flint*, 85; Fordham, *Personal Narrative*, 195; W. T. Harris, *Remarks Made during a Tour*, 96.

14. Cist, *Cincinnati Miscellany*, 1:126, 128, 156; Neville, "The Last of the Boatmen," in J. Hall, ed., *Western Souvenir*, 117 (1828); J. Flint, "Letters from America," in Thwaites, *Early Western Travels*, 9:92; Brackenridge, *Recollections*, 175–187; Schultz, *Travels*, 2:114.

15. Schoolcraft, *Scenes and Adventures*, 26; Brackenridge, "Journal," in Thwaites, *Early Western Travels*, 6:72; Cuming, "Sketches," in Thwaites, *Early Western Travels*, 4:147; Chittenden, *American Fur Trade*, 1:62; Kentucky, *Statute Law*, 1:262. The *Missouri Gazette* (St. Louis) of October 12, 1808, recounts in detail the proceedings at the trial of George Druillard, who had in the performance of his duty shot and killed a deserter. He was pronounced not guilty.

16. Cist, *Cincinnati Miscellany*, 2:134. See also Hulbert, *Ohio River*, 208. Other boasts are found in Schultz's *Travels*, 2:145, and two or three specially embroidered examples occur in Samuel L. Clemens, *Life on the Mississippi*, 18–20 (New York, 1904). A typically exaggerated western description of Davy Crockett is in Richard G. A. Levinge, *Echoes from the Backwoods*, 2:12 (London, 1846): "His voice was so rough it could not be described—it was obliged to be drawn as a picture. He took hailstones for life pills when he was unwell—he picked his teeth with a pitchfork—combed his hair with a rake—fanned himself with a hurricane, wore a cast iron shirt, and drank nothing but creosote and aquafortis."

17. Cramer, *Navigator*, 306 (1814); Wilkeson, "Early Recollections of the West," in *American Pioneer*, 2:271–273 (1843); Melish, *Travels*, 2:180; Hulbert, *Ohio River*, 209, 221.

18. Wilkeson, "Early Recollections of the West," in *American Pioneer*, 2:273 (1843); J. Hall, *Letters from the West*, 229; Strickland, *Pioneers of the West*, 198; Neville, "The Last of the Boatmen," in J. Hall, ed., *Western Souvenir*, 116–118 (1828); *Mississippi Messenger* (Natchez), August 30, 1805.

19. Cramer, *Navigator*, 33, 307 (1814).

20. Hildreth, "Voyage from Marietta to New Orleans," in *American Pioneer*, 1:134 (1842); J. Flint "Letters from America," in Thwaites, *Early Western Travels*, 9:113; Howe, *Historical Collections of the Great West*, 1:80; Schultz, *Travels*, 2:136; Charles B.

Galloway, "Thomas Griffin," in Mississippi Historical Society, *Publications,* 7:160 (1903). Writers on the early West are reticent as to whether or not the boatmen were accompanied on their voyages by prostitutes, but it seems likely that they often were. There is an oblique statement that the young women of the Illinois were too ready to take passage on the boats, in T. Flint, *Recollections,* 98. Mike Fink, was apparently always accompanied by a mistress. For the relations of the boatmen with the Indian women, see Bradbury's "Travels," in Thwaites, *Early Western Travels,* 5:61, 140, and Brackenridge, "Journal," in Thwaites, *Early Western Travels,* 6:129.

21. *Historical Sketch Book and Guide to New Orleans,* 201; John A. Paxton, *New Orleans Directory,* 22 (New Orleans, 1822); *Western Spy* (Cincinnati), September 12, 1804; *Pittsburgh Gazette,* February 28, 1817; Cist, *Cincinnati Miscellany,* 1:126. Probably there were not very many flatboatmen in the Battle of Chalmette, since only five flatboats had arrived in December, 1814. Ten barges arrived during the month.

22. Ludlow, *Dramatic Life as I Found It,* 237.

23. Clark to the secretary of war, September 12, 1813, Clark Papers; *Niles' Weekly Register,* 6:242, 390 (June 11, August 6, 1814); *Pittsburgh Gazette,* August 19, 1814; Perkins, *Annals of the West,* 911–913; Stevens, *Black Hawk War,* 47–51. The accounts differ as to the number of killed and wounded.

24. Stevens, *Black Hawk War,* 52; Kingston, "Early Western Days," in *Wisconsin Historical Collections,* 7:311; Anderson, "Personal Narrative," in *Wisconsin Historical Collections,* 9:198, and Anderson, "Journal," in *Wisconsin Historical Collections,* 9:219–233, 254. The last account presents the British side of the picture. Statements as to the number of boats conflict; eleven are mentioned in one source, and eight in several others. According to one account, the American flagship was pierced with portholes for twelve guns.

25. "Early Days at Prairie du Chien," in *Wisconsin Historical Collections,* 5:144–152.

26. The material on Sedley and Girty is based on accounts in *Historical Sketch Book and Guide to New Orleans,* 201; Cist, *Cincinnati Miscellany,* 1:126, 128. Cist claimed that Girty's last job

was steering a boat up the Cumberland for him and that Girty died at Nashville at the end of this voyage in 1820.

27. The material on Mike Fink in this and the following paragraphs is based on Casseday, *Louisville*, 72–81; Neville, "The Last of the Boatmen," in J. Hall, ed., *Western Souvenir*, 107–122 (1828); Howe, *Historical Collections of Ohio*, 1:321; Cist, *Cincinnati Miscellany*, 1:156; Chittenden, *American Fur Trade*, 2:709–712; Blair and Meine, *Mike Fink, King of Mississippi Keelboatmen*. The last-named work follows the development of the Mike Fink legend and gives a complete bibliography.

28. T. Flint, *Recollections*, 15.

Notes to Chapter V

RIVER PIRATES AND THE NATCHEZ TRACE

1. Firmin A. Rozier, *History of the Early Settlement of the Mississippi Valley*, 59 (St. Louis, 1896); Howe, *Historical Collections of the Great West*, 1:171; Scharf, *Saint Louis*, 2:1092; Logan U. Reavis, *Saint Louis*, 22 (St. Louis, 1871).

2. T. Flint, *Western Monthly Review*, 3:354–359 (1830).

3. Rothert, *Outlaws of Cave-in-Rock*, 17–20. Near the middle of the ceiling of the cave there is a cleft about three feet by ten in which a person may with difficulty maintain a footing on the narrow ledge that runs around the bottom, but which even imagination would be hard put to it to define as a room. Nevertheless, Ashe, in his *Travels*, 225–230, gives an amazing description of his visit to the pirate's vast treasure room and slaughterhouse above the cave, and others have followed his example.

4. Cramer, *Navigator*, 45 (1806); Rothert, *Outlaws of Cave-in-Rock*, 44.

5. From this tavern were derived the terms often attached to the cave, *Rock-Inn-Cave*, and *Rocking Cave*.

6. Rothert, *Outlaws of Cave-in-Rock*, 49–53; L. Collins and R. H. Collins, *Kentucky*, 2:147; Ashe, *Travels*, 228. The end of the story as recited in the old accounts is too fanciful for belief. The stamp of fiction is conclusively placed upon it by the statement that sixty-five skeletons were found in the upper room of the cave.

7. Guild, *Old Times in Tennessee*, 94; Rothert, *Outlaws of Cave-in-Rock*, 157–173, 237–245; Cuming, "Sketches," in Thwaites, *Early Western Travels*, 4:267. Francis Baily, who visited the cave in 1797, saw and heard nothing of robbers, but his visit was made during high water. See Baily, *Journal*, 246–248.

8. Rothert, *Outlaws of Cave-in-Rock*, 55–156.

9. Audubon, *Delineations of American Scenery*, 20; Rothert, *Outlaws of Cave-in-Rock*, 177, 195.

10. The material on the Natchez Trace in this and the following four paragraphs is based on Baily, *Journal*, 332–404; Guild, *Old Times in Tennessee*, 93–104; Cotterill, "The Natchez Trace," in *Tennessee Historical Magazine*, 7:27–35 (1921); *Mississippi and Louisiana Almanac*, 57 (Natchez, 1819).

11. Guild, *Old Times in Tennessee*, 93–104; Cotterill, "The Natchez Trace," in *Tennessee Historical Magazine*, 7:27–35 (1921); Dunbar Rowland, *Encyclopedia of Mississippi History*, 567 (Madison, 1907); F. A. Michaux, "Travels," in Thwaites, *Early Western Travels*, 3:245; *Historical Sketch Book and Guide to New Orleans*, 201; John F. H. Claiborne, *Life and Times of Gen. Sam. Dale*, 85 n. (New York, 1860). Estimates of the length of the trace differ between five hundred and six hundred miles, depending on the route taken.

12. Guild, *Old Times in Tennessee*, 92–96.

13. Rothert, *Outlaws of Cave-in-Rock*, 183; Guild, *Old Times in Tennessee*, 96; *Kentucky Gazette* (Lexington), September 14, 1801.

14. Rothert, *Outlaws of Cave-in-Rock*, 188.

15. Rothert, *Outlaws of Cave-in-Rock*, 200–205, 207–247; Guild, *Old Times in Tennessee*, 97.

16. Rothert, *Outlaws of Cave-in-Rock*, 247–251, 254–263.

17. *Pittsburgh Gazette*, July 22, 1807; Scharf, *Saint Louis*, 2:1092; Gould, *Fifty Years on the Mississippi*, 58. John Parsons was told in Indiana in 1840 that the Natchez Trace in the earlier days was called the Bloody Path because of the highwaymen's activities. See John Parsons, *Tour Through Indiana in 1840*, 28, 330 (New York, 1920).

18. Cramer, *Navigator*, 203 (1814); Sampson, "The New Madrid and Other Earthquakes in Missouri," in Mississippi Valley Historical Association, *Proceedings*, 6:232; Nuttall, "Journal," in Thwaites, *Early Western Travels*, 13:295; Ludlow, *Dramatic Life as I Found It*, 126.

Notes to Chapter VI

THE IMMIGRANT

1. Cramer, *Navigator*, 28 (1814).

2. Temple Bodley, *George Rogers Clark*, 157 (Boston and New York, 1926); Clarence W. Alvord, ed., *Kaskaskia Records 1778–1790*, 421–423, 443–445 (*Illinois Historical Collections*, vol. 5—Springfield, 1909); Clarence W. Alvord, ed., *Cahokia Records, 1778–1790*, xxviii (*Illinois Historical Collections*, vol. 2—Springfield, 1907).

3. T. M. Harris, "Journal," in Thwaites, *Early Western Travels*, 3:344; Imlay, *Topographical Description*, 81; Melish, *Travels*, 2:84; Cramer, *Navigator*, 15 (1806); Hulbert, *Pioneer Roads*, 2:72; David Thomas, *Travels through the Western Country in the Summer of 1816*, 214 (Auburn, N.Y., 1819).

4. Cramer, *Navigator*, 35 (1814); Buttrick, "Voyages," in Thwaites, *Early Western Travels*, 8:56–58; J. Flint, "Letters from America," in Thwaites, *Early Western Travels*, 9:97; T. Flint, *Recollections*, 13.

5. Schultz, *Travels*, 2:100.

6. Emilius O. Randall and David J. Ryan, *History of Ohio*, 2:457 (New York, 1912); *Pittsburgh Gazette*, November 2, 1793; *Centinel of the Northwestern Territory* (Cincinnati), November 23, 1793.

7. Sealsfield, *The Americans as They Are*, 53–76.

8. Melish, *Travels*, 2:86; Thomas Hulme, "Journal Made during a Tour in the Western Countries of America," in Reuben G. Thwaites, *Early Western Travels*, 10:39 (Cleveland, 1904); Collot, *Journey*, 1:42, 94.

9. Buttrick, "Voyages," in Thwaites, *Early Western Travels*,

8:56–58; Gilpin, "Journal of a Tour from Philadelphia," in *Pennsylvania Magazine of History and Biography*, 51:353 (1927); J. Hall, *Letters from the West*, 87; Howells, *Recollections*, 84.

10. J. Hall, *Letters from the West*, 138–140.

11. Draper MSS, 11J43; L. Collins, *Kentucky*, 31–33, 41–46. Contemporary newspapers and travel accounts give numerous fragmentary figures on immigration, but they are of little value in computing the total number of immigrants.

12. *Kentucky Gazette* (Lexington), May 7, 1791; Pope, *Tour*, 18; L. Collins, *Kentucky*, 217; Denny, *Military Journal*, 137; Heckewelder, "Journey to the Wabash in 1792," in *Pennsylvania Magazine of History and Biography*, 12:37 (1888); Jacob Burnet, *Notes on the Early Settlement of the North-Western Territory*, 94 (Cincinnati, 1847). In 1792 the mouth of the Scioto was a mile west of the "Watch Tower."

13. L. Collins, *Kentucky*, 433–438, 511. For another account of an escaping white man, see "Notes of a Journey from Philadelphia to New Madrid, Tennessee, 1790," in *Pennsylvania Magazine of History and Biography*, 36:213 (1912).

14. *Kentucky Gazette* (Lexington), April 4, 1788; May 17, July 12, 1790; *Pittsburgh Gazette*, July 5, 1788; Cresswell, *Journal*, 91–93; L. Collins, *Kentucky*, 434, 511; Antoine F. Saugrain, "Saugrain's Relation of His Voyage down the Ohio," in American Antiquarian Society, *Proceedings*, new series, 11:369–380.

15. L. Collins, *Kentucky*, 365; Willard R. Jillson, *Tales of the Dark and Bloody Ground*, 96–98 (Louisville, 1930).

16. L. Collins, *Kentucky*, 217–221; Howe, *Historical Collections of the Great West*, 1:146–150.

17. L. Collins, *Kentucky*, 510–515.

18. "It was a tradition among the Cumberland folk that the Chickamaugas suffered retribution in losses from small-pox from infection by the unfortunate emigrants." Williams, *Early Travels in the Tennessee Country*, 236 n.

19. Donelson, "Journal," in Williams, *Early Travels in the Tennessee Country*, 232–242. Among the voyagers on this trip was Rachel Donelson, who later became the wife of Andrew Jackson.

20. The material in this and the following two paragraphs is gathered from T. Flint, *Recollections,* 21, 32; J. Flint, "Letters from America," in Thwaites, *Early Western Travels,* 9:92; Melish, *Travels,* 2:87, 112–114; A. Wilson, "Letter from Lexington," in *Port Folio,* third series, 3:505 (1810).

21. Baily, *Journal,* 163–186.

22. Latrobe, "The First Steamboat Voyage on the Western Waters," in Maryland Historical Society, *Fund Publications,* no. 6, p. 8, 10.

23. T. Flint, *Recollections,* 286–288; Kirkpatrick, *Timothy Flint,* 298–300.

24. T. Flint, *Recollections,* 40; A. Wilson, "Letter from Lexington," in *Port Folio,* third series, 3:505 (1810).

Notes to Chapter VII

SHIPBUILDING ON THE WESTERN WATERS

1. Henry Clay, *Works,* 1:193; 6:50 (New York, 1904). The true identity of the ship and port will probably never be known. Howe, in his *Historical Collections of Ohio,* 2:785, ascribes the incident to a Marietta vessel and names the port as St. Petersburg. James T. Lloyd, in *Lloyd's Steamboat Directory and Disasters on the Western Waters,* 41 (Cincinnati, 1856), gives the ship as the brig "Dean" and the port as Leghorn. James L. Bishop, in *A History of American Manufactures from 1608 to 1860,* 2:111 (third edition, Philadelphia, 1868), speaks of "an East Indian port." Cist's *Cincinnati Miscellany,* 1:234, names the "Western Trader" as the ship, Marseilles as the port, and Captain John Brevoort as commander. Gould, in his *Fifty Years on the Mississippi,* 99, characteristically embellishes Clay's speech; he states that the customs officer closed with "I knew America could show many wonderful things, but a fresh water sea port is something I never dreamed of."

2. Abraham Weatherwise, pseud., *Father Abraham's Almanac,* not paged (Philadelphia, 1761); T. M. Harris, *Journal,* 210. See also Cramer, *Navigator,* 358 (1814). The statement does not appear in the standard collections of Franklin's writings.

3. "The Trenton Circular," in *Quarterly Publication of the His-*

torical and Philosophical Society of Ohio, 5:90 (1924); Ohio in
1788: A Description . . . of that Portion of the United States Situ-
ated between Pennsylvania, the Rivers Ohio and Scioto and Lake
Erie, 43, 48 (translated by John H. James—Columbus, 1888);
Pittsburgh Gazette, April 28, 1787; Jervis Cutler, A Topographical
Description of the State of Ohio, Indiana Territory and Louisiana,
21 (Boston, 1812); F. A. Michaux, "Travels," in Thwaites, Early
Western Travels, 3:160.

4. Albert Gallatin, report on "Roads and Canals, Communicated
to the Senate, April 6, 1808," in American State Papers, Miscellaneous, 1:732 (Washington, 1834); Baily, Journal, 330.

5. Pittsburgh Gazette, August 25, 1800; Tree of Liberty (Pittsburgh), March 28, 1801.

6. Elizabeth Herald, June 7, 1900; Pittsburgh Gazette, May 1,
15, 1801; Louisiana Gazette (New Orleans), August 23, December
30, 1808; Josiah S. Johnston, ed., Memorial History of Louisville
from Its First Settlement to the Year 1896, 1:245 (Chicago and
New York, [1896]). The Walker family, engaged in boatbuilding
for generations at Elizabeth, always claimed that John Walker
sailed the first ocean vessel built on the western waters. In "Ship
and Brig Building on the Ohio and its Tributaries," in Ohio
Archæological and Historical Publications, 22:54–64, Richard T.
Wiley argues that the existence of a Spanish passport dated July
17, 1795, authorizing John Walker to sail for Philadelphia on the
schooner "Polly" shows that the first ocean vessel was the "Polly."
He cites Thaddeus Mason Harris' statement at Elizabeth, April 14,
1803, that "the Monongahela Farmer and other vessels of considerable burden built here and laden with the produce of the adjacent
country, were sent to the West India islands." See T. M. Harris,
Journal, 34. Ambler, in his Transportation in the Ohio Valley, 84,
thinks the "Polly" may have been the ship mentioned by Gallatin.
It may be suggested here that the passport may have been issued
to Walker as a passenger, not as master, of the "Polly." There is
considerable difference of opinion as to the tonnage of the "Monongahela Farmer," the foregoing accounts giving variously 92, 120,
and 250 tons.

7. Elizabeth Herald, June 7, 1900; Palladium (Frankfort, Ky.),

May 19, 1804; Cramer, *Navigator,* 66 (1814); *Pittsburgh Gazette,* May 25, 1804.

8. Memorandum Book, dated May 19, 1794, Craig Papers; Neville B. Craig, *The History of Pittsburgh,* 285 (Pittsburgh, 1851); *Pittsburgh Gazette,* March 30, 1799.

9. Sherman Day, *Historical Collections of the State of Pennsylvania,* 82 (Philadelphia, c1843).

10. *Pittsburgh Gazette,* January 21, March 18, 1803; Cramer, *Navigator,* 21 (1814); *Liverpool Saturday's Advertiser,* July 9, 1803, quoted in *Western Spy* (Cincinnati), October 5, 1803.

11. *Pittsburgh Gazette,* February 11, April 29, May 6, 13, 20, 1803; March 30, April 6, May 25, June 22, 1804; *Tree of Liberty* (Pittsburgh), January 7, April 21, 1804; *Louisiana Gazette* (New Orleans), April 16, 1805; Cist, *Cincinnati Miscellany,* 1:234; James T. Lloyd, *Lloyd's Steamboat Directory and Disasters on the Western Waters,* 41 (Cincinnati, 1856). A partial list of Pittsburgh ships reads as follows:

1798 Gunboat "President Adams."

1799 Gunboat "Senator Ross."

1803 Brig "Dean" (*Pittsburgh Gazette,* January 21, 1803); schooner "Amity," 103 or 120 tons (*Pittsburgh Gazette,* April 29, 1803); ship "Pittsburgh," 250 or 270 tons (*Pittsburgh Gazette,* February 11, April 29, May 6, 13, 20, 1803); schooner ——, 120 tons (*Pittsburgh Gazette,* May 20, 1803).

1804 Brig or schooner —— (*Tree of Liberty* [Pittsburgh], January 7, 1804). The last two might possibly have been the "Mildred," 150 tons, and the "Beebe," 120 tons, mentioned in Hulbert's "Western Ship-Building," in *American Historical Review,* 21:724 (1915–16). Brig "Nanina," 132, 150, or 200 tons (*Pittsburgh Gazette,* March 30, May 25, 1804); Sherman Day, *Historical Collections of the State of Pennsylvania,* 82 (Philadelphia, c1843); (*Tree of Liberty* [Pittsburgh], January 7, 1804); brig, brigantine or ship "Louisiana," 169, 300, or 350 tons (*Pittsburgh Gazette,* April 6, May 25, 1804); schooner "Conquest," 126 tons (*Pittsburgh Gazette,* April 6, May 25, 1804); schooner or brig "Allegheny," 150 tons (*Pittsburgh Gazette,* April 6, 1804; *Tree of Liberty* [Pittsburgh], January 7, 1804).

1805 Ship or brig "General Butler," 400 tons (Cist, *Cincinnati Miscellany,* 1:234; *Louisiana Gazette,* April 16, 1805); brig "Fayett" (Masson, "Plan of Pittsburgh").

1806 Ship "Western Trader," 400 tons (Sherman Day, *Historical Collections of the State of Pennsylvania,* 82 [Philadelphia, c1843]); Cramer, *Navigator,* 66 (1814); brig "Black Walnut" (or "Black Warrior"?) (*Palladium* [Frankfort, Ky.], April 3, 1806); William G. Lyford, *Western Address Directory,* 60 (Baltimore, 1837); brig "Betsy O'Hara," probably from Pittsburgh (William G. Lyford, *Western Address Directory,* 60 [Baltimore, 1837]).

1810 Brig ——, 160 tons (Cramer, *Navigator,* 21, [1814]).

12. Mrs. C. Simpson, "Reminiscences of Early Pittsburgh," in *Western Pennsylvania Historical Magazine,* 4:244 (1921).

13. *Pittsburgh Gazette,* April 6, 1804; papers of the "Louisiana" now in possession of Marietta College; Hulbert, "Western Ship-Building," in *American Historical Review,* 21:726 (1915–16).

14. Howe, *Historical Collections of Ohio,* 2:792.

15. Hildreth Papers, 4:151. A different version is given in Hildreth's *Early Pioneer Settlers of Ohio,* 160.

16. Hildreth Papers, 2:33; Hildreth, *Early Pioneer Settlers of Ohio,* 159; Cist, *Cincinnati in 1841,* 181; *Pittsburgh Gazette,* August 14, 1801.

17. Schultz, *Travels,* 1:143; Cist, *Cincinnati Miscellany,* 1:205; Hildreth, *Early Pioneer Settlers of Ohio,* 254, 309, 457; Hildreth Papers, 2:33; *Palladium* (Frankfort, Ky.), July 4, 1802; *Pittsburgh Gazette,* March 18, 1803.

18. Following is a list of Marietta ships, reconstructed as accurately as the surviving notices will permit. The years given were probably in most cases the dates of the laying of the keels.

1801 Brig "St. Clair," 110 tons; ship "Muskingum," 230 tons; brig "Eliza Green," 126 tons.

1802 Brig "Dominic," 100–140 tons; schooner "Indiana," 75 tons; brig "Marietta," 150 tons; brig "Mary Avery," 150 tons.

1803 Schooner "Whitney," 75 tons; schooner "McGrath," 75 tons; brig "Orlando," 150 tons; brig "Galett," 185 tons; brig "Minerva" (*Kentucky Gazette* [Lexington], May 17, 1803).

1804 Ship "Temperance," 230 tons; brig "Ohio," 150 tons; schooner "Nonpareil," 70 tons.

1805 Brig "Perseverance," 160 tons.

1806 Ship "Rufus King," 300 tons; ship "John Atkinson," 320 tons; ship "Tuscarora," 320 tons; brig "Sophia Green," 100–144 tons; two gunboats.

1807 Ship "Francis," 350 tons; ship "Robert Hall," 300 tons; brig "Rufus Putnam," 300 tons; brig "Collatta," 140 tons.

1808 Schooner "Belle," 100–144 tons.

1809 Schooner "Adventurer," 60 tons.

1812 Schooner "Maria," 75 tons.

1816 Schooner "Maria," 50 tons (*Pittsburgh Gazette*, April 27, 1816).

19. *Pittsburgh Gazette*, April 22, 1803; Cist, *Cincinnati Miscellany*, 1:205; *Liberty Hall* (Cincinnati), February 24, 1807; Cramer, *Navigator*, 275 (1814).

20. Wheeling—"Dorcas and Sally," 50 or 70 tons (*Kentucky Gazette* [Lexington], May 17, 1803). Frankfort and vicinity—Schooner "Go-by" (*Kentucky Gazette* [Lexington], May 17, 1803); schooner "Ceres," 85 tons, owned by Instone (*Pittsburgh Gazette*, May 25, 1804); schooner "Jane," 80 tons, owned by Mullamphy (*Pittsburgh Gazette*, May 25, 1804); ship "General Scott," 260 tons (*Kentucky Gazette* [Lexington], May 28, 1805). Prestonville, Kentucky—Brig ——, 150 tons; schooner ——, 116 tons (*Western Spy* [Cincinnati], July 31, 1805). Charleston, Kentucky—Schooner "Mary Anne," 100 tons, owned by Houghley (*Pittsburgh Gazette*, May 25, 1804). Limestone—"Maysville," 180 tons, owned by Gallegher (*Pittsburgh Gazette*, May 25, 1804). Belville—Ship "Belville," 170 tons, owned by Avery (*Pittsburgh Gazette*, May 25, 1804). Louisville—"Catherine," 180 tons (*Pittsburgh Gazette*, May 25, 1804). Columbia—Brig "Cincinnatus," 170 tons (*Niles' Weekly Register*, 12:70 [March 7, 1817]); two gunboats (*Liberty Hall* [Cincinnati], February 24, 1807). Port Gibson,

Mississippi Territory—two or more (*Natchez Gazette,* August 31, 1808). Eddyville, Kentucky—3 schooners, 160 tons. One of them probably mentioned later as the brig "Melinda." See Bedford, "A Tour in 1807 down the Cumberland, Ohio and Mississippi Rivers from Nashville to New Orleans," in *Tennessee Historical Magazine,* 5:50 (1919). Uncertain origin—"Kentucky," lodged on falls in 1803 (*Pittsburgh Gazette,* May 25, 1804); brig "Kentucky," chartered by J. W. Hunt & Co., and bound for Charleston, South Carolina (*Kentucky Gazette* [Lexington], May 28, 1805). Possibly the same boat as the preceding. "Penrose," at the falls in 1807 (*Western Spy* [Cincinnati], May 18, 1807). At least four gunboats were built at Eddyville, and an unknown number at other points, probably Pittsburgh and Louisville. See Bedford.

21. *Pittsburgh Gazette,* December 9, 1803; *Tree of Liberty* (Pittsburgh), December 17, 1803. James Whitney's calculations of tonnage were based on ninety-five cubic feet to the ton. See Hildreth Papers, 2:14.

22. Hildreth Papers, 2:34; Schultz, *Travels,* 1:191.

23. Schultz, *Travels,* 1:191; Cramer, *Navigator,* 127 (1814).

24. Hulbert, "Western Ship-Building," in *American Historical Review,* 21:732 (1915–16). Cist, in his *Cincinnati Miscellany,* 1:205, mentions both the embargo and the disasters at the falls as the reasons for the decline of western shipbuilding.

25. Hildreth, *Early Pioneer Settlers of Ohio,* 309; Jervis Cutler, *A Topographical Description of the State of Ohio, Indiana Territory and Louisiana,* 19 (Boston, 1812); Ambler, *Transportation in the Ohio Valley,* 101–106.

26. This statement of tonnage, an estimate, but certainly not an overestimate, is based upon the New Orleans wharf register, 1806–23. During that time over twelve thousand flatboats, to say nothing of other craft, landed at that city. The average flatboat carried a burden of forty or fifty tons. The best surviving statistics on the value of the traffic are in Walker, "Commerce of the Mississippi River," in 50 Congress, 1 session, *House Executive Documents,* no. 6, part 2, p. 184, 191, 199 (serial 2552). According to this estimate, over ninety-two million dollars worth of goods were received at New Orleans in the two periods of 1801–8 and 1815–20.

Notes to Chapter VIII

THE BOATMAN HAS HIS DAY

1. Advertisements, "Ohio Packet Boats," in *Pittsburgh Gazette,* November 2 to November 30, 1793; *Centinel of the Northwestern Territory* (Cincinnati), November 23, 1793, January 11, 1794, quoted in J. Hall, *Notes on the Western States,* 223–225; *Kentucky Gazette* (Lexington), December 7, 1793. It is possible that Myers' venture did not outlast the winter. The next May, Isaac Craig in discussing the proposed Ohio mail-boat line stated as his opinion that "the idea of Passenger Packet-Boats ought at present to be abandoned." See Craig to Pickering, May 9, 1794, "Letter Book B," Craig Papers.

2. Craig to Finley, July 2, 1794, "Letter Book B"; instructions to Elijah Martin, boat master of Mail Boat No. 1, July 5, 1794; Charles Mills's receipt for Mail Boat No. 2, July 12, 1794, "Invoice of Stores Forwarded"; disbursements, no. 1127, all in Craig Papers; Pickering to the postmaster at Gallipolis, June 20, 1794, United States, Territorial Papers, 6266 PO–2; Shelby to Randolph, March 14, 1795, "Miscellaneous Papers, 1793–1798," Durrett Collection. The Craig Papers are rich in letters and accounts relating to the mail boats, and no attempt is made here to cite or paraphrase all the material contained in them.

3. Cramer, *Navigator,* 25, 63–65, 110 (1814); Walker, "Commerce of the Mississippi River," in 50 Congress, 1 session, *House Executive Documents,* no. 6, part 2, p. 185 (serial 2552); J. Hall, *Notes on the Western States,* 236; J. Hall, *The West,* 13; Robinson & Barber, advertisement in the *Pittsburgh Gazette,* June 3, 1814; Charles F. Goss, ed., *Cincinnati, The Green City, 1788–1912,* 2:105 (Cincinnati, 1912). In the *Pittsburgh Gazette,* January 21, 1815, John Walker advertised that "the fast sailing boat Torpedo has commenced running between Elizabethtown and Pittsburgh. She will leave Elizabethtown every Tuesday Morning at 9 o'clock, and arrive at Pittsburgh the same Evening; will leave Pittsburgh on Wednesday at 2 o'clock, P.M. and arrive at Elizabethtown on Thursday." Walker was trying to attract the business of wagoners and offered to carry a wagonload one way for five dollars, or both ways for seven dollars. Loads of iron were transported at the same rates.

4. Cramer, *Navigator*, 46, 49–72 (1814); *Harris' Pittsburgh Business Directory for the Year 1837*, 176 (published by Isaac Harris—Pittsburgh, 1837); J. Hall, *Letters from the West*, 70; numerous advertisements in the *Pittsburgh Gazette*.

5. Robert Stubbs, *Ohio Almanac* (Cincinnati, 1810); Jacob Burnet, *Notes on the Early Settlement of the North-Western Territory*, 200 (Cincinnati, 1847); Cramer, *Navigator*, 252 (1814); *Liberty Hall* (Cincinnati), May 29, 1811; October 30, 1811; January 8, 1816; December 2, 1816; *Niles' Weekly Register*, 12:70 (March 29, 1817); *Cincinnati Gazette*, July 15, 1815; *Louisville Correspondent*, March 11, 1816; *Pittsburgh Gazette*, April 1, 1815. Other barges having Cincinnati as a home port about this time were the "Nonsuch," Smith, master, 100 tons, owned by Noble and Moore; the "Fox," Awl, master, 40 tons, owned by John Smith; the "Triton," owned by Baum, Sloo and Company; the "Expedition," William Adams, master, 80 tons, owned by Jeremiah Reeder and Adam Moore; the "Adventurer," 60 tons, owned by James W. Byrn and Company. In addition, the "Ohio" and the "Industry," Craig, master, may have been owned there.

6. Palmer, *Journal*, 66; "Ship News," in *Louisiana Gazette* (New Orleans), August 27, 1805; March 28, 1806; January 13, 1807. The falls pilot kept a record of boats passing the falls, but every effort to unearth it has failed.

7. Cramer, *Navigator*, 275 (1814); Sherman Day, *Historical Collections of the State of Pennsylvania*, 82 (Philadelphia, c1843); A. Michaux, "Journals," in Thwaites, *Early Western Travels*, 3:31; *Louisiana Gazette* (New Orleans), April 2, May 21, 1805; February 21, March 11, April 18, 25, October 7, November 4, 1806; January 6, April 10, 17, June 30, 1807.

8. Statistics on the number of barges and keelboats are scarce and fragmentary. The New Orleans "List of Flats and Barges in Port" for the period from April, 1806, to March, 1823, has survived, but it was too carelessly kept to be of great value. The *Louisiana Gazette* (New Orleans), from about January, 1805, to June, 1807, kept under "Ship News" a fairly full record of arrivals and clearances of river craft together with the ports from which they had arrived or to which they were clearing. Statistics are found in the

following: Cramer, *Pittsburgh Magazine Almanack,* 53 (1814), and Cramer, *Louisiana and Mississippi Almanac for 1814,* 52 (Natchez, 1819); *Pittsburgh Gazette,* October 17, 1834; Morris Birkbeck, *Notes on a Journey in America,* 77 (London, 1818); United States, Engineer Department, Board of Engineers for Rivers and Harbors, *Transportation in the Mississippi and Ohio Valleys,* 167 (transportation series, no. 2—Washington, 1929); Gould, *Fifty Years on the Mississippi,* 204.

9. *American State Papers, Commerce and Navigation,* 1:493; *Pittsburgh Gazette,* May 28, 1802.

10. De Bow, *Industrial Resources,* 2:149.

11. *Pittsburgh Gazette,* September 17, 1802; Sample, "Sketches of Western Settlements," in *American Pioneer,* 1:159 (1842).

12. Jefferson County, Kentucky, "Bond and Power of Attorney," no. 1, February, 1783, to May 1, 1797; Kentucky, *Statute Law,* 3:25; *Kentucky Gazette* (Lexington), April 30, 1802; February 7, 1809; *Pittsburgh Gazette,* June 4, 1802; *Louisiana Gazette* (New Orleans) from 1807 to 1812. On May 5, 1807, the rate on flatboats from above the falls was 10 per cent, and below the falls, 9 per cent; on barges from above the falls it was 6 per cent, and below, 5 per cent. From Natchez it was 1½–2, from the Arkansas 2–2½, from Illinois 3½–4 per cent. These rates remained fairly constant until 1810. The next figures given are for May 18, 1812, when the rate for flats and barges from Kentucky, either above or below the falls, was 5 per cent, from Natchez 1½, from Arkansas 2, and from Illinois 3½.

13. *Pittsburgh Gazette,* November 22, 1814; January 27, 1816; September 8, 1826; Collot, *Journey,* 1:39; F. A. Michaux, "Travels," in Thwaites, *Early Western Travels,* 3:158; *Louisville Correspondent,* September 25, 1815; J. Hall, *Letters from the West,* 52; Cramer, *Navigator,* 15 (1814). Robert Mills gives some figures for 1820 that are interesting if true: "Between Philadelphia and Pittsburgh, there are employed annually 3650 wagons, the freight of which amounts to $730,000; and the quantity carried to 91,250 hundredweight, which, fixing an average of the value of the merchandise at $200 per hundredweight round, gives the enormous sum of $18,250,000 wagoned out every year from Philadelphia to Pitts-

burgh." Robert Mills, *A Treatise on Inland Navigation,* 89 (Baltimore, 1820).

14. Manuel Lisa's receipt for cargoes, St. Louis, September 14, 1813, is in the Chouteau Papers. The most valuable sources of freight-rate statistics are the *Louisiana Gazette* (New Orleans) and its successors from 1804 to 1812, which occasionally published the freight rates along with the prices current. The figure quoted for New Orleans to Pittsburgh is taken from Fearon, *Sketches of America,* 262, with the deduction of a dollar to allow for the continuous haul. The *Pittsburgh Gazette,* September 8, 1826, gives the following downstream keelboat freight rates from Pittsburgh to the points named: St. Louis, $1.62½; Nashville, $1.50; Louisville, $.75; Cincinnati, $.62½; Maysville, $.50; Marietta, $.40; Wheeling, $.18¾.

15. Filson, *Kentucke,* 45; Collot, *Journey,* 1:118–123; 2:198; Winsor, *Westward Movement,* 413.

16. Schultz, *Travels,* 1:139; *Pittsburgh Gazette,* January 21, 1815; Schoolcraft, *Scenes and Adventures,* 240.

17. W. T. Harris, *Remarks Made during a Tour,* 98; Cuming, "Sketches," in Thwaites, *Early Western Travels,* 4:116, 135; A. Wilson, "Letter from Lexington," in *Port Folio,* third series, 3:499–518; T. Flint, *History and Geography,* 1:156; Palmer, Journal, 62; Lyell, *Second Visit to the United States,* 2:131; Basil Hall, *Travels in North America,* 3:357 (Edinburgh, 1829); Hulbert, *Ohio River,* 233; J. Hall, *Letters from the West,* 133; Henry L. Ellsworth, *Illinois in 1837,* 30 (1819); John Parsons, *Tour through Indiana in 1840,* 28 (New York, 1920); T. Flint, *Recollections,* 105. Cist, in his *Cincinnati Miscellany,* 2:341, says: "It was thought a few years since that Charles Carroll of Carrollton was the last of the signers to the Declaration of Independence. This must be a mistake. A late *Vicksburgh Intelligencer* says—'The signers to the Declaration of Independence are on board a flatboat at the foot of Jackson Street. Visit them—they are worth seeing.' "

18. Draper MSS, 30J73, 30J74; J. A. James, *Clark Papers, 1781–1784,* 143; McCully to Craig, June 20, 1793, in "Letter Book A," Craig Papers; *Pittsburgh Gazette,* April 8, 1814; Cramer, *Navigator,* 84 (1814); Savelle, *George Morgan,* 25.

19. Cramer, *Navigator,* 21 (1811); *Franklin Magazine Almanac,*

52, (Pittsburgh, 1820); Gilleland, *Ohio and Mississippi Pilot,* 178 (1820); *Louisiana Gazette* (St. Louis), March 15, 1810.

20. New Orleans, City Council, "An Ordinance Concerning the Port . . . of New-Orleans," article 4; New Orleans, City Council, "Regulations for the Port of New-Orleans"; Gould, *Fifty Years on the Mississippi,* 194; *Historical Sketch Book and Guide to New Orleans,* 201; William C. C. Claiborne, *Official Letter Books 1801–1816,* 1:334, 338 (Jackson, Miss., 1917).

21. T. Flint, *History and Geography,* 1:154.

22. Cramer, *Navigator,* 32 (1811); *Pittsburgh Gazette,* October 18, 1811. According to the *Liberty Hall* (Cincinnati), June 25, 1805, a steamboat built by Captain McKeever was on its way to New Orleans where the steam engine and machinery waited. See also Gould, *Fifty Years on the Mississippi,* 150. According to Emerson Hough, "The Settlement of the West: A Study in Transportation," in *Century Magazine,* 63:202 (1901), a steamboat was built at Pittsburgh in 1806, but it failed to go upstream. Hough gives no citation.

23. Flagg, "Far West," in Thwaites, *Early Western Travels,* 26:150; Robert Buchanan, in the *Cincinnati Gazette,* c1878, from a newspaper clipping copied and preserved in Neville Craig's scrapbook in the Craig Papers. Buchanan was born about 1796 and became a steamboat captain in 1821.

24. David Thomas, *Travels through the Western Country in the Summer of 1816,* 61 (Auburn, N.Y., 1819); Cist, *Cincinnati Miscellany,* 1:151; L. Collins and R. H. Collins, *Kentucky,* 2:361.

25. L. Collins and R. H. Collins, *Kentucky,* 2:362; Cist, *Cincinnati Miscellany,* 1:152; J. Flint, "Letters from America," in Thwaites, *Early Western Travels,* 9:286; J. Hall, *The West,* 133; Audubon, *Delineations of American Scenery,* 28. *Niles' Weekly Register,* 25:95 (October 11, 1823) gives a fare schedule for 1823. Sketches of the career of Captain Shreve are in Hardin, "The First Great Western River Captain," in *Louisiana Historical Quarterly,* 10:25–67 (1927), and in Pfaff, "Henry Miller Shreve: A Biography," in *Louisiana Historical Quarterly,* 10:192–240 (1927).

26. Drake, *Natural and Statistical View,* 148; Benjamin Drake and E. D. Mansfield, *Cincinnati in 1826* (Cincinnati, 1827).

27. Samuel Jones, *Pittsburgh in 1826*, 89 (Pittsburgh, 1826); J. Hall, *The West*, 96; scrapbook of Isaac Craig, Jr., Craig Papers; *Harris' General Business Directory of the Cities of Pittsburgh and Allegheny*, 127, 129 (published by Isaac Harris—Pittsburgh, 1841); Wilson, *Pittsburg*, 49, 177, 180; Cist, *Cincinnati Miscellany*, 1:125; *Historical Sketch Book and Guide to New Orleans*, 200.

Bibliography

THE footnotes contain bibliographical data for printed works that are cited only once or twice, and then incidentally, and that are not essential to an understanding of the keelboat age; these works are not included in the following bibliography. Of the newspapers noted below, the author consulted, in most instances, all available issues published up to 1820. For details of the changes in the titles of newspapers during this period and for the present locations of files, see Clarence S. Brigham's "Bibliography of American Newspapers, 1690–1820," published in the American Antiquarian Society's *Proceedings, 1913–27.*

SOURCE MATERIAL

MANUSCRIPTS

ARCHIVES NATIONALES. *See* France. Archives Nationales.

CHOUTEAU, AUGUSTE. Papers. Missouri Historical Society. St. Louis.

CHOUTEAU-MAFFITT PAPERS. Missouri Historical Society. St. Louis.

CLARK, WILLIAM. Papers. Missouri Historical Society. St. Louis.

CRAIG PAPERS. Carnegie Library of Pittsburgh.

DENNY-O'HARA PAPERS. In the custody of the Historical Society of Western Pennsylvania. Pittsburgh.

DRAPER COLLECTION. State Historical Society of Wisconsin. Madison.

DURRETT COLLECTION. University of Chicago.

FRANCE. Archives Nationales, Archives des Colonies. Paris. Transcripts in the Clements Library. University of Michigan.

HILDRETH PAPERS. Marietta College. Marietta, Ohio.

INNES PAPERS. Library of Congress. Photostats in the Newberry Library. Chicago.

JEFFERSON COUNTY, KENTUCKY. "Bond and Power of Attorney." Record of the county clerk. Courthouse. Louisville.

BIBLIOGRAPHY

JEFFERSON COUNTY, KENTUCKY. County court minute book, no. 5, 1796–1801. Courthouse. Louisville.

LESUEUR, CHARLES A. Sketches. Le Muséum d'histoire naturelle du Havre. France. Photographs in the Howard Memorial Library. New Orleans.

MASSON, WILLIAM. "Plan of Pittsburgh with the Allegany and Monongohaley Rivers. Shewing There Connection into the Ohio. Likewise the Different Vessels Built at Pittsburgh, Octor 10th, 1805." Historical Society of Western Pennsylvania. Pittsburgh.

MORGAN, GEORGE. Letter Books, 1769–79, numbered 1, 2, and 3. Carnegie Library of Pittsburgh.

UNITED STATES. Consular Letters. Department of State.

UNITED STATES. Territorial Papers. Department of State.

VOORHIS, E. G., MEMORIAL COLLECTION. Missouri Historical Society. St. Louis.

NEWSPAPERS

BALTIMORE. *Niles' Weekly Register,* 1811–49. 75 vols.

CINCINNATI. *Centinel of the Northwestern Territory.*

Cincinnati Gazette.

CINCINNATI. *Liberty Hall.*

CINCINNATI. *Western Spy.*

Elizabeth (Pa.) *Herald.*

FRANKFORT, KY. *Argus of the Western World.*

FRANKFORT, KY. *Palladium.*

LEXINGTON. *Kentucky Gazette.*

Louisville Correspondent.

Natchez Gazette.

NATCHEZ. *Mississippi Herald and Natchez Gazette.*

NATCHEZ. *Mississippi Messenger.*

NEW ORLEANS. *Courrier de la Louisiane.*

NEW ORLEANS. *Louisiana Gazette.*

NEW ORLEANS. *Orleans Gazette.*

PITTSBURGH. *Commonwealth.*

BIBLIOGRAPHY

PITTSBURGH. *Tree of Liberty.*

ST. LOUIS. *Louisiana Gazette.*

ST. LOUIS. *Missouri Gazette.*

OTHER PRINTED SOURCES

ALVORD, CLARENCE W., and CLARENCE E. CARTER, eds. *The Critical Period, 1763–1765.* Springfield, 1915. lvii, 597 p. (*Illinois Historical Collections,* vol. 10).

ALVORD, CLARENCE W., and CLARENCE E. CARTER, eds. *The New Régime, 1765–1767.* Springfield, 1916. xxviii, 700 p. (*Illinois Historical Collections,* vol. 11).

ALVORD, CLARENCE W., and CLARENCE E. CARTER, eds. *Trade and Politics, 1767–1769.* Springfield, 1921. xviii, 760 p. (*Illinois Historical Collections,* vol. 16).

American State Papers. Documents, Legislative and Executive, of the Congress of the United States. Washington, 1832–61. 38 vols.

ANDERSON, ISAAC. "Diary," in Indiana Historical Society, *Publications,* 2:111–117 (1896).

ANDERSON, THOMAS C. "Journal, 1814," in *Wisconsin Historical Collections,* 9:207–261 (1882).

ANDERSON, THOMAS C. "Personal Narrative," in *Wisconsin Historical Collections,* 9:135–206 (1882).

Annals of Congress; the Debates and Proceedings in the Congress of the United States . . . from March 3, 1789 to May 27, 1824; compiled by Joseph Gales, Sr., and W. W. Seaton. Washington, 1834–56. 42 vols.

ASHE, THOMAS. *Travels in America, Performed in 1806.* London, 1809. 316 p.

AUDUBON, JOHN J. *Delineations of American Scenery and Character.* New York, 1926. xlix, 349 p.

"AUSTIN PAPERS." Edited by Eugene C. Barker, in American Historical Association, *Annual Report,* vol. 2 (1919).

BAILY, FRANCIS. *Journal of a Tour in Unsettled Parts of America in 1796 & 1797.* London, 1856. xii, 439 p.

BAXTER, FRANCES, ed. "Rafting on the Alleghany and Ohio, 1844,"

237

BIBLIOGRAPHY

in *The Pennsylvania Magazine of History and Biography*, 51:27–78, 143–171, 207–243 (1927).

BEATTY, ERKURIES. "Diary," in *The Magazine of American History*, 1:175–179 (1877).

BEDFORD, JOHN R. "A Tour in 1807 down the Cumberland, Ohio and Mississippi Rivers from Nashville to New Orleans," in *Tennessee Historical Magazine*, 5:40–68 (1919).

BOUQUET HENRY. "Bouquet Papers," in *Michigan Pioneer and Historical Collections*, 19:27–295 (1911).

BRACKENRIDGE, HENRY M. "Journal of a Voyage up the River Missouri; Performed in Eighteen Hundred and Eleven," in Reuben G. Thwaites, ed., *Early Western Travels*, 6:22–166. Cleveland, 1904.

BRACKENRIDGE, HENRY M. *Recollections of Persons and Places in the West*. Philadelphia and Pittsburgh, 1868. 331 p.

BRACKENRIDGE, HENRY M. *Views of Louisiana; Together with a Journal of a Voyage up the Missouri River, in 1811*. Pittsburgh, 1814. 304 p.

BRADBURY, JOHN. "Travels in the Interior of America, in the Years 1809, 1810, and 1811," in Reuben G. Thwaites, ed., *Early Western Travels*, vol. 5. Cleveland, 1904. 320 p.

BUTTRICK, TILLY. "Voyages, Travels, and Discoveries," in Reuben G. Thwaites, ed., *Early Western Travels*, 8:15–89. Cleveland, 1904.

BYARS, WILLIAM V., ed., *B. and M. Gratz, Merchants in Philadelphia, 1754–1798*. Jefferson City, Mo., 1916. 386 p.

CHOUTEAU, FREDERICK. "Reminiscences," in Kansas State Historical Society, *Transactions*, 8:423–434 (1903–4).

CLARK, DANIEL. *Proofs of the Corruption of Gen. James Wilkinson, and of His Connexion with Aaron Burr, with a Full Refutation of His Slanderous Allegations in Relation to the Character of the Principal Witness against Him*. Philadelphia, 1809. 199 p.

COLLOT, GEORGES H. V. *A Journey in North America*. Translated by J. Christian Bay. Florence, 1924. 2 vols.

CRAMER, ZADOK. *The Navigator: Containing Directions for Navigating the Monongahela, Alleghany, Ohio, and Mississippi Rivers; with an Ample Account of These Much Admired Waters, from the Head of the Former to the Mouth of the Latter; and a Concise Description of Their Towns, Villages, Harbours, Settlements, &c. With Accurate Maps of the Ohio and Mississippi. To Which is Added an Appendix, Containing an Account of Louisiana, and of the Missouri and Columbia Rivers, as Discovered by the Voyage under Captains Lewis and Clark.* Sixth edition, Pittsburgh, 1808. 156 p. Preceding editions were those of 1801, 1802, 1804 (?), and 1806; those following were of 1811, 1814, 1817, 1818, 1821, and 1824, with title pages almost unchanged from that of 1808. A reprint of all but about eighty pages of the edition of 1814 is in Ethel C. Leahy, *Who's Who on the Ohio River*, 83–201 (Cincinnati, 1931).

CRAMER, ZADOK. *Louisiana and Mississippi Almanack for the Year of Our Lord 1814.* New Orleans, 1814.

CRAMER, ZADOK. *Pittsburgh Magazine Almanack for the Year of Our Lord 1814.* Pittsburgh, 1814. 72 p.

CRAMER, ZADOK. *Pittsburgh Magazine Almanack for the Year of Our Lord 1816.* Pittsburgh, 1816. 72 p.

CRESSWELL, NICHOLAS. *The Journal of Nicholas Cresswell, 1774–1777.* New York, 1924. ix, 287 p.

CRÈVECŒUR, M. G. ST. JOHN DE. *Lettres d'un cultivateur américain addressées à Wm. S. . . on, esqr. depuis l'année 1770 jusqu'en 1786.* Paris, 1787. 3 vols.

CUMING, FORTESCUE. "Sketches of a Tour to the Western County," in Reuben G. Thwaites, ed., *Early Western Travels*, vol. 4. Cleveland, 1904. 377 p.

CUMINGS, SAMUEL. *The Western Navigator; Containing Directions for the Navigation of the Ohio and Mississippi and . . . Information Concerning the Towns, &c. on Their Banks.* Philadelphia, 1822. 2 vols.

CUMINGS, SAMUEL. *The Western Pilot, Containing Charts of the Ohio River, and of the Mississippi from the Mouth of the Missouri to the Gulf of Mexico, Accompanied with Directions for Navigating the Same, and a Description of the Towns on Their Banks, Tributary Streams, &c. Also, a Variety of Matter Interesting to All Who Are Concerned in the Navigation of Those Rivers.* Cincinnati, 1825. 143 p.

BIBLIOGRAPHY

DENNY, EBENEZER. *Military Journal.* Philadelphia, 1859. 288 p.

DEWEES, MARY. "Journal from Philadelphia to Kentucky, 1787–1788," in *The Pennsylvania Magazine of History and Biography,* 28:182–198 (1904).

DONELSON, JOHN. "Journal of a Voyage Intended by God's Permission in the Good Boat Adventure from Fort Patrick Henry of Holston River to the French Salt Springs on Cumberland River," in Samuel C. Williams, ed., *Early Travels in the Tennessee Country, 1540–1800,* 231–242. Johnson City, Tenn., 1928.

DRAKE, DANIEL. *Natural and Statistical View, or, Picture of Cincinnati, and the Miami Country.* Cincinnati, 1815. ix, 251 p.

DUNBAR, WILLIAM. "Journal of a Voyage, 1804, October," in Eron Rowland, ed., *Life, Letters, and Papers of William Dunbar,* 216–320. Jackson, Miss., 1930.

"EARLY DAYS AT PRAIRIE DU CHIEN," in *Wisconsin Historical Collections,* 5:123–153 (1867–69).

EVANS, ESTWICK. "A Pedestrious Tour of Four Thousand Miles through the Western States and Territories during the Winter and Spring of 1818," in Reuben G. Thwaites, ed., *Early Western Travels,* 8:91–364. Cleveland, 1904.

FEARON, HENRY B. *Sketches of America: A Narrative of a Journey of Five Thousand Miles through the Eastern and Western States of America.* London, 1818. vii, 462 p.

FILSON, JOHN. *Filson's Kentucke.* Louisville, 1930. (*Filson Club Publications,* no. 35).

FLAGG, EDMUND. "The Far West: or, a Tour Beyond the Mountains," in Reuben G. Thwaites, ed., *Early Western Travels,* vol. 26, 27:19–121. Cleveland, 1904.

FLINT, JAMES. "Letters from America," in Reuben G. Thwaites, ed., *Early Western Travels,* vol. 9. Cleveland, 1904. 333 p.

FLINT, TIMOTHY. *The History and Geography of the Mississippi Valley.* Cincinnati, 1832. 2 vols. in 1.

FLINT, TIMOTHY. *Recollections of the Last Ten Years, Passed in Occasional Residences and Journeyings in the Valley of the Mississippi.* Boston, 1826. 395 p.

BIBLIOGRAPHY

FLINT, TIMOTHY, ed. *Western Monthly Review.* Cincinnati, 1827–30. 3 vols.

FORDHAM, ELIAS P. *Personal Narrative of Travels in Virginia, Maryland, Pennsylvania, Ohio, Indiana, Kentucky; and of a Residence in the Illinois Territory . . . 1817–1818.* Edited by Frederic A. Ogg. Cleveland, 1906. 248 p.

GILLELAND, J. C. *The Ohio and Mississippi Pilot, Consisting of a Set of Charts of Those Rivers . . . to Which is Added a Geography of the States and Territories West and South of the Allegheny Mountains.* Pittsburgh, 1820. xii, 274 p.

GILPIN, JOSHUA. "Journal of a Tour from Philadelphia thro the Western Counties of Pennsylvania in the Months of September and October, 1809," in *The Pennsylvania Magazine of History and Biography,* 50:64–78, 163–178, 380–382; 51:172–190, 351–375; 52:29–58 (1926–28).

HALL, BASIL. *Forty Etchings, from Sketches Made with the Camera Lucida, in North America, in 1827 and 1828.* Edinburgh, 1829. ii, 21 p.

HALL, JAMES. *Letters from the West; Containing Sketches of Scenery, Manners, and Customs.* London, 1828. 385 p.

HALL, JAMES. *Notes on the Western States.* Philadelphia, 1838. xxiii, 304 p.

HALL, JAMES. *The West: Its Commerce and Navigation.* Cincinnati, 1848. vii, 328 p.

HALL, JAMES, ed. *Western Monthly Magazine, and Literary Journal.* Cincinnati, 1833–37. 6 vols. in 5.

HARRIS, THADDEUS M. *The Journal of a Tour into the Territory Northwest of the Alleghany Mountains Made in the Spring of the Year 1803.* Boston, 1805, 271 p.

HARRIS, THADDEUS M. "The Journal of a Tour into the Territory Northwest of the Alleghany Mountains Made in the Spring of the Year 1803," in Reuben G. Thwaites, ed., *Early Western Travels,* 3:307–382. Cleveland, 1904.

HARRIS, WILLIAM T. *Remarks Made during a Tour through the United States of America, in the Years 1817, 1818, and 1819 . . . in a Series of Letters to Friends in England.* London, 1821. 196 p.

BIBLIOGRAPHY

HECKEWELDER, JOHN. "Narrative of John Heckewelder's Journey to the Wabash in 1792," in *The Pennsylvania Magazine of History and Biography*, 11:466–475; 12:34–54, 165–184 (1887–88).

HILDRETH, SAMUEL P. "History of a Voyage from Marietta to New Orleans in 1805," in *The American Pioneer*, 1:89–105, 128–145 (1842).

HOUCK, LOUIS, ed. *The Spanish Régime in Missouri; a Collection of Papers and Documents Relating to Upper Louisiana.* Chicago, 1909. 2 vols.

IMLAY, GILBERT. *A Topographical Description of the Western Territory of North America.* London, 1797. xii, 598 p.

JAMES, EDWIN. "Account of an Expedition from Pittsburgh to the Rocky Mountains, Performed in the Years 1819, 1820," in Reuben G. Thwaites, ed., *Early Western Travels,* vols. 14–17. Cleveland, 1904.

JAMES, JAMES A., ed. *George Rogers Clark Papers, 1771–1781.* Springfield, 1912. clxvii, 715 p. (*Illinois Historical Collections,* vol. 8).

JAMES, JAMES A., ed. *George Rogers Clark Papers, 1781–1784.* Springfield, 1926. lxv, 572 p. (*Illinois Historical Collections,* vol. 19).

KELLOGG, LOUISE P., ed. *Frontier Advance on the Upper Ohio, 1778–1779.* Madison, 1916. 509 p. (*Wisconsin Historical Collections,* vol. 23).

KELLOGG, LOUISE P., ed. *Frontier Retreat on the Upper Ohio, 1779–1781.* Madison, 1917. 549 p. (*Wisconsin Historical Collections,* vol. 24).

KENTUCKY. *The Statute Law of Kentucky, 1809–1819.* Frankfort, 1809. 5 vols.

KER, HENRY. *Travels through the Western Interior of the United States, from the Year 1808 up to the Year 1816.* Elizabethtown, N. J., 1816. viii, 376 p.

KEYSER, PETER D., ed. "Memorials of Col. Jehu Eyre," in *The Pennsylvania Magazine of History and Biography,* 3:296–307, 412–425 (1879).

LEWIS, HENRY. *Das illustrirte Mississippithal, dargestellt in 80 nach*

BIBLIOGRAPHY

der natur aufgenommenen ansichten vom wasserfalle zu St. Anthony an bis zum Golf von Mexico. Leipzig, 1923. xii, 431 p.

LEWIS, MERIWETHER, and JOHN ORDWAY. *The Journals of Captain Meriwether Lewis and Sergeant John Ordway.* Madison, 1916. 444 p. (*Wisconsin Historical Collections,* vol. 22).

LYELL, CHARLES. *A Second Visit to the United States of North America.* New York and London, 1849. 2 vols.

MAXIMILIAN, PRINCE OF WIED. "Travels in the Interior of North America," in Reuben G. Thwaites, ed., *Early Western Travels,* vols. 22–25. Cleveland, 1905.

MAY, JOHN. *Journals and Letters . . . Relative to Two Journeys to the Ohio Country in 1788 and 1789.* Cincinnati, 1873, 160 p. (Ohio Historical and Philosophical Society, *Publications,* new series, vol. 1).

MELISH, JOHN. *Travels in the United States of America in the Years 1806 & 1807, and 1809, 1810, & 1811.* Philadelphia, 1812. 2 vols.

MICHAUX, ANDRÉ. "Journals of André Michaux's Travels into Kentucky, 1793–1796," in Reuben G. Thwaites, ed., *Early Western Travels,* 3:25–104. Cleveland, 1904.

MICHAUX, FRANCOIS A. "Travels to the West of the Alleghany Mountains," in Reuben G. Thwaites, ed., *Early Western Travels,* 3:105–306. Cleveland, 1904.

NEW ORLEANS. City Council. "An Ordinance Concerning the Port and the Levee of New-Orleans." Broadside dated December 11, 1816. The Cabildo. New Orleans.

NEW ORLEANS. City Council. "Regulations for the Port of New-Orleans." Broadside dated January 18, 1808. The Cabildo. New Orleans.

NEW ORLEANS. List of flats, barges, and steamboats arriving at the New Orleans levee from upriver from April, 1806, through March 1823. Register kept by the levee authorities. City Hall.

Niles' Weekly Register. See Newspapers. Baltimore.

"NOTES OF A JOURNEY FROM PHILADELPHIA TO NEW MADRID, TENNESSEE, 1790," in *The Pennsylvania Magazine of History and Biography,* 36:209–216 (1912).

"Notes of a Voyage from Pittsburgh to New Orleans, Thence by Sea

BIBLIOGRAPHY

to Philadelphia, in the Year 1799, Made by a Gentleman of Accurate Observation, a Passenger in a New Orleans Boat," in Reuben G. Thwaites, ed., *Early Western Travels*, 4:354–377. Cleveland, 1904.

NUTTALL, THOMAS. "A Journal of Travels into the Arkansa Territory, during the Year 1819, with Occasional Observations on the Manners of the Aborigines," in Reuben G. Thwaites, ed., *Early Western Travels*, vol. 13. Cleveland, 1905. 366 p.

PALMER, JOHN. *Journal of Travels in the United States of North America, and in Lower Canada, Performed in the Year 1817.* London, 1818. vii, 456 p.

PECK, JOHN M. *Forty Years of Pioneer Life. Memoir of John Mason Peck.* Edited by Rufus Babcock. Philadelphia, 1864. 360 p.

PERRIN DU LAC, FRANÇOIS M. *Voyage dans les deux Louisianes et chez les nations sauvages du Missouri, par les Etats-Unis, l'Ohio et les provinces qui le bordent.* Paris, 1805. x, 479 p.

POPE, JOHN. *A Tour through the Southern and Western Territories of the United States of North America; the Spanish Dominions on the River Mississippi, and the Floridas.* New York, 1888. 104, iv p.

SCHOOLCRAFT, HENRY R. *Scenes and Adventures in the Semi-Alpine Region of the Ozark Mountains of Missouri and Arkansas.* Philadelphia, 1853. xii, 256 p.

SCHOOLCRAFT, HENRY R. *A View of the Lead Mines of Missouri . . . Including Journal of a Voyage up the Mississippi from the Mouth of Ohio to St. Louis, with an Account of That Place.* New York, 1819. 299 p.

SCHULTZ, CHRISTIAN, JR. *Travels on an Inland Voyage . . . in the Years 1807 and 1808.* New York, 1810. 2 vols.

SEALSFIELD, CHARLES [Karl Postl]. *The Americans as They Are; Described in a Tour through the Valley of the Mississippi.* London, 1828. x, 221 p.

SHEPHERD, WILLIAM R., ed. "Papers Bearing on James Wilkinson's Relations with Spain, 1787–1789," in *The American Historical Review*, 9:748–766 (1904).

SIBLEY, JOHN. "Journal of Dr. John Sibley, July-October, 1802," in *The Louisiana Historical Quarterly*, 10:474–497 (1927).

BIBLIOGRAPHY

STODDARD, AMOS. *Sketches, Historical and Descriptive, of Louisiana.* Philadelphia, 1812. viii, 488 p.

THWAITES, REUBEN G., and LOUISE P. KELLOGG, eds. *Frontier Defense on the Upper Ohio, 1777–1778.* Madison, 1912. xvii, 329 p. (Draper Series, vol. 3).

THWAITES, REUBEN G., and LOUISE P. KELLOGG, eds. *The Revolution on the Upper Ohio, 1775–1777.* Madison, 1908. xix, 275 p. (Draper Series, vol. 2).

UNITED STATES. *The Public Statutes at Large of the United States of America, from the Organization of the Government in 1789, to March 3, 1845.* Boston, 1850. 6 vols.

WHITAKER, ARTHUR P., ed. "James Wilkinson's First Descent to New Orleans in 1787," in *The Hispanic-American Historical Review,* 8:82–97 (1928).

WILKESON, SAMUEL. "Early Recollections of the West," in *The American Pioneer,* 2:139–143, 158–164, 203–217, 269–273, 368–371 (1843).

WILKINSON, JAMES. *Memoirs of My Own Times.* Philadelphia, 1816. 3 vols.

WILLIAMS, SAMUEL C., ed. *Early Travels in the Tennessee Country, 1540–1800.* Johnson City, Tenn., 1928. xi, 540 p.

WILSON, ALEXANDER. "Letter from Lexington," in *The Port Folio,* third series, 3:499–519 (1810).

WOODS, JOHN. "Two Years Residence in the Settlement on the English Prairie," in Reuben G. Thwaites, ed., *Early Western Travels,* 10:79–357. Cleveland, 1904.

SECONDARY MATERIAL

ALBIG, W. ESPY. "Early Development of Transportation on the Monongahela River," in *The Western Pennsylvania Historical Magazine,* 2:115–124 (1919).

ALVORD, CLARENCE W. *The Illinois Country, 1673–1818.* Chicago, 1922. 524 p. (*Centennial History of Illinois,* vol. 1).

AMBLER, CHARLES H. *A History of Transportation in the Ohio Valley.* Glendale, Calif., 1932. 465 p.

BALDWIN, LELAND D. "The Rivers in the Early Development of

BIBLIOGRAPHY

Western Pennsylvania," in *The Western Pennsylvania Historical Magazine*, 16:79–98 (1933).

BLAIR, WALTER, and FRANKLIN J. MEINE. *Mike Fink, King of Mississippi Keelboatmen*. New York, 1933. xiv, 283 p.

BUTLER, MANN. *A History of the Commonwealth of Kentucky*. Louisville, 1834. xi, 396 p.

CARSON, W. WALLACE. "Transportation and Traffic on the Ohio and the Mississippi before the Steamboat," in *The Mississippi Valley Historical Review*, 7:26–38 (1920).

CARTER, CLARENCE E. *Great Britain and the Illinois Country, 1763–1774*. Washington, 1910. ix, 223 p.

CASSEDAY, BENJAMIN. *Bargemen of the Western Waters*. New York, 1928.

CASSEDAY, BENJAMIN. *The History of Louisville from Its Earliest Settlement till the Year 1852*. Louisville, 1852. 255 p.

Catalog of the Watercraft Collection in the United States National Museum. Compiled and edited by Carl W. Mitman. Washington, 1923. v, 298 p. (United States National Museum, *Bulletin 127*).

CAUGHEY, JOHN. "Willing's Expedition down the Mississippi, 1778," in *The Louisiana Historical Quarterly*, 15:5–36 (1932).

CHAPPELL, PHILIP E. "A History of the Missouri River," in Kansas State Historical Society, *Transactions*, 9:237–294 (1905–6).

CHITTENDEN, HIRAM M. *The American Fur Trade of the Far West*. New York, 1902. 3 vols.

CIST, CHARLES. *Cincinnati in 1841: Its Early Annals and Future Prospects*. Cincinnati, 1841. xi, 300 p.

CIST, CHARLES, comp. *The Cincinnati Miscellany, or, Antiquities of the West*. Cincinnati, 1845–46. 2 vols.

CLAIBORNE, JOHN F. H. *Mississippi, as a Province, Territory and State, with Biographical Notices of Eminent Citizens*. Jackson, 1880. Vol. 1.

COLLINS, LEWIS. *Historical Sketches of Kentucky*. Cincinnati, 1847. xvi, 500 p.

COLLINS, LEWIS, and RICHARD H. COLLINS. *Collins' Historical Sketches of Kentucky . . . to the Year 1874*. Covington, 1882. 2 vols.

BIBLIOGRAPHY

COTTERILL, R. S. "The Natchez Trace," in *Tennessee Historical Magazine,* 7:27–35 (1921).

COX, ISAAC J. "General Wilkinson and His Later Intrigues with the Spaniards," in *The American Historical Review,* 19:794–812 (1913–14).

DAHLINGER, CHARLES W. *Pittsburgh; a Sketch of Its Early Social Life.* New York, 1916. vii, 216 p.

DE BOW, JAMES D. B. *The Industrial Resources, etc., of the Southern and Western States.* New Orleans, 1852–53. 3 vols.

DUNBAR, SEYMOUR. *History of Travel in America.* Indianapolis, c1915. 4 vols.

ESKEW, GARNETT. *The Pageant of the Packets.* New York, 1929. xiv, 314 p.

FOREMAN, GRANT. "River Navigation in the Early Southwest," in *The Mississippi Valley Historical Review,* 15:34–55 (1928).

GOULD, EMERSON W. *Fifty Years on the Mississippi.* St. Louis, 1889. xv, 749 p.

GUILD, JOSEPHUS C. *Old Times in Tennessee, with Historical, Personal, and Political Scraps and Sketches.* Nashville, 1878. 503 p.

HABERMEHL, JOHN. *Life on the Western Rivers.* Pittsburgh, 1901. 222 p.

HAMY, JULES T. E. *Les voyages du naturaliste Ch. Alex. Lesueur dans l'Amérique du Nord (1815–1837) d'après les manuscrits et les œuvres d'art conservés au Muséum d'histoire naturelle de Paris et au Muséum d'histoire naturelle du Havre.* Paris, 1904. III p. (La Société des Américanists de Paris, *Journal,* vol. 5).

HARDIN, J. FAIR, ed. "The First Great Western River Captain," in *The Louisiana Historical Quarterly,* 10:25–67 (1927).

HILDRETH, SAMUEL P. *Biographical and Historical Memoirs of the Early Pioneer Settlers of Ohio.* Cincinnati, 1852. xii, 539 p.

Historical Sketch Book and Guide to New Orleans and Environs. New York, 1885.

HOAGLAND, H. E. "Early Transportation on the Mississippi," in *The Journal of Political Economy,* 19:111–123 (1911).

HOUCK, LOUIS. *A History of Missouri from the Earliest Explorations and Settlements until the Admission of the State into the Union.*

BIBLIOGRAPHY

Chicago, 1908. 3 vols.

HOWE, HENRY. *Historical Collections of the Great West.* Cincinnati, 1851. 2 vols. in 1.

HOWE, HENRY. *Historical Collections of Ohio.* Columbus, 1890. 2 vols.

HOWELLS, WILLIAM C. *Recollections of Life in Ohio, from 1813 to 1840.* Cincinnati, 1895. xiv, 207 p.

HULBERT, ARCHER B. *The Ohio River, a Course of Empire.* New York, 1906. xiv, 378 p.

HULBERT, ARCHER B. *Pioneer Roads and Experiences of Travelers.* Cleveland, 1904. 2 vols. (*Historic Highways,* vols. 11, 12).

HULBERT, ARCHER B. *Waterways of Western Expansion.* Cleveland, 1903. 220 p. (*Historic Highways,* vol. 9).

HULBERT, ARCHER B. "Western Ship-Building," in *The American Historical Review,* 21:720–733 (1915–16).

JAMES, JAMES A. *The Life of George Rogers Clark.* Chicago, 1928. xiii, 534 p.

KINGSTON, JOHN T. "Early Western Days," in *Wisconsin Historical Collections,* 7:297–344 (1876).

KIRKPATRICK, JOHN E. *Timothy Flint, Pioneer, Missionary, Author, Editor, 1780–1840.* Cleveland, 1911. 331 p.

LATROBE, JOHN H. B. "The First Steamboat Voyage on the Western Waters," in Maryland Historical Society, *Fund Publications,* no 6. Baltimore, 1871.

LEAHY, ETHEL C. *Who's Who on the Ohio River and Its Tributaries.* Cincinnati, 1931. xiv, 868 p.

LELAND, WALDO G. "Lesueur Collection of American Sketches in the Museum of Natural History at Havre, Seine-Inférieure," in *The Mississippi Valley Historical Review,* 10:53–78 (1923).

LOIR, ADRIEN. *Charles-Alexandre Lesueur, artiste et savant francais en Amérique de 1816 à 1839.* Le Havre, 1920. 108 p.

LUDLOW, NOAH M. *Dramatic Life as I Found It.* St. Louis, 1880. xix, 733 p.

MACGILL, CAROLINE. *History of Transportation in the United States before 1860.* Washington, 1917. xi, 678 p.

BIBLIOGRAPHY

McMURTRIE, DOUGLAS. "Early Printing in Pittsburgh, 1786–1830." Typescript lent by the author to the Historical Society of Western Pennsylvania, Pittsburgh.

MARTINDALE, CHARLES. "Loughery's Defeat and Pigeon Roost Massacre," in Indiana Historical Society, *Publications,* 2:97-127 (1895).

MONETTE, JOHN W. "Progress of Navigation and Commerce on the Mississippi and Great Lakes, A. D. 1700 to 1846," in Mississippi Historical Society, *Publications,* 7:479–523 (1903).

MUSICK, JOHN R. *Stories of Missouri.* New York, 1897. 288 p.

NEVILLE, MORGAN. "The Last of the Boatmen," in James Hall, ed., *The Western Souvenir, a Christmas and New Year's Gift for 1829,* 107–122. Cincinnati, 1828.

Pageant of America; a Pictorial History of the United States. [Edited by Ralph H. Gabriel.] New Haven, 1925–26. 15 vols.

[PERKINS, JAMES H.] *Annals of the West.* Pittsburgh, 1856. xl, 1016 p.

PETERSEN, WILLIAM J. "The Lead Traffic on the Upper Mississippi, 1823–1848," in *The Mississippi Valley Historical Review,* 17:72–97 (1930).

PFAFF, CAROLINE S. "Henry Miller Shreve: a Biography," in *The Louisiana Historical Quarterly,* 10:192–240 (1927).

QUICK, HERBERT, and EDWARD QUICK. *Mississippi Steamboatin'.* New York, c1926. xiv, 342 p.

ROTHERT, OTTO A. *The Outlaws of Cave-in-Rock.* Cleveland, 1924. 364 p.

SAMPLE, GEORGE. "Sketches of Western Settlements," in *The American Pioneer,* 1:157–160 (1842).

SAMPSON, FRANCIS A. "The New Madrid and Other Earthquakes in Missouri," in the Mississippi Valley Historical Association, *Proceedings,* 6:218–238 (1912–13).

SAVELLE, MAX. *George Morgan, Colony Builder.* New York, 1932. xiv, 266 p.

SCHARF, J. THOMAS. *History of Saint Louis City and County.* Philadelphia, 1883. 2 vols.

BIBLIOGRAPHY

SCROGGS, WILLIAM O. "Early Trade and Travel in the Lower Mississippi Valley," in Mississippi Valley Historical Association, *Proceedings*, 2:235–256 (1908–9).

SHEPHERD, WILLIAM R. "Wilkinson and the Beginnings of the Spanish Conspiracy," in *The American Historical Review*, 9:490–506 (1904).

SIEBERT, WILBUR H. "The Loyalists in West Florida and the Natchez District," in *The Mississippi Valley Historical Review*, 2:465–483 (1916).

STEVENS, FRANK E. *The Black Hawk War, Including a Review of Black Hawk's Life*. Chicago, 1903. 323 p.

STRICKLAND, WILLIAM P. *The Pioneers of the West; or, Life in the Woods*. New York, 1868. 403 p.

TRAVIS, IRVEN. "Navigation on the Muskingum," in *Ohio Archæological and Historical Publications*, 14:408–424 (1905).

VERHOEFF, MARY. *The Kentucky River Navigation*. Louisville, 1917. 257 p.

VOLWILER, ALBERT T. *George Croghan and the Westward Movement, 1741–1782*. Cleveland, 1926. 370 p.

WALKER, NORMAN. "Commerce of the Mississippi River from Memphis to the Gulf of Mexico," in 50 Congress, 1 session. *House Executive Documents*, no. 6, part 2, p. 136–389 (serial 2552).

WHITAKER, ARTHUR P. *The Mississippi Question, 1795–1803*. New York and London, c1934. ix, 342 p.

WHITAKER, ARTHUR P. *The Spanish-American Frontier: 1783-1795*. Boston and New York, 1927. viii, 255 p.

WILEY, RICHARD T. "Ship and Brig Building on the Ohio and Its Tributaries," in *Ohio Archæological and Historical Publications*, 22:54–64 (1913).

WILSON, ERASMUS, ed. *Standard History of Pittsburg, Pennsylvania*. Chicago, 1898. xvi, 1074 p.

WINSOR, JUSTIN. *The Westward Movement*. Boston and New York, 1897. viii, 595 p.

Index

251

INDEX

INDEX

Campbell, Lieut., in Indian raid, 106, 107

Canadian boatmen. *See* Creole boatmen

Canoes, types of, 41; prices of, 53; used by immigrants, 200n.13

Carondelet, Francisco L. H., baron de, governor of Louisiana, attitude toward immigrants, 35; and St. Louis rebels, 36

Carpenter, ——, and Mike Fink, 113, 114

Carter, Capt. Thomas, keelboat commander, 72

Cartwright, Robert, immigrant, 151

Cash River, pirate base, 117

Cave-in-Rock (Ohio River), 162; pirate base, 117, 122, 123, 119–121, 218n.6, 219n.7; described, 119, 218n.3

Cave-in-Rock Island (Ohio River), 119

Céleron de Blainville, 6

Chalmette, battle of, boatmen in, 105, 217n.21

Charleston (Ky.), boatbuilding center, 52; shipbuilding at, 169, 226n.20

Charlestown (Va.), warehouse, 188

Chenoweth, Capt., 19

Chester, Joseph, shipyard of, 162

Chickasaw Indians, receive Natchez fugitives, 14; on Natchez Trace, 126

Chittenden, H. M., describes Creoles, 99

Choctaw Indians, on Natchez Trace, 126

Cincinnati, tavern scene, 2; boatbuilding center, 52; shipping statistics, 66, 178, 179, 229n.5; founded, 142; immigrants in, 157; celebrates arrival of "St. Clair," 168; packet service, 176; freight rates, 185; warehouse, 188

"Cincinnati" (barge, *1811*), makes record speed, 66; in Cincinnati trade, 179

"Cincinnati" (vessel, *1806*), in Cincinnati trade, 179

"Cincinnati" (vessel, *1815*), in Cincinnati trade, 66, 179

"Cincinnatus" (brig), launched, 173

Claiborne, W. C. C., governor of Louisiana, and pirates, 131

Clark, Daniel, influences Spanish officials, 26; quoted on Wilkinson, 28

Clark, George Rogers, 10, 12, 13, 187; expedition to the Illinois, 16, 17; and Col. Lochry, 18; contracts for flour at St. Louis, 22

Clark, William, governor of Missouri Territory, estimates navigable waters, 39; expedition, *1814*, 106

Clary, ——, pirate, exploits of, 133

Clay, Henry, speech on port of Pittsburgh, 159, 222n.1

"Clem Hall" (vessel), in Tennessee trade, 180

Clemens, Samuel, describes river water, 87; describes flatboatmen, 96

Colbert, James, half-breed, ferryman on Natchez Trace, 127

Colbert, James, outlaw, leads Natchez fugitives, 14; captured by traders, 16

Colbert family, piracies of, 117

Collot, Gen. Georges H. V., 81; stirs revolutionary sentiment in St. Louis, 36; quoted on boat prices, 53; describes boatmen, 95; calculates freight rates, 185

Columbia (Ohio), shipbuilding at, 169, 173, 226n.20

Commerce. *See* Trade and commerce

"Commodore McDonough" (barge), 98

Conemaugh River, as trade route, 178

Conestoga wagons, in eastern trade, 184

"Conquest" (schooner), built, 165

Coody, Archy, half-breed, 149

Cordelles, 61; described, 64

Cornice Rocks (Mississippi River), 64, 70

Cotton, John, immigrant, 151

Cottonwood Creek, scene of raid, 15; pirate base, 116, 117

Craig, Mr. ——, trader, 32, 33

Craig, Maj. Isaac, provisions Wayne's army, 34; boat contracts of, 47, 49;

INDEX

INDEX

227n.26; in military use, 34; described, 47–50, 137, 155, 206n.11; names for, 47, 205n.10; period of use, 47, 52; disposal of, 49; prices of, 53, 54; navigation of, 67; speed of, 67; number of, 181, 227n.26; places of origin of, 182; seasons for arrival of, 182; insurance rates on, 183, 230n.12; as trading boats, 186, 187; passenger rates on, 186; theaters on, 187; at New Orleans wharf, 189; first, on Mississippi, 201n.24

Flint, Rev. Timothy, describes boatmen, 65, 95, 96, 98; recollections of, 67, 68, 74, 81, 83, 187; voyage of, *1819*, 156; describes immigrants, 157; describes waterfront scene, 189, 190

"Floating stores," described, 9, 186, 187

Floods, 67, 77

Florida, Spanish domination of, 22

Flour trade, in *1782–84*, 20, 21; in *1790*, 29

Fluger, Col., boat wrecker, exploits of, 118

Forbes, Gen. John, 7

Fordham, E. P., describes boatmen, 98

Ford's Ferry (Ohio River), 120

Fort Duquesne, provisioned, 6, 7

Fort Granville, attacked, 6

Fort Jefferson, 14

Fort Massac, rebuilt, 7

Fort Panmure, captured, 14

Fort Pitt, supplies Detroit, 7; boatbuilding at, 8, 50

Fort Shelby, captured, 106

Fort Washington, flatboats used in construction of, 49

Fox Indians, attack boats, 106

Frankfort (Ky.), founded, 24; shipbuilding at, 169, 226n.20; shipping port, 180

Franklin, Benjamin, quoted, 160

Franks and Company, merchants, in Illinois trade, 8, 9

Frenau, Philip, quoted, 3

French, oppose English trade, 6

French and Indian War, events on western waters, 6, 7

French Creek, supply route to Detroit, 7; guide to, 59

French Salt Springs (French Licks, Tenn.), 149, 153

Frontier conditions, 1–5, 158

Fur trade, in Mississippi region, 36

Gallatin, Albert, quoted, 161

Galleys, 162; in Clark's expedition, 16; used in Revolution, 18, 19; described, 19, 163, 169; used by Spain, 36; used by immigrants, 138

Gallipolis (Ohio), boatbuilding center, 52

Gálvez, Bernardo de, governor of Louisiana, conquers Natchez, 14

Gardoqui, Diego de, Spanish minister to U. S., 31; encourages immigration, 30

Gayoso de Lemos, Manuel, governor of Natchez district, characterized, 33; policy toward trade, 35, 36

"General Butler" (brig), launched, 165

George, Capt. Robert, 13, 14; commands galley, 19

Gibson, Capt. George, expedition to Wheeling, 10, 11

Gilman, B. I., shipowner, 168

Girty, James, boatman, 109, 217n.26; and Andrew Jackson, 104; adventures of, 110

Gould, Emerson, quoted, 49

"Governor Clark" (gunboat), attacked, 106, 107

Grand Chain of the Mississippi, towline at, 61, 64; described, 70

Grand Gulf (Mississippi River), 74

Grand Tower (Mississippi River), 70; initiations held at, 94; pirate base, 116

Grandpré, Carlos de, commandant at Natchez, 25

Gratz family, in Kentucky trade, 34

Great Raft (Red River), 80

INDEX

Greathouse, Capt., in Indian raid, 147

Green, Charles, shipowner, 168

Griffin, Rev. Thomas, in Natchez, 104

Grindstone Ford (Miss.), 126

Guild, J. C., quoted, 128

Gunboats, built, 10, 51, 106, 163, 169, 224n.11, 225n.18, 226n.20; used in Revolution, 12, 18, 19, 51; in Clark's expedition, 16, 17; effect of, 20; used by Spain, 36; used in War of *1812*, 106

Hall, James, describes Falls of Ohio, 69; quoted, 87; describes fiddler, 90; describes immigrants, 141

Harpe, Micajah, pirate, exploits of, 122–124

Harpe, Wiley (John Setton), pirate, 129; exploits of, 122–124, 130; death of, 131

Harris, W. T., describes boatmen, 98

Harrison, Lieut., and Natchez rebels, 13; name of, 200n.16

Harrison, Reuben, immigrant, 149

Harrison, William Henry, 49

Heckewelder, John, describes wreck, 82; quoted, 143

Helm, Capt. Leonard, 17

Henderson, Richard, 148

Henderson (Red Banks, Ky.), outlaws at, 122

Henry, Patrick, governor of Virginia, 11

Hildreth, Samuel P., 172

Honoré, John, trading ventures of, 21

Horton, Jonathan, boatowner, 179

Hospital boat, in army use, 34

Howard, Carlos, expedition of, *1796*, 36

Hubbell, Capt. William, battle with Indians, 146, 147

Hulbert, Archer B., describes riot, 102

Hunt, Wilson P., 93, 100

Hunter and Beaumont, publishing firm, 57

"Hunters of Kentucky," poem, quoted, 105

Hurricane Island (Ohio River), 119, 120, 121

Hutchins, Col. Anthony, 12; resists Willing, 13; leads Natchez revolt, 14

Illinois country, trading ventures in, 7–9, 20, 50; Clark's expedition to, 16, 17; immigration to, 136, 153

Immigrants, economy of, 4; accompany Clark's expedition, 16; treatment of, in Spanish territory, 23, 30; travel methods of, 42, 142, 148, 186; character of, 134, 144, 145, 154; aims of, 135; embarkation points for, 136; seasons favored by, 136; craft used by, 137–140; descriptive scenes of, 137, 140, 157; types of, 141, 158; experiences of, with Indians, 142–148, 149–153; voyages of, 148–153, 155–157; occupations of, 154, 155; on arrival, 157, 158. *See also* Immigration

Immigration, to Natchez, 9; during Revolution, 10, 134; to Falls of Ohio, 16; Spanish policy toward, 30, 31, 35; routes to West, 35, 135, 142; to Kentucky, 135, 142, 153; to Illinois country, 136, 153; north of Ohio River, 142; to Tennessee, 148; to Ohio, 153; to West Virginia, 153. *See also* Immigrants

Indians, traders' influence on, 5; in Ohio Valley, 6; revolt under Pontiac, 7; harass traders, 14, 20, 21, 32; attack Rogers' expedition, 17; attack Lochry's expedition, 18; effect of cannon on, 20; incited by Spain, 23; expeditions against, increase river traffic, 34; raids, War of *1812*, 106–109; capture keelboat, 116; on Natchez Trace, 126, 127; harass immigrants, 142–148, 149–152; contract smallpox from immigrants, 221n.18

Iroquois Indians, in Ohio Valley, 6

Irvine, Gen. William, describes flour trade, 20

Islands, number of, 59; formation of, 73

256

INDEX

INDEX

Monongahela Company, shipbuilding firm, 162

"Monongahela Farmer" (vessel), built, 162; voyages of, 162, 163; tonnage of, 223n.6

"Monongahela Packet" (packet boat), passenger rates on, 186

Monongahela River, as trade route, 20; boatbuilding on, 51, 52; guide to, 59; shipyards, 161, 162; packet service on, 175

Moore, ——, boatmaster, 179

Morgan, George, trading ventures in Illinois country, 8, 9; builds gunboats, 10; founds New Madrid, 31; complains of boats, 51; builds warehouse, 188

Morris, Robert, 12

Morrison, William, trader, 34

Murray, William, trade agent, 8, 9

Muscle Shoals, 148, 152; name, 97

"Muskingum" (brig), 164; launched, 168; voyage of, 169

Myers, Jacob, establishes packet service, 176

"Nanina" (brig), launched, 165

Napoleon, sells Louisiana to U.S., 37, 38

Napoleon (Ohio), marine hospital at, 90

Nashville (Tenn.), trade of, 180; freight rates, 185

"Nashville Packet" (vessel), in Tennessee trade, 180

Natchez (Miss.), British trade at, 9; Willing's expedition at, 12; settlers of, resist Willing, 13; revolt in, 14; flour trade of, 21; traders held at, 23; Spanish policy in, 32; American rule established at, 37; boatmen's hospitals in, 90; boatmen in, 103, 104, 110

"Natchez Packet" (barge), 81

Natchez rebels, river raids of, 14–16; pardoned, 16

Natchez Trace, described, 124–127; piracies on, 126, 128, 129, 131–133; length of, 219n.11; name for, 219n.17

Navarro, Martin, intendant at New Orleans, relations with Wilkinson, 26, 27; encourages immigration, 30

Navigation, interrupted by raids, 14–16, 18; interfered with by Spain, 22–24, 35, 37; effect of Wilkinson's activities on, 25–30; rights conceded by Spain, 35; opened by Louisiana Purchase, 38; of shallow waters, 39; of bullboats, 40; of pirogues, 41; of bateaux, 42; of barges, 45, 61, 66, 76; of keelboats, 45, 61–65; of flatboats, 48, 67; accidents in, 54, 73, 78, 79, 80, 81, 82, 83, 207n.19; guides to river, 57–61; distances, 59, 66; methods of, 41, 42, 45, 48, 61–65, 68, 69–71; perils of, 61, 68–83, 161, 173, 212n.26, 27; speed statistics of, 61, 65, 66, 67, 68; endangered by piracies, 116–124; of ocean craft, 162, 164–169, 170–172, 173, 222n.1, 223n.6; insurance statistics of, 183, 230n.12; of steamboats, 191, 192. *See also* Trade and commerce; various types of boats

Navigation of the Mississippi, pilot book, 58

Navigator, pilot book, advice to boat buyers, 54; described 57–60; discontinued, 61; quoted, 66, 67, 77, 82, 120, 163, 190, 191; *1814* edition, 208n.3

"Neptune" (British brig), 12

Neville, Morgan, quoted, 178, 193

New Madrid (Mo.), founded, 31; earthquakes, 60, 82; waterfront scene, 189, 190

New Orleans, as market for pioneers, 4, 5; trade of, 20, 21, 25, 28, 29, 31, 37, 174, 178, 179, 180; freight rates, 22, 185; Wilkinson's activities in, 26, 27, 28, 29; Spanish duty at, lifted, 35; shipping statistics, 37, 66, 174, 178, 179, 180, 181–183, 227n.26, 229n.8; purchased by U.S., 38; flatboats used in construction at, 49; harbor affected

INDEX

by storms, 81; hospital facilities for boatmen, 89, 90; boatmen in, 97, 104, 105, 109; market hazards, 182; shipping agents, 183; waterfront described, 189; threatened by westerners, 201n.26

New Orleans boats, described, 47. *See also* Flatboats

Newspapers, carried by packet, 175, 176; report western trade, 178

Nicholson, Capt. Charles, 161

North Carolina, and Spanish restriction, 23

Northwest, economic development of, 4

Notes on the Navigation of the Mississippi, pilot book, 60; described, 208n.5

Nuttall, Thomas, experiences of, 60, 67, 78, 83; describes pirates, 132, 133

O'Hara, James, trades with St. Louis, 34; shipowner, 165; in charge of mail packets, 177

Ohio, immigration to, 153

Ohio and Mississippi Navigator, pilot book, 58

Ohio Navigator, pilot book, described, 57

Ohio River, as military route, 6, 7, 10, 11; as trade route, 8; trade of, stimulated by Wilkinson, 28; traffic on, stimulated by Indian expeditions, 34; types of boats used on, 40, 41, 44, 47; character of, 56, 60, 61, 68, 71, 74, 81; guides to, 57, 58–61; distances on, 59; islands in, 59; floods in, 67, 77; pirate bases on, 117, 119–124; settlement on, 153; as shipbuilding center, 160–174; packet service on, 176, 177, 228n.1. *See also* Falls of the Ohio; Immigration; Navigation; Trade and commerce

Olean (N. Y.), embarkation point, 137

"Oliver H. Perry" (keelboat), 108

"Orleans" (steamboat), 156, 191

Orleans boats. *See* New Orleans boats

Ottawa Indians, in Ohio Valley, 6

Pack horses, displaced by boats, 7; used in trade, 8

Packet boats, 175, 228nn.1,3; described, 176, 177

Paducah (Ky.), marine hospital at, 90

Palladium (Frankfort, Ky.), quoted, 53, 88; advertises pilot book, 57

Palmer, John, observations of, 87, 180

"Parassena" (vessel), in St. Louis trade, 180

Patten, James, falls pilot, 210n.18

Patterson, ——, Wilkinson's agent, 26

Patterson, Capt. Robert, militia commander, 19

"Penrose" (ship), at Falls of the Ohio, 171

Pensacola, siege of, 14

Perrie, Col., trader, 25

"Perseverance" (vessel), in Tennessee trade, 180

Pfluger, Col. *See* Fluger, Col.

Philadelphia, trade interests in West, 7, 22, 31, 33, 34, 179, 184, 230n.13; freight rates from, 22, 184, 185

Pickawillanee (Piqua, Ohio), trading post, 6

Pilot books, 208nn.2,3; described, 57–61, 208n.5

Pilots, at Falls of the Ohio, 69, 210n.18, 229n.6

Pinckney, Charles C., negotiates with Spain, 35

Pioneers, characterized, 1–4. *See also* Immigrants

Piqua (Pickawillanee), trading post, 6

Pirates, river exploits of, 116–124; at Cave-in-Rock, 119–122; on Natchez Trace, 126, 128–133; at Stack Island, 132, 133

Pirogues, described, 41; prices of, 53; names for, 204n.3

Pittsburgh, boatbuilding at, 8, 10, 42, 49, 50, 51, 52; trade interests of, 8, 20, 34, 177–179, 184, 230n.13; embarkation point, 10, 12, 58, 135, 136; at close of Revolution, 25; headquarters

INDEX

for military shipments, 34; publishing interests at, 57; rating in *Navigator*, 59; marine hospital at, 90; as seaport, 159, 160, 164, 222n.1; as shipbuilding center, 160, 163–165, 169, 173, 224n.11; packet service, 175–177, 228n.3; shipping statistics, 177–179, 184, 185, 194; industrial development of, 178; freight rates, 184, 185, 231 n.14; warehouse, 188; wharfs, 188

"Pittsburgh" (ship), launched, 164

Pittsburgh Gazette, advertisements in, 52, 175, 176, 183; delivered by packet, 175, 176; quoted, 117, 184, 191

Pittsburgh Navigator. See *Navigator*

Plug, Col. *See* Fluger, Col.

Point Coupée (Mississippi River), 212 n.27

Pollock, Oliver, aids Revolutionary cause, 10, 11, 12; aids Clark's expedition, 16

"Polly" (schooner), 223n.6

Pontiac's War, 7

Pope, John, voyage of, *1791, 32, 33*

Pope, William, boatbuilder, 53

Port Gibson (Miss.), shipbuilding at, 169, 226n.20

Porter, David R., election celebration, 194

Pourée, Capt., merchant, attacked by Natchez rebels, 15

"President Adams" (galley), 54, 162; launched, 163

Prestonville (Ky.), shipbuilding at, 226n.20

Push boats, 195

Pyatt, Capt. Jacob, marine commander, 19

Rafting industry, 41

Rafts, used by immigrants, 42, 138

Railroads, effect on shipping, 195

Randolph, John, quoted, 56

"Rattletrap" (gunboat), 12

"Rebecca" (British vessel), 12

Rector, Lieut., in Indian raids, 107, 108

Red Banks (Henderson, Ky.), outlaws at, 122

Red River, Great Raft of, 80

Redstone (Brownsville, Pa.), embarkation point, 16, 21, 58, 136; boatbuilding center, 52

"Redstone" (schooner), built, 162

Reed, ——, merchant, 179

Reed and Forde, trading firm, 34

Reeder, Jesse, warehouse owner, 188

Religion, Spanish policy toward, 31

Revolutionary War, events of, on western waters, 10–22, 117; effect on boatbuilding, 51; effect on immigration, 134

Rice, Sally, 123

Richardson, Justice Andrew, decision on boat wreck, 54, 55

Riggs, Lieut., in Indian raid, 107

Roberts, Betty, 123

Roberts, Susan, 123

Robertson, Capt. James, 148, 152

Rock River, engagements, *1814,* 106, 107

Rogers, Col. David, attacked by Indians, 17

Rogers, Capt. John, 16

Roosevelt, Nicholas, traveling experiences of, 156

Ross, Hugh, boatbuilder, 53

Rowan, ——, immigrant, encounters Indians, 145

Rozier, F. A., quoted, 116

"Rufus King" (ship), at Falls of the Ohio, 170–172

"Running Fly" (galley), 17

Sails, on bateaux, 42; on barges and keelboats, 45; on flatboats, 48

"St. Clair" (brig), 162; launched, 167; voyage of, 168

St. Louis, trade of, 34, 180; revolutionary sentiment in, 36; marine hospital at, 90; freight rates, 185; wharfage charges, 188; shipping statistics, 194

INDEX

Ste. Marie (La.), wharfage facilities at, 189

San Ildefonso, treaty of, 37, 38

Sanders, John, banker, 22

Sargent, Winthrop, 169

Sarpy, Capt., 132

Sauk Indians, attack boats, 106

Schoolcraft, H. R., describes boatmen, 98, 99

Schooners, built, 161, 162, 164, 165, 224n.11, 225n.18, 226n.20

Schultz, Christian, observations of, 53, 57, 62, 75, 88, 99, 137, 172, 186

Scioto River, mouth of, 143, 221n.12

Scott, John, shipbuilder, 162

Sealsfield, Charles, describes keelboat, 139

Sedley, Bill, boatman, adventures of, 109

"Senator Ross" (galley), 54, 162; launched, 164

Setting poles, 42; described, 62–64

Setton, John. See Harpe, Wiley

Sevier, John, 121

Shawnee Indians, in Ohio Valley, 6

Shipbuilding, prophecies concerning, 159, 160; at Pittsburgh, 160, 163–165, 169, 173, 224n.11; materials available for, 160; factors adverse to, 161, 170–173; at Elizabeth, 162, 163; at Marietta, 166–169, 172, 173, 225n.18; prices for, 168; localities engaged in, 169, 226n.20; tonnage statistics of, 169, 170, 173, 227nn.21,26; decline of, 170–173, 227n.24; evaluated, 173, 174

Shipping. See Shipbuilding; Trade and commerce

Shippingport (Ky.), anchorage facilities at, 188

Shreve, Capt. Henry, dislodges raft, 80; builds steamboat, 192

Skiffs, 42; prices of, 53; used by immigrants, 140. See also Bateaux

Sloops, built, 161

Smith, James, 60

"Smoke House" (trader's boat), voyage of, 32, 33

Southwest, economic development of, 4

Spain, policy of, toward colonial expedition, 10, 11; deals with Natchez rebels, 14, 16; restricts American commerce on Mississippi, 20–24, 35, 37; policy of, influenced by Wilkinson, 25–30; encourages American immigration, 30–32; grants American navigation rights, 35; attitude of, toward British traders, 36; cedes Louisiana to France, 37; attitude of, toward pirates, 117, 124

Spears, Solomon, 145

Spriggs, ——, merchant, 180

Stack Island (Mississippi River), pirate base, 132, 133

Steamboatmen, characterized, 192

Steamboats, built, 173, 232n.22; inaugurated, 190, 191; effect of, 191–194; freight rates on, 192, 193

Stump, Capt., 131

"Susan Amelia" (keelboat), makes record speed, 66

Swaine, Capt., 33

Swaney, John L., mail carrier, on Natchez Trace, 127, 128

Symmes, J. C., advertises ships, 160

Talbot, ——, and Mike Fink, 113, 114

Tarascon Brothers, James Berthoud & Co., merchants, establish business in Pittsburgh, 34; shipbuilding ventures of, 164, 165; wharfage charges of, 188

Tardiveau, Barthelemi, encounters Natchez rebels, 16; trading ventures of, 21, 22

Taylor, John (John Setton). See Harpe, Wiley

Taylor, Maj. Zachary, directs expedition against Black Hawk, 107

Teatman, J. and W., boatowners, 179

Tennessee, pirates in, 122, 123; immigration to, 148; trading ports, 180

INDEX

Tennessee River, as military route, 7; as immigration route, 35, 148

Tensaw settlements, resist Willing, 13

Tobacco, prices of, 24, 29; shipped by Wilkinson, 25; sale privilege to immigrants, 30

Toorner, Juan. *See* Turner, John

"Torpedo" (packet), 228n.3

Tower Rock (Ohio River), 119

Towlines, 61; described, 64

Trade and commerce, established in Ohio Valley, 5–7; of Illinois country, 7–9, 20; of Pittsburgh, 8, 20, 34, 177–179, 184, 185; British, 9, 36; in Mississippi region, 9, 36; of Louisiana, 9; of Natchez, 9, 21; on trading boats, 9, 186, 187; during Revolution, 14, 20–22; flour trade, *1782*, 20; of Kentucky, 20, 27, 29, 34, 180; of Louisville, 21, 22, 178, 180, 185; of New Orleans, 20, 21, 22, 25, 27, 28, 29, 31, 35, 37, 174, 178, 179, 180, 181–183, 185, 189, 227n.26; on Monongahela River, 20; Spanish interference with, 22–31, 35–37; Wilkinson's influence on, 25–30; expansion, *1790*'s, 29–31, 32–34; of St. Louis, 34, 180; in *1801*, 37; opened by Louisiana Purchase, 38; ocean, 160, 161, 164–166, 168, 169, 173, 174; effect of embargo on, 172; number of boats employed in, 177, 178, 180–182; of Cincinnati, 178, 179, 185, 229n.5; of Tennessee ports, 180; price fluctuations of, 182; handled by agents, 183; stimulates marine insurance, 183; freight rates of, 184–186, 192, 193, 228n.3, 231n.14; with Philadelphia, 184, 230n.13; warehouses established for, 187, 188; wharfage facilities for, 188, 189; reflected in waterfront scene, 189, 190; effect of steamboats on, 191–193

Traders, penetrate West, 5, 6, 7; English, on Mississippi, 199n.4. *See also* Trade and commerce

Trading boats, described, 9, 186, 187

Transportation, flatboat (ark) chief means of, 4, 47; by bateau, 7, 8; routes of, 7, 8, 10, 22, 34, 185; costs of, 8, 22, 24, 36; of goods to the Illinois, 8; on routes from East, 8, 184, 185, 230.13; of flour, *1782*, 20; by barge, 34, 178, 180, 191, 192; by flatboat, 34, 181, 184; types of craft used for, 40–50; by ship, 161, 162, 164–166, 167, 173; by packet, 176, 177, 228n.3; by keelboat, 177, 178, 180, 181, 184, 191, 193–195; agents, 183; rates, 184–186, 192, 193, 228n.3; by steamboat, 191–193. *See also* Immigrants; Navigation; Travel

Travel, accounts, 32, 33, 139, 148–153, 155–157; on Natchez Trace, 125–127; on packets, 138, 176; rates, 186. *See also* Immigrants

Tree of Liberty (Pittsburgh), 58, 70

"Triton" (vessel), in Cincinnati trade, 179

Trollope, Anthony, quoted, 2

Tupper, E. W., shipowner, 168

Turner, John, leads river raid, 15

"Tuscarora" (ship), at Falls of the Ohio, 170–172

Twain, Mark. *See* Clemens, Samuel

"Union" (barge), in New Orleans trade, 180

Unzaga, Luis de, governor of Louisiana, 10

Vernon and Skidmore, shipping agents, 183

"Vigilina" (vessel), in St. Louis trade, 180

Vigo, François, trader, 34

Villiers, Capt. Coulon de, 6

Vincennes, Clark's expedition to, 16, 17

Virginia, authorizes powder expedition, 10; plans construction of gunboats, 18

263

INDEX